Exploring Learning Ecologies
Norman J Jackson

lifewide education

Second Edition October 2019

Published by
Chalk Mountain 15/03/16
Chalk Mountain 15/10/19

Distributed through LULU

Cover Image 'Ecological Thinking' by Tom Chalkley

ISBN 978-0-9935759-1-4

*'an explorer can never know what he is exploring
until it has been explored' (Gregory Bateson 1972)*

For all the people who have helped me on my journey

Contents

Acknowledgements

I am grateful to so people who have helped me develop to the ideas of lifewide learning and learning ecologies. I would particularly like to thank all the people whose narratives of learning I have drawn upon in this work, including John Cowan, Peter Rawsthorne, Neda Tomlinson, Yalda Tomlinson, Navid Tomlinson, John Tomlinson, Jenny Willis, Lisa Mann, Elaine Woods, Barbara Lee, Hayley York, Emilie Crapoulet, Francesca Oh, Donovan Anani, Manmit Rahis, Callum Strong, Gideon Coolin, Jenny Willis, Lisa Mann, Andrew Doig, Helen Carmichael, Anita Esser, Shirley Manzi, Paula Nottingham, Gary Hearn, Melissa Shaw, Russ Law and Sue Wattling. You have all been an important and inspirational part of my learning ecology. I am also grateful to talented illustrator Kiboko Kamau who turned some of my ideas into pictures. He has been an important presence in my learning ecologies for the last seven years and the process we go through to imagine and design an illustration has often enhanced my understanding.

Writing can be a lonely business and it's great to receive support in the form of encouragement and feedback on your ideas. I would like to sincerely thank Professor John Cowan, Graham Morgan, Robyn Philip Andrew Middleton, Hazel Messenger, Mark Langan, Nikos Mouratoglou and Victoria Wight, who reviewed draft chapters and give me constructive criticisms and suggestions.

I would also like to say a special thank you to three people who have helped me along the way. Professor Ronald Barnett continues to encourage me to explore the concept of lifewide learning and education and provides a supportive and insightful Foreword to the book. Ron always adds value to ideas through his own knowledgeable and imaginative perspectives. Professor John Cowan has, over many years, acted as a 'guide by my side' and, at times, a 'meddler in the middle' with his provocative but always caring and constructive feedback when I have invited him to comment on my ideas. I count myself fortunate indeed to have such a caring and thoughtful mentor who teaches me to be more critical about my ideas. The third person I would like to thank is Dr Jenny Willis. She has been an important ally and partner in enabling me to explore and communicate ideas through the Lifewide Education and Creative Academic Magazines and she helped in the proof reading of the manuscript for this book.

I have been fortunate to have participated in an amazing transformation of higher education over the last 30 years and I've been privileged to work in a number of different organisations that have helped shape and support this transformation. Thanks to HEFCE's Centre's for Excellence in Teaching and Learning (CETL) initiative between 2005-11, and the opportunity provided by the University of Surrey to lead its CETL, I was able to work in a university environment with students to understand how they learned and developed across all the domains of their life. This started me on a journey to explore, develop and implement the idea of lifewide learning and education: a journey involving many different learning ecologies, that eventually led me here. The CETL evaluation report (HEFCE 2011) noted that 'the legacy of the [CETL] programme rests largely in individual staff' who were involved in the programme. This book, and the lifewide learning and education network that has grown around these ideas, are examples of how that legacy is still being realised and demonstrates that it might take a while for the full effects of an intervention to be revealed.

Last but not least I would like to thank my family. I am blessed with a large family and my wife and children never cease to amaze me as they tackle the challenges and discover opportunities in their lives. You have provided me with endless sources of inspiration and your stories about your lives have enriched my understanding of the core ideas explored in this book.

Preface to second edition

This second edition is a shortened version of the first which can be downloaded from https://www.lifewideeducation.uk/books.html It aims to provide a more succinct introduction to the idea of a learning ecology.

There is always a context to the things we do and there are two contexts for this second edition. The first relates to the development of my thinking. In the 3 years since the first edition was published I have refined ideas. While not wishing to re-write this book I wanted to include a refined conception of a learning ecology. A learning ecology is a related, connected and interdependent set of practices (thinking and doings) that the creator is weaving together in order to learn, so it is more accurate to define a learning ecology as an *ecology of practice for the purpose of learning*. This construct recognises that while learning may be the main purpose of an ecology of practice, in some situations, for example work, its main purpose is to perform. In such cases learning, although not the priority, might be an essential or necessary aspect of the performance. The second edition includes a new chapter on mapping ecologies of practice.

The second reason for producing this second edition is to make the book more accessible to a wider audience. While the first edition was aimed primarily at educators working in higher education, this shortened version has in mind the people who support learning and development in organisations that are not primarily educational. In October 2019 I participated in an event organised by the Harvard Learning Innovations Laboratory (LILA) that explored the idea of learning ecologies with Chief Learning Officers (CLO's). This edition is intended to be more relevant to their interests and needs.

Norman Jackson
October 7th 2019

Foreword

The idea of ecology is a rich concept. At once, it alerts us to certain features of the world: it intimates not just interconnectedness but also a complex system of interactions. It alerts us, too, to a fragility in a system: the connections between the elements that constitute an ecology might become impaired in some way. An ecology may be 'disrupted' (as we see here) and it might even fall apart. And the idea of ecology alerts us, also, to an interconnected setting having worthwhile properties, that it requires continual maintenance, and that human beings collectively have a responsibility in that direction. In this admirable book by Norman Jackson, we can see all of these elements in learning ecologies. We assuredly gain a sense of a complex of factors at work (in a learning ecology), a sense too of there being elements of serendipity in the way in which matters play out but also of there being spaces in which learning ecologies can be buttressed with wise actions and policies. Learning ecologies may falter but they can also be strengthened.

Among this book's many virtues, for me, three in particular stand out. *Firstly*, Norman Jackson provides us with a schema that depicts the 'components of an individual's learning ecology' (introduced in figure 2.5, p71). Nine components are identified - the past, present and emerging relationships, processes, contexts, a person, space, resources, affordances and the future. That these nine components interact with each other produces an unpredictable setting but one which is full of possibilities. *Secondly*, a learning ecology is particular to a person. We can speak quite naturally, therefore, of an individual's learning ecology. *Thirdly*, we gain a sense here that, while a person's learning ecology presents itself to some extent, so individuals can 'create their own ecologies for learning, development and achievement'. A learning ecology, in other words, is nothing less than a space in which individuals can open paths for their own renewal, and their unfolding. In the process, especially through reflection on the journey they are taking, individuals can forge a narrative of themselves. And it is perhaps in the personal stories that individuals tell of themselves in these pages that many readers will find the greatest value in this volume.

Key concepts in this book, it will be already evident, as well as ecology itself, are those of narrative, journey, learning and trajectory. So far as the idea of journey is concerned, in this book, we are treated not just to one journey but to multiple journeys. We have a journey in and around the very idea of learning ecologies, we have the personal journeys of individuals and we have the autobiographical journey of the author, Norman Jackson. And these journeys weave in and out of each other, so enriching the overall effect. But there is another term which is supremely significant: it is 'I'. For, as stated, a great virtue of this book is the space that it offers to a number of individuals – who Norman Jackson has encountered at some point in his own biography – to reflect on their own learning journey and to disentangle their own learning ecology. Just what were the elements (of the nine components) of the learning ecology that were significant? How did they cope with imminent disruption? How and which new opportunities opened and how did they take advantage of those opportunities?

It follows that in the aptly chosen title for this book – that of *'Exploring Learning Ecologies'* – each of the three terms is doing work. *'Ecologies'* is the central concept in this book, 'learning' is the particular location of the ecological perspective, and 'exploring' indicates the open-ended approach taken here. On the idea of ecologies, I would just reflect that much has been made and is still being made in the literature of the 'structure-agency' relationship, with different positions being taken over the nature of that relationship and the relative influence exerted respectively by social structures and by persons (or groups) as have 'agentic' powers for themselves. The idea of ecology, especially as deployed here by Norman Jackson, seems to me to offer a far superior way of understanding human beings in their environments. Rather than two forces being pitted against each other (structure and agency), here – in the idea of ecology – we can gain a sense of human beings as being embedded in a complex environment and as being able to play a part in affecting that environment.

The second term in the title, that of *learning*, is also treated to a particularly open-ended conception. For here, learning becomes a matter of a whole-life narrative, both through life and at any point in time. 'Lifewide learning' comes crucially into view here, reminding us that individuals possess learning moments and learning opportunities aplenty: contemporaneously, many individuals find themselves learning in organisations, in formal learning settings and informally. Sometimes, it is not easy to distinguish these learning moments. Informal learning can take places in educational institutions and quite structured learning can be experienced in apparently informal settings. (In an interview which I conducted, I remember hearing from a music student - dissatisfied with his formal programme of study - how he had set up a group in which music students could compose for, and receive critical comment from, each other.) The recognition of such 'lifewide learning' opens awkward questions for formal institutions of 'learning': just what kind of learning are *they* offering, to what extent might a student's extra-curricula learning (which may well be highly regulated and structured) be recognized, and to what extent do the different spaces of learning contribute to a harmony in an individual's own learning ecology?

In other words, there are large implications of this book for formal educational institutions. The idea of learning ecologies, as worked out here by Norman Jackson, turns out to be a radical concept. If taken seriously, it would call for a fundamental reappraisal of the curriculum so that it promotes an ecology for learning; and just that, I take it, is part of the thesis of this important book, not least in the proposal here for a 'co-curriculum'. Here, there would be recognition not just sporadically of a student's serendipitous learning moments and achievements but rather a recognition that a student has a total learning life, a learning ecology, in which the educational institution plays but a part.

The third and last term in the title, that of *exploration*, is evident both in the crafting of the book and in the personal narratives it contains. On one level, Norman Jackson is himself exploring the validity and value of the nine-fold schema of what it is to be a learning ecology; on the other hand, the individuals whose stories we encounter reveal themselves as engaged in a personal process of self-exploration. Ultimately, an ecology is lived. It is lived-in and lived-through, in all manner of meanings. And it gains special traction - if such a term may be used here - when an individual is able and is enabled to reflect upon themselves and reveal themselves, if only to themselves. That Norman Jackson has the authenticity and composure to share himself with us in these pages, as he reveals and reflects upon his own learning ecology, is a yet further strand in the making of this book. It is a book from which we can all learn.

Ronald Barnett
UCL Institute of Education
October 2016

CHAPTER 1
Journey With An Idea

Starting Point

In December 2005 I reached what I would eventually see as an inflection point in my life. I gave up a role I had enjoyed at the Higher Education Academy and became Director of the Surrey Centre for Excellence in Professional Training and Education (SCEPTrE) at the University of Surrey. In my new role I embarked on an entirely new career pathway that opened up many new affordances and adventures for professional learning and my own development.

The problem that I and my team invented for ourselves was something like, *'How can we add value to the educational opportunities and 1experiences that the university already provides?* We began a journey to explore the idea of 'a more complete education.' Our first step was to speculate that a more complete education would embrace the whole of a student's life while they were studying at university rather than only their academic experience. We used the terms *lifewide learning and development* to represent the learning and personal growth that would be associated with such an enterprise and *lifewide education* to describe the encouragement, support and recognition that an institution might provide to underpin learners' lifewide learning enterprises. We considered that a *lifewide curriculum* would offer a comprehensive framework for viewing the affordances for learning across a learner's life.

Between 2008-11, helped by students and colleagues from inside and outside the university, we engaged in many research studies, development projects, workshops, conferences and educational interventions to try to understand and give practical meaning to these ideas and what we learnt was documented in 'Learning for a Complex

World: a lifewide concept of learning, education and personal development (Jackson 2011a).

So began a journey that continues today: a journey through which I carry and develop my ideas, beliefs and important aspects of my own identity as a learner and human being. Gregory Bateson (1972 xxiv) got it right when he said, 'an explorer can never know what he is exploring until it has been explored': each step of the exploration lays the foundation for the next. From these explorations of lifewide learning a new awareness began to emerge that learning is an ecological phenomenon. We cannot participate in the world without interacting with it and our learning emerges from and through this process. The book sets out to explore the idea of learning ecologies. Ideas are at best provisional they are not particularly refined. The book should be viewed as an initial attempt to document and organise thoughts - lest I forget them. But I am happy to share them as readers may find some of my ideas useful and may wish to develop them for themselves.

Universal Challenge

How we prepare learners and enable them to develop themselves for a lifetime of learning and adapting to the continuous stream of situations they create or encounter in their lives, is to my mind the universal challenge facing higher education all over the world. Fundamentally it's a developmental challenge that we tried to capture in a picture (Figure 1.1) drawn on the wall of the SCEPTrE Centre.

For higher education teachers, the developmental challenge is associated with a question like, *'how do we prepare our students for an ever more complex world?'* This does not just mean preparing them for their first job when they leave university. It also means how do we prepare them so that they can deal with the many challenges, uncertainties, disruptions and emergent opportunities they will encounter over a lifetime of working, learning and living. The central proposition of this book is that teachers can do much to help learners prepare for these uncertainties if we adopt a more holistic, lifewide and ecological approach to learning and personal development.

Figure 1.1 Symbolic representation of the challenge of learning for a complex world

From a student's perspective the same challenge is embodied in questions like, *'How do I develop myself so I'm better prepared for the rest of my life?' What sorts of things do I need to learn, what sorts of skills, qualities, dispositions and values do I need to develop, and what sorts of experiences do I need to have in order to develop these things?'* Personal and professional development needs to be so much more than simply studying and learning an academic curriculum. My proposition is that by encouraging students to see their learning, development and achievement in a more holistic, lifewide and ecological way, they will be better prepared to engage with the uncertain world outside higher education wherever life takes them and whatever life throws at them.

The challenge for institutional leaders is embodied in the question, *'How do we change our university so that it is better able to meet the challenge of preparing learners for a very complex, uncertain and ever-changing world?'* This leads to further questions about environments, resources and people and their development. The challenge for institutional leaders is how to move from what is still a predominantly industrial provider-designed and directed model of higher education, to a more ecological, social, learner-designed and self-managed model of learning that is more appropriate for the complex world our students will inhabit when they leave university?

Ann Pendleton-Jullian (2015) talks about living and adapting to a 'white water world'. A world that we can only understand if we get into the water and learn how to read its unpredictable flow and navigate the hazards as we meet them. But you can't get into the water unless you have the skill and confidence to do this - so the issue becomes how do we develop enough agency and confidence to get into and cope with the white water world we inhabit. She describes living in the complex world is often about muddling through but that we can design our systems to enable us to muddle through as a strategy of choice. This idea resonates with me and I think our ecologies for learning and developing ourselves are the way in which we 'design our lives', in a conscious but flexible way, in order to muddle through towards the possible solutions for the problems, challenges and opportunities in our lives. So the challenge of how we develop ourselves for a complex, 'white water world' is the educational challenge this book is trying to address, and my argument is that higher education needs to enable learners to become more aware of their own ecologies for learning and more adept at creating them, if they are to sustain themselves through long, complex learning lives.

Lifewide Learning

Most people are familiar with the idea of lifelong learning - the learning we gain as we progress and develop through our lives from childhood and school, to college and university and through our career and beyond. Viewed at the scale of an individual's life course, for most people, formal education occupies only a relatively small part of their lifelong learning activity. The vast majority of their lifespan pre- and post-school, college and university, is conducted in the domain of informal experiential learning and personal development (Banks et al 2007:9): something that higher education has tended to ignore. It is ironic that one of the most important things higher education can do to prepare learners for learning in the rest of their lives is to pay more attention to the informal dimension of their learning lives while they are involved in formal study in higher education. By equipping them with tools and strategies that enhance their self-awareness, by encouraging attitudes that view life experiences as opportunities for learning and development and by valuing and recognising learning and development gained through life experience, universities and colleges can greatly enhance individuals' preparedness for learning through the rest of their life.

Figure 1.2 The lifelong and lifewide dimensions of learning

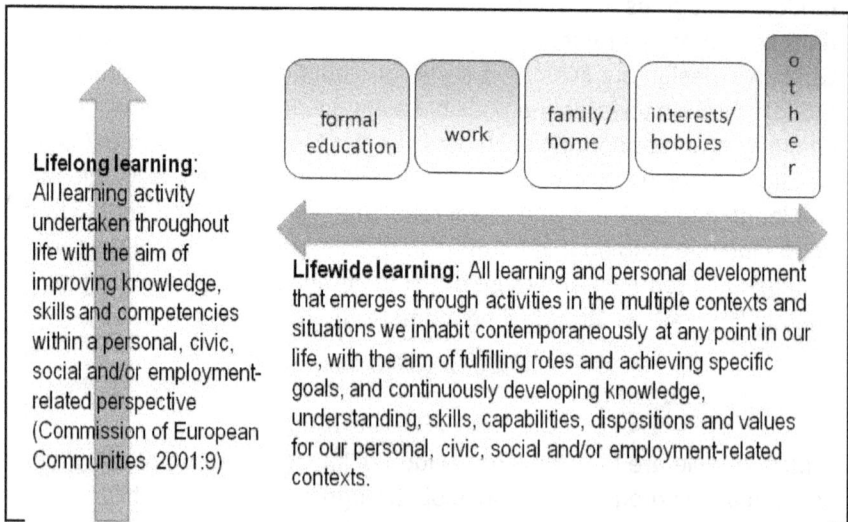

Lifelong learning: All learning activity undertaken throughout life with the aim of improving knowledge, skills and competencies within a personal, civic, social and/or employment-related perspective (Commission of European Communities 2001:9)

formal education   work   family/ home   interests/ hobbies   other

Lifewide learning: All learning and personal development that emerges through activities in the multiple contexts and situations we inhabit contemporaneously at any point in our life, with the aim of fulfilling roles and achieving specific goals, and continuously developing knowledge, understanding, skills, capabilities, dispositions and values for our personal, civic, social and/or employment-related contexts.

'Lifewideness' adds value to the 'lifelongness' dimension of learning (Jackson 2011c) by recognising that most people, no matter what their age or circumstances, simultaneously inhabit a number of different contextual spaces - like work or education, running a home, being a member of a family and or caring for others, being involved in a club or society, travelling and taking holidays and looking after their own wellbeing mentally, physically and spiritually (Figure 1.2). We also inhabit different psychological (cognitive and emotional) spaces within and across these physical spaces. We live our lives in this multitude of spaces each with its own temporal rhythm for the activities we perform so the *timeframe* of our lifelong journey and the multiple *spaces, places and timeframes* of day to day existence across our lives, intermingle and connect and as we accumulate and learn from our experiences, who we are and who we are becoming are the consequences of this complex intermingling and sense making.

In the different spaces we inhabit we make decisions about what to be involved in, we meet and interact with different people, have different sorts of relationships, adopt different roles and identities, and think, behave and communicate in different ways. In these different spaces we encounter different sorts of challenges and problems, seize, create or miss opportunities, and aspire to live and achieve our purposes and our ambitions. These different spaces also provide affordances for our creativity. Affordances that we can seize because we are motivated and inspired by our interests and the possibilities they hold. So the spaces that provide the contexts for our life enable us to create the meaning that is our life and develop the purposes and values that motivate or inspire us to lead a certain sort of life.

Lifewide learning is a powerful concept because it embraces all forms of learning and learning in all situations. The concept embraces learning in formal educational environments, work and all other social environments. It accommodates learning through directed (instructed) and self-managed activity, learning that is intentional or unintended, learning that is driven by our needs, interests and ambitions. To be a competent lifewide learner requires the awareness to recognise and take advantage of opportunities, and the will and capability to get involved in situations arising from these opportunities. It also requires the ability to think about and extract meaning and significance from experiences to use in future imaginings, decision making and activity. It is this consciousness that lifewide education seeks to develop: what Rogers (2003) calls learner conscious learning.

Learning Ecologies

Emerging from this exploration of the idea of lifewide learning and education is the idea that we create our own ecologies for learning, developing and achieving.

I first encountered the idea of learning ecologies when I read John Seely Brown's (JSB) influential paper 'Growing Up Digital: How the Web Changes Work, Education, and the Ways People Learn' (Brown, 2000). Here was one of the great contemporary thinkers working across the education business interface, providing insights into the way our learning lives were changing. He likened the way people were using the web to a new ecology of learning which he characterised as:

> an open, complex, adaptive system comprising elements that are dynamic and interdependent - a collection of overlapping communities of interest (virtual), cross-pollinating with each other, constantly evolving and largely self-organising. (Brown, 2000:19)

In his view, the learning ecology was an emergent property of the internet Web 2.0 as people with diverse backgrounds found and interacting with each other driven by the interests, passions and needs they shared.

> Let's consider a learning ecology, particularly one that might form around or on the Web.......consider the Web as comprising a vast number of "authors" who are members of various interest groups, many of which embody a lot of expertise in both written and tacit form.

7

Given the vastness of the Web, it's easy these days to find a niche community with the expertise you need or a special interest group whose interests coincide exactly with your own..............................
    informal learning often involves the joint construction of understanding around a focal point of interest, and one begins to sense how these cross-linked interest groups, both real and virtual, form a rich ecology for learning. (Brown 2000:19)

I admired the way JSB linked the conceptual points he was making to the real world through stories he told about the learning lives of real people: something I have tried to emulate in this book.

A second trigger for my thinking about learning ecologies emerged as I was editing 'Learning for a Complex World'. One of the contributors Maret Staron used the idea of learning ecologies in her exploration of how to support vocational education and training (VET) in the knowledge era. The conception she and her research team developed was called 'life-based learning' (Staron et al 2006, Staron 2011). This located the idea of learning ecologies in the everyday learning and enterprise of people. The ecological metaphor made sense to me and I knew that at some point I must explore the idea for myself.

A learning ecology metaphor is: dynamic - with ever-shifting relationships and interdependence informing learning and doing; adaptive - which is a key survival capability within an ecology; and diverse - a core requirement in knowledge work... It enables a move away from seeking the 'one way to get it right' to a more open *orientation* to learning - including *multiple* ways of working, learning and living. A learning ecology metaphor also invites us to work with apparently contradictory concepts that often challenge us, such as using an anticipative approach rather than a predetermined approach; using approximations rather than exactness; seeing fuzziness as a strength; and watching self-organisation happen even though there may be no explanation for where the self-organising pattern comes from. (Staron *et al.* 2006:26).

In 2011, I left the University of Surrey and decided to establish a social enterprise formed around the idea of lifewide learning and education. Not surprisingly I went through a significant transition as I left the professional environment I knew and moved into the uncertain space of creating my own environment for learning and achieving things I cared about. Over the years it has gradually dawned on me that I inhabit a perpetual liminal space (Turner 1967), a state of being 'betwixt and between'. No longer an academic in practice in a university but still clinging on to my academic identity and investing time and effort into maintaining it, but nevertheless uncertain of where my journey is taking me. Perhaps because of this uncertain and sometimes ambiguous mental, physical and virtual space I inhabit, I have become more conscious that it is essentially down to me to decide how I am going to spend my time and what I am going to try and achieve, at least in my professional domain.

The continuous challenge of motivating myself and constructing my own trajectories for learning has made me more aware of the 'ecological' relationships I have with my world. By that I mean that what and how I learn, perform and develop in all the different contexts and situations in my everyday life, feels more like a living, emergent, organic process involving me, my purposes and goals, and my relationships with the physical, virtual and social worlds I inhabit, rather than something that I plan, design and implement according to my plan. I feel I, and my learning, are part of an ecosystem which I help create and maintain but do not control and sometimes I'm pushed and pulled in all sorts of unforeseen directions. I am faced with abundant choice and the decisions I make take me in different directions but regardless of the decisions I make I seem to move in the general direction in which I want to go. The idea that I am part of an ecology and I help create my own ecology intuitively feels right so over the last few years I have thought about this idea in the context of my own life and the lives of people I know, and also tried to find out how others have thought about it too. So this book combines the result of my own experiments with myself in my everyday contexts and also the result of experiments that others have conducted with themselves in their own lives.

Once I embarked on my exploration I discovered a significant body of literature that engages directly or indirectly with the idea of learning ecologies which I have drawn upon throughout this book.

Threshold Concept

For me the idea of learning ecologies has been, and continues to be, a threshold concept.

> concepts, practices or forms of learning experience can act in the manner of a portal, or learning threshold, through which a new perspective opens up for the learner. The latter enters new conceptual terrain in which things formerly not perceived come into view. This permits new and previously inaccessible ways of thinking and practicing ....They provoke a state of 'liminality'–a space of transformation in which the transition from an earlier understanding (or practice) to that which is required is effected. This transformation state entails a reformulation of the learner's meaning frame and an accompanying shift in the learner's ontology or subjectivity. The latter tends to be uncomfortable or troublesome for, in many respects, we are what we know. (Land et al 2014:200).

Trying to understand a new concept is a struggle so I appreciate that the idea of learning ecologies may also be uncomfortable and troublesome for others who experience the idea as a threshold concept.

Learning from Nature

Every organism inhabits an ecosystem - the complex set of interactions among the residents, resources and habitats of an area for the purpose of living (Tansy, 1935). Every organism within an ecosystem develops a unique ecology for living/surviving and reproducing. This also applies to humans, but we differ from other organisms in the extent to which we collaborate to adapt existing ecosystems and make our own ecosystems and develop our own ecologies not simply to sustain and reproduce ourselves, but to make our lives more interesting, meaningful and fulfilling. Underlying our unique characteristics as an organism capable of destroying, modifying and creating ecosytems, is our need, desire and ability to learn and develop ourselves and our world through our learning.

Figure 1.3 A wonderful example of the ecology of life in the natural world. The coral reef is a highly dynamic and productive natural ecosystem. Each organism develops its own ecology for living within this ecosystem, Source: Coral Reef Image Bank an organisation that is supporting the fight to save coral reefs. The photo was taken by Warren Baverstock in the Gulf of Aqaba, Jordon.

Every organism has an environment: the organism shapes its environment and environment shapes the organism. So it helps to think of an indivisible totality of 'organism plus environment' - best seen as an ongoing process of growth and development (Ingold 2000:20).

Ingold's insight is more relevant for human's than any other organism. Look at the way we have modified the world around us through our physical and virtual constructions and reflect on how this affects our behaviour. From an environmental perspective it does not make sense to talk about the environment in which we are learning without reference to ourselves as the organism that is perceiving and interacting with the environment we inhabit in order to learn.

Formalised education tends to treat learning as something separate from the rest of life. Applying the idea of ecology to learning, personal development and achievement is an attempt to view a person their purposes, ambitions, goals, interests, needs and circumstances, and their social and physical relationships with the world they inhabit, as inseparable and interdependent. The idea of a learning ecology encourages us to think more holistically and more dynamically about the way we inhabit and relate to the world. It encourages us to think in a more holistic way about our life: how we connect up the moments in our lives to form experiences and achievements that mean something to us.

Growing out of this exploration is a belief that our ecologies for learning embrace all the physical and virtual places and spaces we inhabit in our everyday lives and the learning and the meaning we gain from the contexts and situations that constitute our lives. They are the product of both imagination and reason and they are enacted using all our capability and ingenuity. They are therefore one of our most important sites for our creativity and they enable us to develop ourselves personally and professionally in all aspects of our lives. If this belief is well founded then surely, our ability to create our own ecologies for learning and development must be one of the most important capabilities we need for sustaining ourselves, achieving our purposes and maintaining our sense of wellbeing in a complex, ever changing and often disruptive world. Yet to date, there has been little consideration of these ideas in the higher education curriculum or teaching and learning process. One of the purposes of this book is to encourage teachers and curriculum designers to explore and use the ideas in their own learning and teaching contexts.

Ecology of Human Development

Urie Bronfenbrenner, a developmental psychologist, introduced his ecological paradigm for interpreting human development in the 1970's in a series of papers. He argued:

> in order to understand human development, one must consider the entire ecological system in which growth occurs. This system is composed of five socially organized subsystems [A to E below] that help support and guide human growth. They range from the microsystem, which refers to the relationship between a developing person and the immediate environment, such as school and family, to the macro-system, which refers to institutional patterns of culture, such as the economy, customs and bodies of knowledge (Bronfenbrenner, 1994:1643).

Bronfenbrenner's (1994) conceptual framework highlights the nested nature of ecosocial systems. He identified four levels of interaction (Figure 1.4).

A) The *microsystem* contains the factors within someone's immediate environment, the day-to-day situations they encounter and their relationships and communications with the people they meet or interact with using communications technology. This is the level of our lifewide learning experiences, the level at which our individual situations and our responses to these situations matter to us and to the people they affect. This is the level at which we make decisions and plan what to do and how to do it and the level at which we act and use our capability (everything we can bring to a situation). This is the level at which we reflect on our experiences and the effects of our actions. This is the level of our learning ecology - the contexts, tools, technologies and resources we are able to draw upon to do what we have to do and the level at which we create new ecologies for learning, performing and creating new value.

B) The *mesosystem* encompasses the interrelations of two or more settings for example a learner's wider experiences in life and the university course they are studying. It involves people who have an interest in promoting and supporting learning. It is the level at which guidance and tools are provided to help learners fulfil the requirements for their programme. Appropriately organised activities in the mesosystem, for example a teacher designing and teaching a module, enables people to learn more and better in their own microsystem.

Figure 1.4 Interpretation of Bronfenbrenner's model of an ecosystem using higher education as the example of an ecosocial system

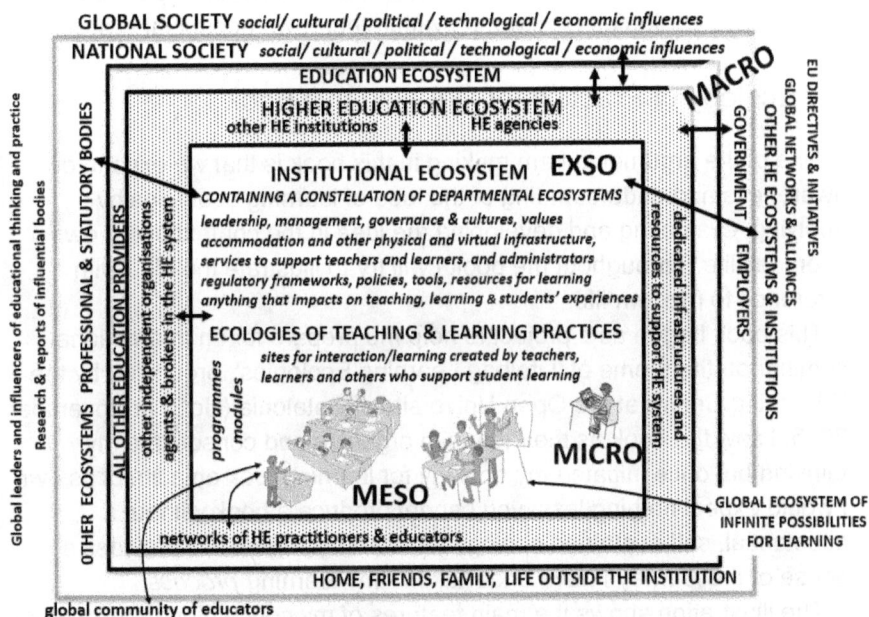

C) The *exosystem* consists of settings that do not involve us directly, but which contains events that impact on us. This is the ecological level at which, for example, an institution adopts and embeds certain policies that affect the way a programme is designed or determine in a broad sense the types of attributes the institution wants to see as an outcome of the education it provides.

D) The *macrosystem* is the wider society in which all other settings are nested including the socio-economic, cultural and political contexts. It includes government policies and strategies for promoting and supporting lifelong learning. This is the ecological level of the higher education system and the vision is that one day the system as a whole will embrace the idea of lifewide education.

The ecological paradigm requires us to be aware of all these levels of activity and interaction in an eco-social system but this book is primarily concerned with the microsystem and individual's personally constructed ecologies for learning within their own ecosocial system.

My Ecology of Practice for Creating this Book

One of the arguments I am making in this book is that we expand our awareness and understanding of the idea of learning ecologies by applying, evaluating and developing the idea in the context of our own everyday life. Throughout the book I will try to illustrate the idea with reference to my own life.

This book began as a project to help me prepare for an international seminar on the theme of 'Lifelong Learning Ecologies', organised by the E-learning Centre at the Open University of Catalonia (UoC) in November 2015. I saw the book as the means to organise and consolidate my thinking but once initiated my ecology for learning took on a life of its own. I would expect nothing less: you cannot produce a book without a substantial, self-sustained ecology for learning. Figure 1.5 provides a sense of the journey I have undertaken - my learning *process*.

The illustration shows the main features of my conception of an ecology of practice for learning and performing - the things I did to create the book. By imagining this book I was creating a new *affordance* in my life i.e. the imagined book invited me to create and engage in a process that would, I hoped, lead to its formation. This idea of imagination creating affordance and opportunity immediately suggests that we are tapping into the domain of creativity and I began to see how the ecologies we create in order to learn and achieve might be both a manifestation of our creativity and the means by which we are able to tap into and use our creativity.

Figure 1.5 The learning ecology I created for this book between August 20 and November 20th 2015

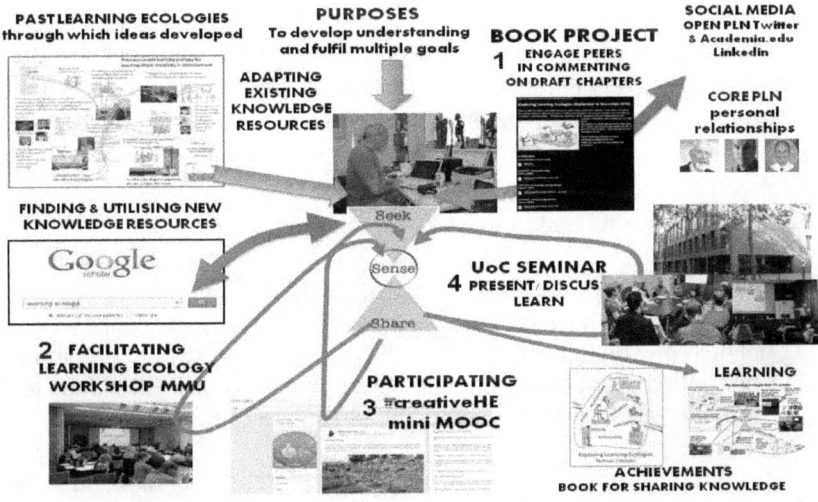

Twelve weeks separate the starting and end points in this visual representation of my learning ecology. At the heart of the learning ecology is the *space* I created for 'exploring the idea'. This *exploratory space* enabled me to think, inquire, imagine and develop ideas, write, share and discuss my ideas, and discover, read, think about and assimilate the ideas of other people.

In this self-determined process I drew on an abundance of information and knowledge *resources* in books, articles and blogs using a range of technological tools. I also drew on my own information resources primarily interview transcripts from research studies I made in the past. I utilised some of my existing *relationships*, for example my collaboration with illustrator Kiboko Camau enabled me to illustrate some of the ideas in pictures. I used some of my *existing relationships* to seek feedback on my ideas and used social media to expand my personal learning network for this purpose (see acknowledgements). At the heart of my process was the writing process through which I organised and curated my resources and tried to make sense of ideas. What emerged from this process - the tangible outcome - is the book, which constitutes the principal but not the only mediating artifact created through the process.

It all seems planned and logical when the words are laid out like this but the reality was very different. The ecological view of exploration is about determining your pathways as you explore them. You respond to what emerges through the process of exploring, and even then what has been explored only seems like a starting point for further exploration. I kept what I wrote when I began writing this chapter 3 months ago.

> Writing this one week into my 'journey with an idea', I am very uncertain as to how it will work out. But I have enough confidence and belief in myself to know that I have the basis for a strong learning and engagement process and if I do certain things to bring the ideas to life, the book will surely be brought into existence

This not only reflects the uncertainty of exploration but also the belief that by creating an ecology for learning the book would emerge through the process I continually created. This brings me to another important point about our ecologies for learning: they are also our ecologies through which we practice and achieve. They are the means through which we bring new order and material things into existence. In other words, they provide the affordance for our creativity. I believe that an important part of our creativity is being able to see affordance to achieve something which we value in the circumstances of our life. What is eventually created is original, at least to us but probably to the world, because 1) no one else cares about the thing we are trying to create like we do and 2) no one else can see this affordance because we are the only people who understand and can influence our life circumstances. The ecologies we create to learn, develop and achieve are therefore the vehicles for our creative self-expression and the means by which we bring new things into existence. Our ecologies are rooted in and grow from the circumstances of our lives, our needs, interests, responsibilities, purposes and ambitions and it is these things that also motivate us to utilise our personal creativity.

The *explorative* space (Law 2008) at the heart of my learning ecology for this book is liminal or transitional in nature - in the sense it represents the space 'betwixt and between' past ecologies through which I have developed understanding and the new representations and formulations that are provided in this book which must always be viewed as provisional. Which brings me back to the idea of a never-ending journey. Never ending because even when I hang my pen up so to speak, there will always be someone else to pick up the ideas and begin their own journey. That is the way ideas develop and how they travel through the minds and practices of people, across cultures and throughout the history of human existence. My ecology for learning is simply one small contribution to the ecology of learning involving all mankind.

Value of an Ecological Perspective

One belief I have come to hold is that our ecologies of practice for learning and performing are the environments within which our creativity emerges and flourishes. Expressed another way - they are the means by which we create new value in the world. So what is the potential value of the ideas explored in this book?

Awareness of the ecological nature of our existence

Gaining a footing in the landscape of learning ecologies begins with an appreciation that we are ecological beings and that we live out our lives in an ecological world: a world that is continually forming and reforming. This "world in formation" affects everything - people, social structures, material and virtual infrastructures, places, institutions and organisations, contexts, ideas, technologies and, of course, us.

The ecologies of practice we create for our learning and our performance are the vehicles for our thinking and feeling. Seeing ourselves as social organisms inhabiting a number of ecosocial systems across our everyday lives, encourages us to think about our relationships and interactions with the world in an ecological way. Underlying our unique characteristics as organisms conscious of our place and role in the world and the effects we have on the world, is our ability to think ecologically - to think with ecological awareness in a manner so brilliantly captured in Tom Chalkley's brilliant cartoon (Figure 2.3) used on the cover of the book. I believe that viewing learning as an ecological phenomenon will change our perception of ourselves and our relationship with the world around us.

Thinking ecologically about learning, practice, achievement, human development and creativity, is consistent with the worldviews developed by psychologist Clare Graves (1974) and used by organisational theorist, Frederick Laloux to develop the concept of a 'Teal organisation' (Laloux 2014). Teal is the colour used for the seventh stage in a seven-stage sequence of human development from hunter-gatherers (Beige) through tribes (Purple), warlord bands (Red), towns and cities (Blue), to a technological-industrial economy (Orange) and the human-oriented response of modern social democracies (Green). Humanity is at the threshold of the seventh (Teal) stage of human-social-organisational development that requires mankind to engage with a complex, interactive, interconnected and uncertain world. The complexity of the world we are now living in, requires an integration of the first six stages and emergence of a new higher level of consciousness. It is a higher level of awareness and understanding about our thinking, doing and learning in the complex world we inhabit that the idea of ecologies for learning and practice is seeking to develop.

Conceptual value

The concept of a learning ecology provides us with the means to visualise the dynamics of a complex self-determined and self-organised learning process and to appreciate how the different elements of the ecology - contexts, process, will and capability, relationships and resources, fit together. The concept provides a more holistic perspective on learning and development than is normally considered in higher education.

An ecological perspective conveys learning and personal development or growth as a living emergent process in which we continuously change our understandings and apply what we know in a continuous stream of new situations.

All too often in formal education, learning is viewed as the acquisition of prescribed codified (book or paper) knowledge in ways that are largely determined by teachers and educational institutions, the retention and abstract use of which is tested through assessment. The reality of everyday learning outside formal education is very different when needs, interests and curiosity drive individual's motivation and they have to find the resources they need to learn from the world around them. This process is necessarily less systematic, more intuitive and organic than the professionally designed and organised world of formalised education this perspective adds value to the way we might visualise and represent lifewide learning and education.

We have argued that learning is not simply scoring high on a test or assignment but should involve increasing possibilities for action in the world. Learning ...is about successfully participating as part of an ecosystem, an intentionally bound network [of affordances], and it fundamentally involves increasing opportunities for action in the world. Life-world expansion, [is] the ultimate trajectory of learning.... (Barab and Roth 2006:11)

The conceptual tool developed in chapter 2 (Figures 2.10 & 2.11) can be used to evaluate, from an ecological perspective, narratives of learning, development and achievement such as those presented in Chapters 3 and 7. Narratives reveal the motivations to create a process for learning and the agencies and capabilities used to form an ecology of practice. They all contain significant relationships through which learning was facilitated or gained and they reveal the self-regulatory nature of learning (chapter 6) as people respond to the situations they are in and the nature of the resources that were found, used and created. Similarly, Figure 7.7 provides a conceptual tool to facilitate the auditing of a curriculum to identify affordances that have been designed so that learners can create their own ecologies for learning.

Value to the learner

The value of an ecological perspective to a learner is that it encourages them to see learning as a process that connects them in a holistic way to other people and to their environment. In particular it enables them to appreciate the ways in which they engage with contexts by creating processes that utilise and develop relationships and resources in order to do what they have to do. The ecological perspective emphasises that this is a living dynamic process which they orchestrate and improvise according to the effects of their actions and the feedback they receive on the effects of their actions. Such an appreciation lends itself to the idea that we continually nurture and grow our learning ecologies rather than starting with a blank sheet of paper each time we have to learn something new. An ecological view of the relationship between learning, developing and living will also help prepare student learners for the ecological worlds of organisations they will inhabit when they progress into work and perhaps raise their awareness of the important link between their learning ecology and living a sustainable life. An ecological perspective will also encourage learners to trust their own instincts.

> We learn in relationship and in context - not in isolation. This is why our learning ecology is so important to us..... It tells us about our learning environment and interrelationships - with others, with our culture, work and with our educational institutions. And importantly, it tells us about our learning relationship with ourselves. We need to trust ourselves to establish a learning ecology that is meaningful, authentic and supportive of our growth and personal wellbeing (Staron 2013:7-8)

Value to a teacher or mentor

The value of an ecological perspective to a mentor or teacher is that it firstly encourages them to appreciate their own learning processes in a holistic way - to appreciate how they use and expand their own learning ecology to meet the challenges of new learning and development projects. Secondly, it might encourage them to view their own strategies for encouraging students' learning as an ecological process that they have designed and resourced and perhaps this may open up new possibilities for contexts, relationships and interactions as they appreciate that the learning ecologies of their learners extend beyond the classroom.

For mentors who are encouraging and supporting lifewide learning, an appreciation of a particular learner's learning ecology may enable them to help their mentees consider other affordances for learning and development in their lives as they engage with specific learning projects. After examining a learner's learning ecology a mentor might reflect on and share their perspectives (Staron 2011:154) on such matters as:

- Assumptions - whether their assumptions about learning help them fulfil their aspirations.
- Strengths - whether their strengths align with their values, goals and purpose.
- Reality - recognise that their reality (or context) is both 'internal' and 'external'.
- What works and what does not work - so that they focus on what works for them and helps achieve their dreams.
- Different perspectives - from which perspective they view their learning ecology, whether mental, emotional, physical and/or spiritual, or whether through a formal, informal or lifewide learning perspective, and what all this tells them about their relationship with their learning environment.

Value to higher education

Sustainability is perhaps the greatest challenge facing mankind. It permeates all aspects of our lives and manifests itself at all levels of society. 'One of the great challenges facing environmental educators is to prepare students to participate effectively as members of sustainable communities in an ecologically healthy world' (Capra 2007: 9). But, as Capra himself points out, this is not only a matter of environmental education it is of concern to everyone who is involved in education. By viewing our learning and development as an ecological process we have the potential to raise learners' awareness of the ecological world they inhabit and help create.

The ecology of our learning and how we develop it for particular purposes is key to knowing how to learn and to our ongoing process of learning how to learn. Knowing how to learn and continuing to develop capability for learning throughout our life (captured in the expression 'learning to learn'), are political as well as educational issues. In 2009 the EU Directorate General for Education and Culture commissioned a foresight study aimed at visualising the Future of Learning (Redecker et. al., 2011) the overall vision emerging from the study is that 'personalisation, collaboration and informal learning will be at the core of learning in the future. The central learning paradigm is characterised by lifelong and lifewide learning and shaped by the ubiquity of Information and Communication Technologies (ICT)'. The key words - personal, collaborative, informal and lifewide - have particular meaning when viewed through the lens of personal learning ecologies.

While the concept of personal learning ecologies does not yet feature in EU and UK educational policy the concept of *learning to learn* has. A report by an EU working group on 'Key Competencies' contains the following definition.

> 'Learning to learn' is the ability to pursue and persist in learning, to organise one's own learning, including through effective management of time and information, both individually and in groups. This competence includes awareness of one's learning process and

needs, identifying available opportunities, and the ability to overcome obstacles in order to learn successfully. This competence means gaining, processing and assimilating new knowledge and skill as well as seeking and making use of guidance. Learning to learn engages learners to build on prior learning and life experiences in order to use and apply knowledge and skills in a variety of contexts: at home, at work, in education and training. Motivation and confidence are crucial to an individual's competence.' (Education Council, 2006 annex, paragraph 5).

The idea of personal learning ecologies is simply another way of representing these essential orientations, dispositions and capabilities that we require in order to undertake significant learning projects. However, the idea of being able to create a learning ecology extends beyond *being aware of one's own learning process and needs* to *creating one's own processes for learning in order to meet those needs.* Furthermore, it adds to this abstract list of learning to learn characteristics in that it embeds them in the specific social contexts, relationships and situations that comprise everyday life and gives them meaning and significance in the contexts of our purposes, values and beliefs.

We live in a world beset by complex problems within which our affordances, if we can only see them, offer hope for the future. But seeing such affordances is dependent an ecological mindset: the complexities of the world can only really be understood in terms of an ecology of ideas (Bateson 1972 xxiii). An ecology that comprehends the way people and society interacts with the world and the way all sorts of stuff emerges from these interactions.

Perhaps the most important tasks for a university is its support, encouragement and facilitation for learners to think with sufficient complexity to understand the complex web of relationships that connect phenomenon and their causes and effects and to develop their awareness, understanding and capabilities to create and sustain their own ecologies for learning when confronted with such complexity. In other words, to think and behave in an ecological way. Such ways of thinking integrate the imaginative and associative and the critical and the analytical. They are by definition creative in so far as they will lead to connections that have not been thought of before and from such connections new solutions can be brought into existence.

Regardless of whether we look at the educational system or the institution as an ecosystem, or a teacher's ecology into which students fit themselves to learn, or a learner's own ecology for the purpose of learning - the idea of a learning ecology has value and it's worthy of exploration and application. I hope that in some small way, the ideas and illustrations
offered in this book will cause the reader to reflect on their own learning life and appreciate the wonderful complexity of their own ecologies for learning, development and achievement.

Value to organisations

The ecologies of practice for learning model provides a powerful heuristic with which to appreciate learning, performance and the creation of value as ecological phenomena. The ecologies of practice heuristic is a tool to aid reflection on how we learn, perform and create new value. There are similarities between this ecological model of learning through work with the thinking that underlies 'Workflow Learning' (Pradnam 2017 a & b). Workflow learning is a concept being used by some developers of organisational learning strategies to describe learning that is a necessary part of work. It's learning that is integral to performance and learning that has the potential to be utilized in future performances. It's also learning that has the potential to be shared with others. Mapping an ecology of practice for learning and performance reveals the dynamics and nuances of learning during the flow of work. Such a map reveals the particular contexts for learning, it reveals what is being learned, how, when and where its being learned, and even why it's being learned. Such a map has the potential to reveal the questions that drive inquiry and how we access the information and knowledge we need, and the tools we use or make to help us solve our problems. It shows the relationships we make and the spaces and places we inhabit. The map celebrates the resourcefulness and inventiveness of individuals as they weave together ideas in order to come to know how to create novel solutions. By developing awareness and capacity to think about learning, performance and the creation of new value as ecological phenomena, individuals build their understanding of how they, as unique individuals, learn and perform in these highly specific contexts, situations and circumstances within their own organisational ecosystems. The mapping of individuals' ecologies of practice for learning and performance could reveal exactly how an organisations tools and resources to support learning are used within an individual's workflow learning.

Value to me

All my books are autobiographical, in the sense that they were written at a particular point in my life and they reflect the roles I performed and the important ideas I was working with and trying to understand. This book is no different. It has grown from the circumstances of my life and it has formed around ideas that are important for me to try to understand. What makes this book different is the extent to which I have shared the details of my life as a means of exploring what these ideas mean in my own contexts and circumstances. In exploring and applying the idea of learning ecologies to my own life I have been able to make more sense of the way I have experienced my life and learnt from it. Furthermore, the more I work with the ideas the more I can appreciate the value of the heuristic device as a meta-framework for incorporating many different theories of learning and practice.

At a personal level I have used the ideas to help me understand and create meaning from my life and I hope that readers will also see the value in using these ideas to reflect upon and learn from their own lives. By sharing the narratives of my life I am hoping that you will see how I have come to know the things I am writing about. More than this, I hope that you can see the value in some of these ideas for your own practices.

CHAPTER 2
Conceptualising Ecologies of Practice for Learning and Performance

Introduction

> How do moments add up to lives? How do our shared moments together add up to social life as such? Every human action, all human activity takes place on one or more characteristic timescales. A heartbeat, a breath, a step, a spoken word takes but a moment; a stroll, a conversation extends over many such moments; and an education or a relationship may be a lifetime project. How do actions or events on one timescale come to add up to more than just a series of isolated happenings?" (Lemke 2000: 273)

These simple but profound questions caused me to think about my own life. Now in my 60's I have had many moments and considerable time to reflect on the many different ways in which I have added up and connected the moments I have experienced to give my life meaning. When I think about the moments that resulted in this book they were grown and connected within the process of imagining, searching, finding and connecting, analysing and synthesising existing ideas, writing and re-writing and creating illustrations to create this new artefact. But they also include many moments that were not directly related to the writing project, for example, participating in a workshop, seminar or mooc, perusing my Twitter feed, reading a newspaper, going for a walk, driving my car, watching TV, being involved in things that are family related or any number of things, because particular thoughts that emerged in these situations were interpreted and given meaning by me in the context of producing this book. The book is the tangible expression of a process of purposefully connecting, integrating and articulating thoughts and actions that emerged from many moments of my life - 'my journey with this particular idea'.

Within the book I describe many processes through which I and others have connected up some of the moments in our lives. Our life is full of such processes that, according to Lemke (2000), provide the fundamental unit of analysis to represent the dynamics in the complex social ecosystems we inhabit. I would like to refine this idea to suggest that our processes are the core element of what I am calling an ecology that connects us in a fundamental way to the environment in which the moments of our life unfold. We connect and give meaning to streams of moments through the stories we tell about how things came to be. How we became a certain sort of person doing particular things in particular ways and in particular contexts and circumstances. Our narratives explain to ourselves and others, how the processes we create to journey through life, connect, combine, integrate and make sense of our moments to give purpose and meaning to our life. The ecologies we create to engage with the situations we encounter or create enable us to experience the world and through these experiences we learn and become different.

> every experience enacted and undergone modifies the one who acts and undergoes, while this modification affects, whether we wish it or not, the quality of subsequent experiences. For it is a somewhat different person who enters into them (Dewey, 1938/2015: 35).

Dewey understood learning to be a phenomenon that emerged through a process that takes place as a person interacts with their social and material world. The learning that emerges through such interactions was not seen as static cognitive effect, rather it was understood as being dynamically constructed as the person transforms themselves through their thinking and actions in particular contexts and circumstances.

Our ecologies for engaging with our world contain ourselves and what we can bring to particular situations - knowledge and skill, the will that motivates us to try, try harder and to persevere when the chips are down, qualities like honesty, empathy, compassion and integrity, and our ability to think - perceive, reason, imagine and reflect. Our processes are sites for action, not just any action but actions that are judged to be appropriate and likely to be effective for the situation. And they are sites for real-time reflection and evaluation on the effects of our actions so that we can change intended actions if necessary. Clearly the processes we create are the vehicles for our everyday practices - actions and behaviours that enable us to perform in particular ways in order to achieve particular things in a particular environment.

Identifying the features of an ecology of practice for the purpose of learning

I have been using the term 'learning ecology' but a more accurate term for what we are exploring is an *ecology of practice for the purpose of learning and performance*, since we are trying to comprehend a related and connected set of practices (thinking and doings) that the creator is weaving together in order to learn and perform. What might such an ecology of practice look like? What is its tangible form and expression?

One way of exploring the form of an ecology of practice for learning is through the narrative of a significant learning experience like 'learning to drive a car'. This is a project that most adults undertake at some point in their life in order to transform themselves from someone who cannot drive to someone who can (Figure 2.1)

The process begins when the person decides they want to learn to drive *(motivation/will)* and take and pass the test to demonstrate proficiency (*the proximal goal*). They will probably have a rough time scale in mind e.g. a few months, but the end point will be adjusted as the learner engages with the challenge and monitors their own progress.

Before they start their learning project, they have significant implicit knowledge derived from *past* experiences. They have been driven along roads before and are broadly familiar with what is involved in driving a car. They are likely to have a level of awareness about how people and traffic behave on roads and they may have familiarity with signs and what they mean. All this is useful background knowledge that provides a foundation on which to construct new understanding.

As their learning project is initiated the learner must perceive the *affordances* (opportunities for action) available to them in their immediate environment in order to learn and develop their knowledge and practical skills and road awareness.

Figure 2.1 Ecology of practice created by a person in order to learn how to perform i.e. drive a car and pass the driving test.

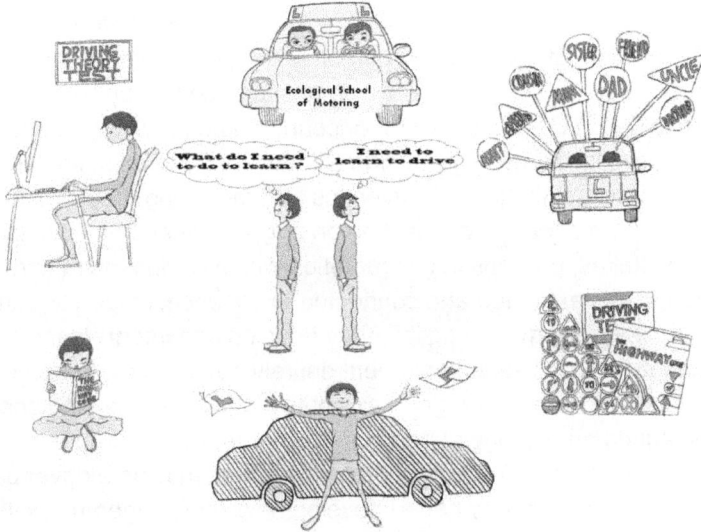

The person, often with parental encouragement and support, creates a *process* containing numerous activities drawing on the affordances in their physical and social environment. They may be fortunate to have access to essential resources, like a car, perhaps a book on 'how to pass the driving test' or more likely on-line resources that prepare the learner for the theory test.

They will probably pay for driving lessons given by an experienced instructor and these will be supplemented with driving experiences accompanied by relatives and / or friends who have passed the driving test. Through this they will learn about insurance. They may drive several different cars on lots of different roads under different conditions *(places)*. Some things can only be learnt in particular places: to learn to drive requires a person to place themselves in the places (roads) that have been designed for people to drive in order to develop their awareness and skills.

The period of preparation for the driving test may last several months and perhaps involve 50-100 hours of *time* and *effort* (physical, intellectual and emotional) which might be distributed over several months or even years. Throughout this time the person is developing an 'epistemology of practice' (Eraut, 1994) much of which has to become semi-automated if we are to be successful i.e. when encountering a (driving) situation we: need to assesses it quickly, decide what action(s) to take, implement the action(s), assessing their effectiveness and modifying them when necessary and afterwards reflecting on our performance to identify and rectify mistakes, perhaps in conversation with a driving instructor!

Through this extended and connected experience, knitted together through their ecology of practice, they develop and integrate their knowledge and skills and implement entirely new driving practices.

This scenario provides a good example of a learner creating and implementing an ecology of practice in order to learn how to perform. The ultimate aim of the ecology is to perform competently as a driver but in order to achieve this they had to develop new knowledge and skill. Their learning and competence emerged through their purposeful interactions with their environment and the material things in it. Learning and development progress along a *trajectory* from little or no knowledge and capability to a level of capability where they can be trusted to drive safely under the conditions and situations they have experienced. There is no doubt that the person who emerges from such an ecology is different to the person who entered it.

The narrative provides a flavour of what an ecology of practice for learning and performing might contain. In the following sections we examine in each of the elements of an ecology of practice for learning and performance in more detail. All must be woven together by the creator if an ecology of practice is to achieve their goals.

Purpose(s)

Creating an ecology of practice for learning takes time, effort and skill so there has to be a good reason for doing it. The reason(s) for its existence are the motivational force for its creation. These may take the form of one or more explicit objectives or be more nebulous e.g. to explore something. Furthermore, short term proximal goals may be nested within longer term distal goals. The network of reasons for doing something influences the will of someone to initiate an ecology of practice and their determination to sustain it. The purpose of purpose is to give meaning and relevance to the actions that will unfold within the ecology of practice.

In the illustration of learning to drive the link between learning and performing is clear: the person has to learn in order to perform as a safe and competent driver. In other examples of an ecology of practice a person may already know how to perform in a particular situation but they need to learn in order to perform in the most effective way. In such cases learning is a necessary bi-product of performance rather than the dominant goal.

Context(s)

Contexts are the circumstances that form the setting for an event, experience, practice, idea or any real or imagined thing in terms that can be understood. Contexts provide meaning for our thinking, including our imaginings, our doings and our learning that emerges from our doings. Luckin (2008:52) describes the context as: 'a situation defined through over time.... in the case of a learner's context we can describe it as 'a situation defined by the social interactions that are themselves historically situated and culturally idiosyncratic.'

Savin-Baden (2008) defined the context for our learning as involving the interplay of all the values, beliefs, relationships, frameworks and external structures that operate within a given learning environment. Contexts are situational and usually social: we are in some way inhabiting them. They can be problems, challenges, opportunities, our work, our programme of study, our doing a jigsaw puzzle with your child.

Barron (2006) applied the idea of personal learning ecologies in her study of how young people developed their digital literacies. Her research discovered that individuals developed their digital fluency through many different activities in many different places and circumstances (contexts) inside and outside school. Her definition of a learning ecology emphasises the happenings and doings in that contextual space.

the set of contexts found in physical or virtual spaces that provide opportunities for learning. Each context is comprised of a unique configuration of activities, material resources, relationships and the interactions that emerge from them' (Barron 2006: 195).

This conceptualisation of a learning ecology resonates with Lemke's notions of the micro-ecologies of people participating in social activity 'persons-in-activity.' The social-cultural arrangement of practices and artifacts and the ecosystem of environmental processes are treated as a single unified system, and the semiotic practices are also regarded as being material processes. The meanings they generate play an essential role in the overall dynamics of the system (Lemke 1997).

Context provides us with certain sorts of knowledge because the things that happen and the knowledge that emerges is situated in that context. Learning ecologies demand that we become contextual knowers.

Contextual knowers construct knowledge claims internally, critically analysing external perspectives rather than adopting them uncritically. Increasing maturity in knowledge construction yields an internal belief system that guides thinking and behaviour yet is open to re-construction given relevant evidence. Cognitive outcomes such as intellectual power, reflective judgement, mature decision making and problem solving depend on these epistemological capacities. (Baxter Magolda 2004b:9)

Time

Our ecologies of practice connect us to our past and all the experiences we have and the things we have learned so that we might draw upon these in our present which itself continually unfolds. And the ecologies of practice we are enacting in our present will become our past with potential to connect to ecologies of practice we create in our future.

Through our ecologies of practice we are able to connect different spaces, contexts, resources, relationships and situations that exist more or less simultaneously and in our past. In this way they form the bridges between past, present and future contexts and situations that we encounter or create in our lives.

Each scale of organization in an ecosocial system is an integration of faster, more local processes (i.e., activities, practices, doings, happenings) into longer-timescale, more global or extended [processes].... It is *relative timescale* that determines the probability and intensity of interdependence....and it is the circulation through the network of *semiotic artefacts* (i.e., books, buildings, bodies) that enables coordination between processes on radically different timescales. In this view the two fundamental questions for analyzing the dynamics of ecosocial systems–and human activities within them–are: What processes, what kinds of change or doing, are characteristic of each relevant timescale of organization of the system/ network? and, How are processes integrated across different timescales? (Lemke 2000: 275).

Our ecologies for learning connect our moments and the thoughts and actions undertaken in such moments and organise them into more significant experiences and networks of thinking and action, through which we can begin to see new patterns of understanding and learning. Comprehending such patterns give us confidence to act in the world and plan our future actions. Our learning ecologies embrace all manner of activities each with their own rhythm of time (Barnett 2011:25) some measured in minutes or hours, others extending over days, weeks, months or even years.

Our learning ecologies - part planned and deliberate, and part intuitive, accidental and opportunistic, result from interactions with the world around us guided by a sense of purpose that has meaning to us. How we think and act reflects our experience, confidence, will and capability. Our own agency and capability is an essential component of the processes we create and the process of imagining, designing, constructing and implementing our learning ecology changes us and our future actions as new ideas and understandings emerge, relationships form and evolve, objects, tools and other artifacts are made, used and invested with meaning, and new opportunities for learning emerge from the circumstances of our lives.

> The most amazing feature of developmental processes is that each step along a developmental trajectory changes the way the system interacts with its environment at the next step. There are no "shortcuts" in development; you must pass through each step in order to be prepared to take the next one because at each step you become a dynamically different system. Different dynamical possibilities are open to you. You have also extended your trajectory to a new timescale on which there are emergent phenomena, both in you and in your interactions with a larger-scale environment. (Lemke 2000: 284).

Our learning ecologies pervade every aspect of our life and are associated with every social interaction. They underlie the contexts we call family, work, study, hobbies, travel and any other significant activity we engage in that involves us in interacting with our environment and the people in it. We create and develop our learning ecologies for particular purposes. The ecologies we develop to accomplish our work will be different to those we create for our hobbies and interests, and those we create with our families and friends. But there may well be connections across these ecologies and things we learn in one learning ecology are available for application in another.

From the above it would seem that our self-created learning ecologies are an essential component of the way we learn and develop outside settings where our learning ecologies are either determined for us or severely constrained. They are the means by which we connect, orchestrate and integrate our lifewide and lifelong experiences and the learning and development we gain from them. They are the means by which we are able to transfer and connect our thinking, learning and development across the contexts that constitute our lives.

Our time is a resource. When we commit to developing an ecology for learning we are committing our time which means we cannot spend that time doing other things. Similarly, when we get involved in other people's ecologies for learning we are giving them our time.

Content, scale and scope

The content of a learning ecology comprises all the things that are within the space created for learning (e.g. Figure 2.1). These include: the person or people who create it, and all the people who are involved; the materials, tools and technologies used, the ideas, information and knowledge resources that are used or created in the process; the process(es) themselves and the thinking and activities that underlie the processes; the environments, spaces and places in which learning takes place, the mediating artifacts that are produced and used, and the products and performances that both demonstrate and effect learning (the learning trajectory).

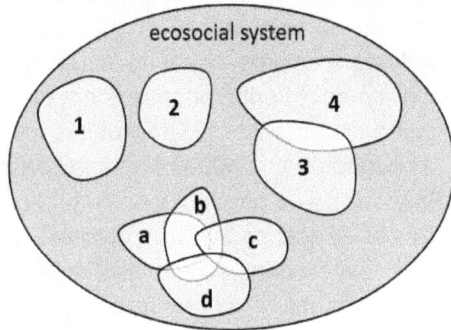

Figure 2.2 Our learning ecologies are located within our broader ecosocial system. They may be 'distinct' (1&2), formed around a particular project, or connected (3&4). They may also be integrated with the learning ecologies of others (a-d).

Our ecosocial system spans the length and breadth of our lives and embraces all the people, contexts, situations, conversations and other social interactions that make up our lives. Our learning ecologies are located within and emerge from our unique ecosocial system (Figure 2.2).

Affordance

An ecological perspective of learning argues that we cannot separate our learning from the physical social-cultural environment in which we are learning.

From an ecological perspective, the learner is immersed in an environment full of potential meanings. These meanings become available gradually as the learner acts and interacts within and with this environment. Learning is not a holus-bolus or piecemeal migration of meanings to the inside of the learner's head, but rather the development of increasingly effective ways of dealing with the world and its meanings (van Leir 2000: 246)

Affordance is a key property of an ecology of practice for learning. It can be found in any of aspect of the components of the ecology. The idea was developed by Gibson (1977, 1979, 1982, 1986) to explain a relationship between an object or an environment and an organism, that affords the opportunity for that organism to perform an action. For example, in the human environment, a floor affords walking upon, a cup affords grasping, water affords drinking and a bed affords lying and the possibility of sleeping.

Affordances provide a way of seeing the world as a meaning laden environment offering countless opportunities for actions and countless constraints on actions. The world is full of potential, not of things.

The meaning or value of a thing consists of what it affords (Gibson, 1982: 407). The original definition (Gibson 1979) described affordance in terms of all actions that are physically possible: *action possibilities* latent in the environment, objectively measurable and independent of the individual's ability to recognize them, but always in relation to agents and therefore dependent on their capabilities.

An *affordance* is an action possibility formed by the relationship between an agent and its environment ...... (Nye and Silverman 2012). It resides neither in the learner nor in the object, technology or environment, but in the relationship between the two. (Williams et al 2008:17)

Greeno (1994) suggested that affordances are "preconditions for activity," and that while they do not determine behavior, they increase the likelihood that a certain action or behaviour will occur. Shaw, Turvey, & Mace (1982) introduced the term effectivities, the abilities of the agent that determined what the agent could do, and consequently, the interaction that could take place.

If an affordance is a possibility for action by an individual, an effectivity is the dynamic actualisation of an affordance......an effectivity set constitutes those behaviours that an individual can..produce so as to realise and even generate affordance networks. When an individual has a particular effectivity set, he or she is more likely to perceive and interact with the world in certain ways–even noticing certain shapes of networks that are unavailable to others (Barab and Roth 2006:6)

Perception and action were co-determined by the effectivities and affordances, which acted 'in the moment' together (Gibson 1986): the agent directly perceives and interacts with the environment, determining what affordances can be picked up, based on his effectivities. This view is consistent with Norman's (1990) theory of "perceived affordances," which emphasizes the agent's perception of an object's utility as opposed to focusing on the object itself. It is the notion of perceived affordances that has particular value to a person who is scanning their environment to identify affordances that they can utilise in their learning ecology.

A *perceived affordance* ....requires an agent to be aware of the affordance, either through direct perception or experience.... a perceived affordance is primarily a relationship between an agent's cognition and the environment
A *perceived affordance* describes a potential for action: in the case of an interaction between a person and their environment the perceived

capacity of an object to enable the intentions of the person. (Nye and Silverman 2012).

The concept of affordance is fundamental to the concept of an ecology of practice for learning. It relates individuals situated in their physical, social, emotional and virtual environments trying to comprehend, resolve problems, challenges and perplexities, and make the most of opportunities, by finding and utilising affordances that their environment provides. Or perhaps by expanding or adapting their environment in order to create and access new affordances.

By realising the action possibilities in their environment, the individual is utilising and developing their effectivities which can be utilised in future situations. In this way we develop our awareness and capabilities for acting and learning ecologically. By improving our effectivities we are better able to sustain ourselves in the world.

A narrative to explain affordance in an unfolding ecology of practice

While I was writing this chapter I was invited to participate in a mini mooc on the theme of Creativity for Learning in Higher Education. The short 'course' was completely on-line using Web 2.0 technologies. My first task was to make sense of the technologies that were being used. I made a map to help me understand the functions and purposes of the different platforms we were using.

The designers of these spaces had created a range of affordances for each piece of technology (*designed affordances*). In addition, participants who had used the platforms had probably discovered further affordances beyond the intentions of the designers (*discovered affordances*). From my initial starting point, with little experience of some of the platforms, I could only appreciate a small number of the possible affordances that were available (*my perception of affordance*). By watching and learning from other participants I was able to extend my understanding of how the technologies complemented each other.

After several weeks of participating in the course and experiencing how the technologies were used by others, I had a much better understanding of the potential for action that was available in these platforms (*realised affordance*). My ignorance had been replaced with knowing gained through the experience of intentionally using the platforms in a social learning process. I had developed my capability or *effectivity* to use the technologies in the situation I was involved in. I had learnt something about the affordances in the technology and the insights and capability I have gained can be drawn upon in future situations. In fact, before the course had finished I used the same platform to begin crowdsourcing content for an issue of Lifewide Magazine. This story illustrates how gaining experience through participation, we can see and exploit affordances in our environment that hitherto had not been recognised.

Spaces

Siemens (2007:63) defined a learning ecology as *'the space in which learning occurs'.* According to Siemens (ibid 62-3) learning ecologies are:

- Adaptive, dynamic and responsive - the ecology enables (or more specifically fosters) adaptation to the needs of the agents within the space.
- Chaotic - diversity generates chaos which is created in dynamic environments and systems
- Self-organising and individually directed - organisation occurs through the ongoing interactions of elements within the ecology
- Alive - features continual changes, newness, activity
- Diverse - with multiple viewpoints and nodes (often contradictory) exist
- Structured informality - structure enables ongoing diversity of openness not restricting development. Minimal control is required to function but no more
- Emerging - the space itself is evolving and adaptive.

But the space of a learning ecology is not a particular sort of physical space like a classroom, office, cafe or garden - it can embrace many sorts of physical spaces simultaneously, rather it is what Savin-Baden (2008: 8-9) describes as a learning space.

the kinds of spaces I am referring to include the physical spaces in which we place ourselves, but what is important, vital even, about learning spaces is that they have a different kind of temporality and different ways of thinking.....[in such spaces]...... flows of capital, information, technology, organizational interaction, images, sounds and symbols go from one disjointed position to another and gradually replace a space of locales 'whose form, function and meaning are self-contained within the boundaries of physical contiguity' (Castells, 1996: 423). Space is inseparable from time; it is 'crystallized time' (Castells, 1996: 411). What I am referring to is not merely about managing time, finding time or rearranging one's day....... Instead I am arguing for locating oneself in spaces where ideas and creativity can grow and flourish, spaces where being with our thoughts offers opportunities to rearrange them in spaces where the values of being are more central than the values of doing. Learning spaces are often places of transition, and sometimes transformation, where the individual experiences some kind of shift or reorientation in their life world. Engagement in learning spaces does not necessarily result in the displacement of identity.........but rather a shift in identity or role perception so that issues and concerns are seen and heard in new and different ways. Learning spaces might also be seen as liminal in nature in that they can be seen as betwixt and between states that generally occur because of a particular need of an individual to gain or create a learning space.

Liminal spaces

Savin-Baden's final point is particularly important. We create our ecologies to learn in order to cope with and traverse the liminal spaces we encounter.

Learning ecology spaces are also liminal spaces. The inquiring space induces a state of 'liminality' (Land et al 2014).
– a space of transformation in which the transition from an earlier understanding (or practice) to that which is required is effected. This transformation state entails a reformulation of the learner's meaning

frame and an accompanying shift in the learner's ontology or subjectivity (Land et al 2014:200)

These authors (2014: 201) suggest that the liminal state performs a progressive function which begins with the encountering and integration of something new. This subsequently entails recognition of shortcomings in the learner's existing view of the phenomenon in question and an eventual letting go of the older prevailing view. At the same time this requires a letting go of the learner's earlier mode of subjectivity. There then follows an envisaging (and ultimate accepting) of the alternative version of self which is contemplated through the threshold space. Meyer and Land (2005: 380) characterise liminality as 'a "liquid" space, simultaneously transforming and being transformed by the learner as he or she moves through it.

Perplexity, uncertainty and ignorance motivate us to act. The ecologies we create are the means we invent to traverse such troublesome spaces. At the heart of such ecologies are the concepts of liminality, transition, adaptation and transformation.

Liminal states and spaces are also induced when we encounter serious disruptions in our life either through circumstances that are not of our own making or intentional acts that take us into contexts and challenges we do not understand.

Space for exploring, inquiring & adventuring
Human affordance includes the potential to create mental spaces for the consideration of ideas, objects and phenomena. Our learning ecologies provide spaces for exploration - for venturing into territory that is not well known or understood. In these spaces we have to deal with uncertainty, ambiguity and perplexity as we encounter things we have not encountered before, 'an explorer can never know what he is exploring until it has been explored' (Bateson 1972 : xxiv),

We often don't know what we need to know when we start a significant new learning project so we have to engage in what John Dewey (1922 cited in Cook and Brown 1999) called 'productive inquiry': finding out what we need to know in order to do the things we need to do. Our ecologies for learning create new spaces for inquiring which Dewey considered to be 'the controlled or directed transformation of an indeterminate situation into one that is so determinate in its constituent distinctions and relations as to convert the elements of the original situation into a unified whole.' The ability to pose and form good questions to help us understand an indeterminate situation and be able to find things out in order to make good decisions about what to do, is an essential capability to be developed if we are to help learners become integrative thinkers and doers. Productive inquiry can be applied to all situations : from scientific investigations to situations that crop up in our daily lives. It is a capability we need in all working contexts. 'Productive inquiry is not a haphazard, random search; it is informed or disciplined by the use of theories, rules of thumb, concepts and the like. These tools for learning are what Dewey understands the term knowledge to mean and using knowledge in this way is an example of that form of knowing which Dewey called productive inquiry' (Cook and Brown 1999:62).

Space for imagining & reflecting
One of our greatest assets as a human being is to be able to create mental spaces for us to think about our past experiences and interpret and draw meaning from the memories we reconstruct. Our ecologies for learning provide the mental space for us to look back on the past and imagine possibilities for the present grown from experiences of the past. We use the term reflection to describe this process but this term seems to conjure up faithful reproductions of situations remembered. But we have the wonderful ability to imagine and ask 'what if,' and generate entirely new possibilities from situations we have experienced. This enables us to create mental models that help us make good decisions and plans about what to do. Through our imagination space we can generate ideas, connect them to all sorts of things, select and synthesise particular thoughts and create entirely new perspectives and possibilities.

Spaces for conversation & discussion
Learning ecology spaces are also dialogic spaces within which conversation and discussion can take place between an individual, themselves and the people involved in their learning ecology. Savin-Baden (2008:51) describe such dialogical spaces in these terms.

> dialogic spaces .... encompass the complex relationship that occurs between oral and written and the way, in particular, that written communication is understood by the reader. Thus, dialogic spaces transcend conceptions of dialogue, which is invariably conceived as the notions of exchange of ideas, and dialectic as the conception of transformation through contestability. This is because dialogic spaces encompass written and verbal communication with others and one's self, but also dialogic spaces have at their core the sense that through encountering and engaging with dialogic spaces (within which conflict and disjunction is likely) transformation will result.

Within our learning ecologies we create spaces for conversation with others and ourselves that are relevant for a particular purpose, goal or learning project.

Smooth and striated learning spaces
Deleuze and Guattari (1987) offer another perspective on space that we can usefully weave into our understanding of learning ecologies. They argue for smooth and striated cultural spaces. For them the notion of smooth space is one of becoming, it is a nomadic space where the movement is more important than the arrival. Smooth learning spaces are open, flexible and contested, spaces. In such spaces learners create their own stance toward knowledge(s). The learning space is not defined, but becomes defined by the creator of the space. In the context of a learning ecology this is the space in which individuals imagine and implement their own learning as autonomous, self-regulating and self-directing individuals.

In contrast, striated learning spaces are characterized by a strong sense of organisation and boundedness. Learning in such spaces is epitomised through course attendance, defined learning places such as lecture theatres and classrooms, and with the use of (often set) books. Savin-Baden (2008: 13) suggests that there is a strong sense of conformity, of authorship, of clear definition, of outcomes, of a point that one is expected to reach in such spaces. For example, students will be expected, to take notes in lectures and learn and subsume disciplinary practices, rather than challenge them.

Therefore, spaces created within an ecology for learning are smooth cultural spaces: an ecological space in which a person can perceive and explore affordances for learning in their own lives. But, according to Savin-Baden (2008) this poses problems for the striated cultural spaces of education, in which people engage in formal learning.

> smooth learning spaces are often seen as suspect, or as privileged spaces for the undisciplined, and to be partisan about such activity can set up challenges to other academics about what counts as legitimate learning space. However, this is not to say that striated spaces cannot contain smooth spaces, yet when they do this presents difficulties about the relationship between the two spaces and the relative value of each. (Savin-Baden 2008: 14)

An ecological view of learning in education provides a framework within which both of these conceptual spaces can flourish.

Spaces for creating, finding/using our voice

All the spaces in our ecologies for learning provide affordance for seeing the world as we experience it and as we imagine it. Providing us with new sorts of information and knowledge with which to make better or different senses of what it means. Our ecologies for learning contain within them the possibility space for synthesising, integrating and reconstructing our understandings and feelings to make entirely new interpretations and meanings by combining and connecting ideas. Our spaces for creating and making are intellectual, emotional, physical and virtual. Affordance is embedded in all of our contexts and our relationships with people, tools and the resources we use. It is the way we perceive our situations that determines how we respond to them and whether they provide us with the challenge or opportunity for creative action and the 'mediums' for creative self-expression. For an artist the medium includes his artistic expression (drawing, painting, sculpture, performance, film or other art form) and it includes the materials and tools he uses to create his art. For a writer his medium for self-expression is the words he writes with a pen and paper in a notebook (old technology) or perhaps using a computer to write a blog (newer technology). For a performer like a footballer, his medium is the football field and ball, and his creativity is expressed in playing the game of football which enables him to interpret and interact with the ebb and flow of the game to utilise his talents and skills to play football.

If we want to live a fulfilled and meaningful life finding affordance for creative self-expression is an important and continuous search through all the circumstances and situations in our life. Our creativity flourishes when we inhabit the particular contexts and challenges in which we can fully utilise our aptitudes, abilities, talents and enthusiasm for doing something, because we care deeply about what we are doing and are motivated to perform in a committed and inspired way to achieve things we value. It happens when we feel what we are doing is in tune with our purposes and our values.

Henry Thoreau wrote, "Most men lead lives of quiet desperation and go to the grave with the song still in them." The song of which Thoreau is speaking is not music, it's the unexpressed authentic self, the creative essence of infinite Intelligence -- life itself -- seeking an outlet..... [But] it requires courage to "sing our song" whatever it may be. That courage will indeed take us to the very edge of our comfort zone, that dark place called fear: fear of rejection, fear of failure, and perhaps, even fear of success. (Jones 2013)

But we don't have to be an artist to feel like this we can find and inhabit a context or situation in any aspect of our life where we can utilise our aptitudes, abilities, talents and enthusiasm for doing something, because we care deeply about what we are doing and are motivated to perform in a committed and inspired way. The ecologies we create to learn, develop and achieve to the things we value are the means we have to give substance to our creativity and our unique voice as long as we have the courage and confidence to try.

> I find that the work that nobody sees is some of my most creative and challenging. This is the type of work that helps streamline process, connect dots, or pulls the right people together.... ....In my role as a producer and project manager, [I am] the connecting cog in the creative machine. Acting as a conduit for the ideas of those around you, and subtly adding your own unique flavour to each project you work on. You can heavily influence the result by creating processes that bring the right people together at the right time. (Kroeger 2016)

Resources

In nature organisms exist and are sustained by accessing flows of energy, food and other nutrients in the ecosystem they inhabit. These *resources* nourish and sustain the essential processes for life. Resources are anything that is of value to the organism and their functioning and survival. Anything can be a resource: it is all a matter of perception (affordance) and the ability to make use of it in a particular context and situation. The resources needed by the surgeon to think and act in an operating theatre are different to those required by a mechanic in a garage. We say someone is resourceful if they are good at finding and harnessing the resources available in their immediate environment.

In an ecology for learning the key resources are information, knowledge and experiences. The knowledge may exist as codified knowledge or be tacit and embodied in a person's know how and practices. Or knowledge might be embodied in artifacts and tools used to facilitate communication or create meaning. Resources also include the technological tools to search for, gather, process and analyse and communicate information.

Luckin (2008:52-5) developed the 'learner centric ecology of resources model of context' describing it as 'an ecology of resources: a set of inter-related resource elements, including people and objects, the interactions between which provide a particular context.' Her model places the learner at the centre but uses their interaction with resources as the essential ecology through which learning takes place.

Information and knowledge

Information can be viewed as a type of input to an organism. Inputs are of two kinds; some inputs are important to the function of the organism via its senses. Dusenbery (1992) calls these causal inputs. Other informational inputs are important only because they are associated with causal inputs.

Figure 2.3 Thinking ecologically. - with the permission of artist Tom Chalkley.

Knowledge is a fluid mix of framed experience, values, contextual information, and expert insight that provides a framework for evaluating and incorporating new experiences and information. It originates and is applied in the minds of knowers (Davenport and Prusak, 1998: 5). The way we use information derived from our experiences of being in the world to create knowledge and wisdom which can be shared, is neatly illustrated in Tom Chalkley's cartoon (Figure 2.3).

The cartoon also reveals the way our thinking is itself ecological in the sense of creating new meaning from the way we connect and relate our knowledge to an imagined future. When we explore and try to understand and solve a challenging problem or encounter a situation that is new to us, we use our perception, imagination and our reasoning in a productive interplay. This can be represented as a continuum (Figure 2.4) in which imagination has the potential to connect to both perception and reasoning in a pragmatic and productive way (Pendleton-Jullian and Brown 2016 and Figure 2.4).

Figure 2.4 The cognitive continuum (Pendleton-Jullian and Brown 2016) the part of the continuum used by our ancestor in Figure 2.3 is highlighted.

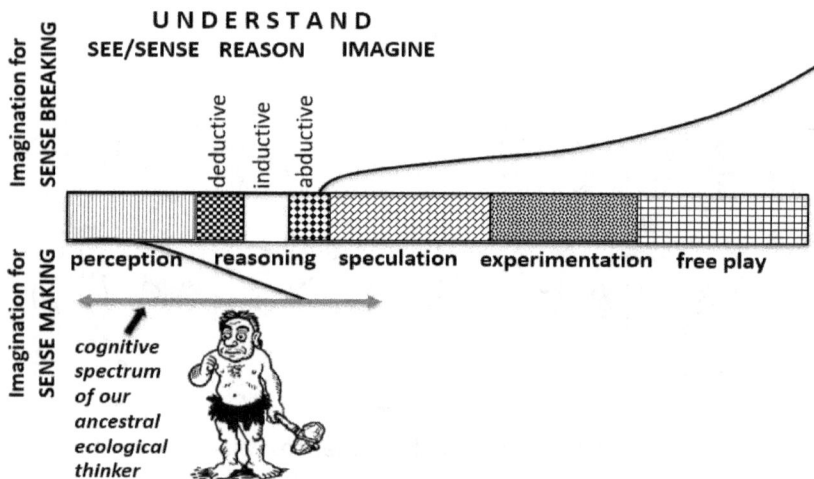

For our ancestor, understanding and making effective use of his environment and all the things in it, was a matter of survival. As he interacted with his environment he tapped into the information flows all around him sensing and perceiving the things in his world and their relationships and interactions. Through his experiences he began to recognize recurrent patterns which he organized into facts (knowledge). By reflecting on his experiences and the knowledge he had gathered, and using his power of reasoning, he was able to synthesize his facts into a theory of how his world worked. Having made this conceptual leap he was able to pass his wisdom on to others.

How we understand what knowledge is and how we develop the knowledge and knowing necessary to learn, develop and accomplish something is important if we are to create our own ecologies of practice for learning. Our epistemology - what is knowledge? how is it acquired? what do I know? how do I come to know what I know? how do I use my knowledge and ways of knowing to develop more knowledge? fundamentally shapes our ability to create ecologies for our own learning.

Boisot (1998) provides a useful conceptual aid for viewing different sorts of knowledge (Figure 2.5).

Figure 2.5 Conceptual framework for viewing knowledge. Adapted from Boisot (1998)

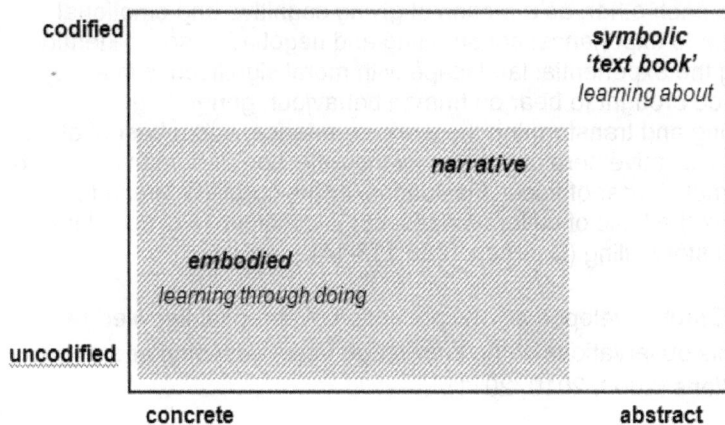

Using the two-by-two matrix of codified/abstract and uncodified/concrete knowledges he shows schematically the relationship between the knowledge that is embodied in everyday thinking and practices - our personalised working knowledge that we use to deal with situations - and more abstract/symbolic and codified knowledge such as that which we find in books, reports and working papers.

Our personal embodied knowledge, and the embodied knowledge of other people, mainly populates the shaded area. It is created or co-created with others through participation in the things we do and the extraction of meaning through our reflections on the situations we have encountered. It includes knowledge that we have gained from codified sources and from every other source (including what we have sensed and felt).

Narrative or storytelling provides a communication medium, often rich in metaphor, that links these two domains the embodied and codified knowledge domains. Bauman (1986) argues that oral narrative is constitutive of social life itself.

> When one looks at the social practices by which social life is accomplished one finds - with surprising frequency - people telling stories to each other, as a means of giving cognitive and emotional coherence to experience; constructing and negotiating social identity; investing the experiential landscape with moral significance in a way that can be brought to bear on human behaviour; generating, interpreting and transforming the work experience; and a host of other reasons. Narrative here is not merely the reflection of human culture, or the external charter of social institutions, or the cognitive arena for sorting out the logic of cultural codes, but is constitutive of social life in the act of storytelling (Bauman 1986:113-14).

Michael Eraut developed a rich conception of personal knowledge based on his observations of the knowledge people develop and use in work situations (2009, 2010, 2011).

> I argue that personal knowledge incorporates all of the following:
> *Codified knowledge* in the form(s) in which the person uses it
> *Know-how* in the form of *skills and practices*

Personal *understandings of people and situations*
Accumulated *memories of cases* and episodic *events*
Other aspects of personal *expertise, practical wisdom* and *tacit knowledge*
Self-knowledge, attitudes, values and *emotions.*

The evidence of personal knowledge comes mainly from observations of performance, and this implies a *holistic* rather than *fragmented* approach; because, unless one stops to deliberate, the knowledge one uses is already available in an *integrated form* and ready for action (Eraut 2010:2).

Cognitive maturity (Baxter Magolda 2004b:6-10) is the capability to make use of these different sources and forms of knowledge and it is necessary for the conscious development and deployment of ecologies for learning. It is characterised by the ability to reason and think critically and creatively, analyse situations and consider the range of perspectives necessary to make good decisions on how to act, and metacognitive and reflective capacity to create deeper meanings and enduring understandings. Cognitive maturity requires knowledge to be viewed as contextual recognising that multiple perspectives exist.

Thomas and Brown (2009, 2011) argue that the traditional model of learning in formal education, which is focused on codified knowledge is based on *thinking and learning about* something i.e. knowledge is something to be studied and accumulated. But the world of outside formal education is more concerned with *learning through doing, making and achieving something in a particular context* and putting the things we learn into action. In the case of work this is often within the context of an epistemic community (Thomas and Brown, 2009).

Homo Sapiens: '(hu)man as knower' is a fundamental statement about what it means to be human. It is also an ontological statement about learning. There are three senses in which learning happens in relation to change. The most basic sense is 'learning about' which corresponds to contexts in which information is stable. We learn about things which are stable and consistent and not likely to change over time. The second sense is 'learning to be,' which requires engagement with an epistemic community and provides a sense of enculturation in practices which allow one to participate and learn how to learn and even shape practices within that community. The third sense, which emerges out of a context of rapid and continual change, is a sense of *becoming*. This sense of learning is itself always in a state of flux, characterised by a sense of acting, participating, and knowing. This sense of knowing requires us to be reflectively aware and reflexively responsive to our learning and to the continuing changes we need to make in order to adapt (Thomas and Brown 2009:5)

These are not just abstract ideas; they are the reality of learning, being and becoming in an ecology for learning and achieving something. Although people may not be able to articulate their understandings in these ways, they will come to realise these things in their own way, through their own experiences of trying to learn something that is not readily available in a book.

Mediating artefacts (tools & signs)

Mediating artefacts are used by individuals to carry out an activity. The concept was developed in the socio-cultural theory of learning developed by Vygotsky (1978) and his co-workers and used by Engstrom (1987) and others in his interpretations of Cultural Historic Activity Theory (Figure 2.6). In Vygotsky's view we learn, think and do through the use and creation of mediating artifacts.

Vygotsky argued that what distinguishes humans from other animals is their use of speech in relation to practical activity (Vygotsky, 1978:24). He argues that words can shape an activity into structure. He describes the analogy of signs as tools. Signs can be used as a means of solving a given psychological problem (to remember, compare, report, choose, etc.) and he argues this is analogous to the use of tools. Therefore, signs act as an instrument of psychological activity in a manner analogous to the role of a tool in labour....He argues that a tool's function is to serve as a conductor of human influence on the object of activity; i.e. it is externally orientated. Whereas a sign changes nothing in the object of psychological operation, it is internally orientated. Therefore, humans use tools that are developed from a culture, such as speech and writing, to mediate their social environment. (Canole 2011:2)

Figure 2.6 The mediational triangle adapted by numerous authors from Vygotsky (1978) utlilised by Engstrom (1987) in his interpretations of Cultural Historic Activity Theory (CHAT). People with intentions (subject) engage in activity which is mediated by tools/artefacts to achieve an objective, which results in outcomes - learning and achievements.

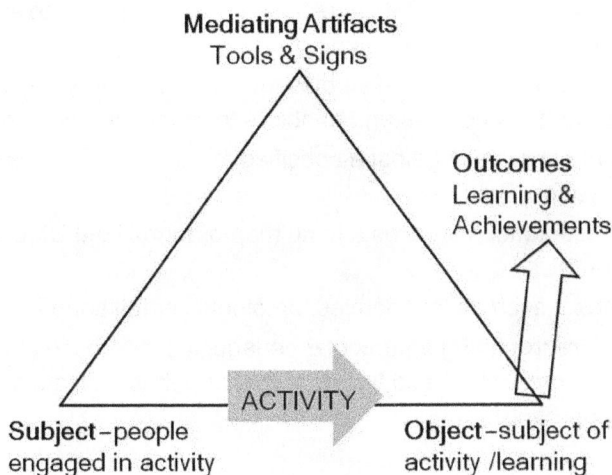

Mediating Artifacts
Tools & Signs

Outcomes
Learning &
Achievements

ACTIVITY

Subject - people
engaged in activity

Object - subject of
activity /learning

There are two types of mediating artefacts - signs and tools. A tool, such as a hammer, pencil, mobile phone or computer, mediates object-oriented material activity, whereas signs (like language) function as a means of social or intrapersonal interaction. The sign acts as an instrument of psychological activity in a manner analogous to the role of a tool in labour (Vygotsky 1978:52).

According to the model of ecological cognition (Bishop 2005a), mediating artifacts have affordances that are perceived by the user, who will use them to engage in planned activity. Mediating artifacts embody knowledge for practice and communicate information for decision making and action. Eraut (2010:12) observed different professional groups using a range of mediating artefacts including: hand over sheets for nurses, accounts used by accountants and engineers using drawings, photos and progress reports. In virtual environments, such as Internet applications, mediating artifacts take the form of text and graphics and in some cases video and other multimedia, which allow users to carry out actions in order to achieve their goals.

Course designers use a range of mediating artefacts (MAs) to support and learning (Canole (2011:3) including:

- textually based narrative case studies, describing the key features of the LA and perhaps barriers and enablers to its implementation,
- more formal narratives against a specified formal methodology such as a Pedagogical Patterns..
- visual representations such as a mind map or formalized UML use case diagram,
- vocabularies....such as taxonomies, ontologies or folksonomies,
- models.....foregrounding a particular pedagogical approach (such as instructivism, problem-based learning or an emphasis on a dialogic or reflective approach).

Canole argues that mediating artifacts can be derived from existing learning activities by a process of abstraction and the same learning activity (LA) can result in a range of abstractions. Indeed, this book constitutes a mediating artifact formed around a powerful metaphorical idea (psychological tool) for transferring and making sense of concepts (Hung 2002). It includes many of the features outlined above eg text-based narratives, visual representations, vocabularies and models

Our tools, including the technologies we use, are an important resource in our learning ecology. Luckin (2008) emphasises the important role of technology in formal learning environments and describes the relationships between learner, resources (like books, pens, paper and ICT and internet technologies), and other supportive individuals and a learner's curriculum through the 'learner centric ecology of resources model of context'.

Over the last decade we have witnessed a significant change in the tools and technologies we use to communicate, learn, develop and achieve our purposes. According to Stodd (2012, 2014a & b) we have entered a new era of human evolution known as the Social Age. The Social Age is defined by the massive global use of social media platforms that are changing behaviours and habits in respect of how we find, use, develop and distribute information and knowledge and create new meaning and understanding. It is being brought into existence as a result of the web 2.0 and web-enabling communication technologies and ever faster broadband, wifi, 3G + 4G technology that enable connectivity almost anywhere at anytime with infinite information resources, personal knowledge residing within personal learning networks. Enhanced connectivity is at the heart of the Social Age might be defined in terms of 'the creation of *value* (knowledge, understanding [or learning] and relationships) by connecting individuals who want to share their interests, knowledge, passions who form a relationship to co-create new understandings.

The Social Age has transformed our relationship with the many forms and sources of knowledge we work with in our daily lives. The use of social media in particular has expanded the range of tools we now have for learning and communicating for example social media - computer-mediated tools that allow people to create, share or exchange information, ideas, and pictures / videos in virtual communities and networks. Social media depend on mobile and web-based technologies to create highly interactive platforms through which individuals and communities share, co-create, discuss, and modify user-generated content. Social media makes it effortless for us to connect, engage, produce, curate, share and distribute information and knowledge. It's virtually synchronous making our encounters more conversational, more about story sharing than publication. Communication is often rich in visual representation to allow more opportunity to create meaning (Stodd 2014 a & b).

Social media gives learners more choice in controlling their own learning, mediated by a raft of technological tools. Web 2.0 software such as blogs, folksonomies, peer-to-peer (P2P) media sharing, and wikis, are providing students with unprecedented opportunities for learning and creative self-expression (McLoughlin and Lee 2008: 672). But social media and other digital tools and environments have necessitated the need for people to develop new literacies in order to access, use, create meaning from and participate in this media (Haythornthwaite 2012).

Relationships

An ecology of practice for learning is a relational concept. By that I mean it embodies the idea that what, how and why we are leaning has a complex and comprehensive set of relationships with our environment and all sorts of things contained within it. For example, it includes - what we know and can do and bring to a situation to deal with it, our past experiences of learning which enable us to learn our way into the future, the particular contexts and situations we are currently inhabiting and the affordances they contain, the sources of information and knowledge we are using, and the tools, technologies and mediating artefacts we are utilising and creating, the people we are interacting with, and our own beliefs, values, attitudes, perceptions, needs and interests. It is through our unique set of relationships that our learning, development and achievement emerge and we are able to give expression to our personal creativity. We might view our learning in the same way that Carl Rogers viewed creativity namely, 'the emergence in action of a [new] relational product growing out of the uniqueness of the individual on the one hand, and the materials, events, people, or circumstances of his life' (Rogers 1961:350). In adapting and appropriating this definition I have simply replaced 'novel' with 'new'. Our relationships with people, objects, events and the circumstances of our life provide affordances for learning.

Personal Learning Networks

In the Social Age, knowledge by itself is no longer power: What is important is our ability to be creative with the knowledge to synthesise and create meaning out of multiple sources, to add value to what exists, and to be able to use our personalised knowledge to effect change and achievement. These are the things that make us influential, that give us authority around a subject. It's not about what we know and hide away, it's about the conversations that we get into and how generous we are and how willing we are to learn with others and to share what we have learnt.

Our Personal Learning Networks (PLN's) are an important component of our learning ecology they comprise the connections we make with the people we believe can help us achieve our particular goals, and beyond this perhaps, who we feel might provide emotional support and enrich our lives. PLNs are like the blood vessels in our body or the roots and capillary vessels of a tree. They provide the structure and means of connecting to others and the means of tapping into the essential nutrients for learning - the flow of information, knowledge, wisdom and creativity within our learning ecology. They connect our ecology for learning with the ecologies developed by others for their learning.

Every time we embark on a new project that requires significant learning we intuitively begin to create a PLN with particular goals and objectives in mind. If we have inhabited a context for a while we will have established a PLN that contains a number of people and resources and tools we can readily draw upon. But if the context and or problems are unfamiliar then we will have to find and develop new relationships with people we do not know.

The Social Age has created new affordances for networking and changed the way we access information and people. Communication technologies enable us to connect to the imaginations, writings, illustrations and conversations of a multitude of people, located anywhere in the world, through the internet, social media, RSS feeds, mail lists, forums, skype and many more technologies.

Figure 2.7 Seek-Sense - Share model of information flow in a personal learning network (Jarche, 2014)

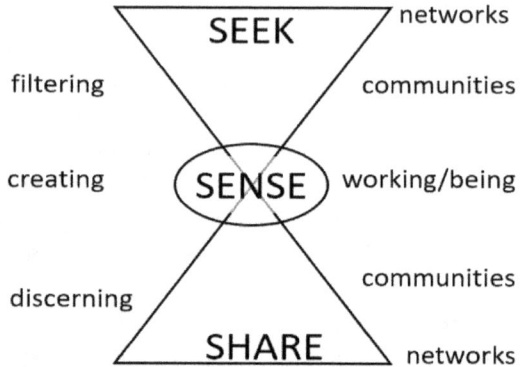

Harold Jarche (2014) developed the Seek-Sense-Share model of information flow (Figure 2.7) to represent the way we set out to find information that is relevant to our learning and development projects, make sense of and use that information then share with others our understandings.

Seeking is finding things out and keeping up to date. Building a network of colleagues is helpful in this regard. It not only allows us to "pull" information, but also have it "pushed" to us by trusted sources. Good curators are valued members of knowledge networks. (Jarche, 2014)

Seeking can be passive ie we connect to people, communities and organisations who share their knowledge freely and wait with 'watchful anticipation' for something to emerge that is of interest. And then there is the more deliberate mode where we invest lots of time and energy seeking out information that has the potential to be useful.

Sensing is how we personalize information and use it. Sensing includes reflection and putting into practice what we have learned. Often it requires experimentation, as we learn best by doing. (Jarche, 2014)

Sensing is about trying to make sense of the information we receive or find. We try to connect it to our own understandings which we may need to alter in the process. It is all about creating meaning and then perhaps learning to use what we have learnt.

Sharing includes exchanging resources, ideas, and experiences with our networks as well as collaborating with our colleagues. (Jarche 2014)

Sharing involves gifting our understandings or personal sense making to the world either by making it accessible in publications like magazines, books, papers, blogs, twitter posts and any other open access publication vehicles. It's also about using it in work or other social practices.

Processes

The way we discover or create new affordances to support our learning is to create new processes and practices. Lemke (2000) argues that social ecologies cannot be defined simply by the spaces they occupy: they must also be defined in terms of their processes - an ecosocial system is a system of interdependent processes within which relationships are developed and enacted, and affordances are accessed and utilised.

In dynamical theories of complex systems, the fundamental unit of analysis is a process... It is in relation to the process that its participants are defined, as filling roles in that process. *Things*, or *organisms*, or *persons*, or *institutions*, as usually defined, are not dynamical notions: they are ordinarily defined in terms of their stable and persistent, or invariant, properties. They are not about dynamics, not about change and doing, but about being what they are. Every process, action, social practice, or activity occurs on some timescale (in complex cases on more than one timescale). In a dynamical theory, an ecosocial system is a system of interdependent processes; an ecosocial or sociotechnical network is described by saying what's going on, what's participating and how, and how one is going-on is interdependent with another (Lemke 2000: 275).

The processes in an ecology for learning and achieving do not happen by themselves they have to be created by people who imagine, orchestrate, enact, encounter, make sense of, and connect up the moments that ultimately form a definable process. Processes have to be imagined, usually in an iterative and emergent way. Actions and activities have to be planned to a greater or lesser degree, choices and decisions have to be made about what or what not to do, effects have to be observed and experienced and actions and thinking have to be modified in response to what happens. In short we are dealing with processes that are the product of individuals, engaging with situations that may or may not be of their making over which they can exert influence through their self-determined or mediated actions. It is therefore necessary for people to develop the capability and insights to be able to create and sustain their ecologies for learning.

The process of creating, connecting and dealing with situations that coalesce over time into a process is fundamentally a process of self-regulation as described Zimmerman (2000). Self-regulation can be represented as a continuous process involving forethought (planning and decision making), action/performance and self-reflection on action/performance Chapter 6 explores this in more detail. Our processes enable us to interact with other people and our environment and through these interactions gain the feedback we need to judge our performance in the world.

Agency - will, confidence, capability, awareness, creativity

You cannot have a learning ecology without a person or persons. Ecologies for learning are willfully constructed by people who have the desire (will) to put time and effort into developing an ecology that is fit for the purpose of learning what they want or need to learn. They must also have the capability and self-awareness to build an ecology that will enable them to achieve their learning goals and self belief that what they are doing stands a good chance of working or, if it doesn't, the belief that they can change what they are doing until they achieve their goal.

Cairns and Stephenson (2009:16) argue that capability is a holistic concept which encompasses both current competence and future development through the application of potential. In their opinion the concept of capability is applicable across individuals and organisations and it includes:

- the capacity to operate in both familiar and unfamiliar situations
- the utilisation of creativity/innovation
- being mindful about change and open to emergent opportunities
- being confident about one's abilities
- being able to engage with social values relevant to actions
- engaging with learning as a self-directed process
- operating to formulate and solve problems.

These authors (ibid:17) identify three elements to capability:

- *ability* - to carry out observable behaviours to a level of acceptable performance and potential skills and attributes that can be realised with effort and opportunity
- *self*-efficacy - defined as the confidence of the individual, acts as a motivational force and with success a confidence builder supporting further risk taking, persistence and capable behaviour
- *values* - the way individuals' actions are guided by a personal set of values and their ability to articulate any values issues associated with that action.

Capable implementation of actions requires (ibid:18):

- *Mindfulness - awareness and openness to change.* Mindful people are conscious of their thinking and working out of solutions and progress
- *Self-management.* All learners need to be self-managing and responsible for their own learning and development.

• *Effective problem formulation and problem solving.*

I would like to emphasise five qualities or characteristics of capable people all of which are important for creating effective learning ecologies.

The first characteristic of capable people is that they have the *will* to try and to keep trying until they succeed. Without the will to try, and determination to persist, nothing is possible. You have to be willing to involve yourself in a situation in order to influence it. Belief in ourselves and our own capacity and ability to effect a change or achieve a result is an integral part of our willingness to try. Knowing that you are able to do something in order to deal with a situation also feeds into our preparedness to try.

The second characteristic is that they are able to think in an integrative way: they are able to think in a way that combines and integrates in a synergistic way their creative imagination and their critical thinking (Puccio et al 2005).

The third dimension of capability is *applied ability.* We have to develop practical skill and knowledge of how and when to use the skill in an appropriate manner to turn ideas into effective action: action that will one way or another achieve their goals. Skill is not a checklist of things we can do but an *integrated set of functionings* that are adjusted in response to the ongoing monitoring or 'sensing' of our effects as the results of our actions emerge. Here we return to the conundrum of what knowledge and skills do we choose to help students' develop for a rapidly changing world? Perhaps the overarching capability is the ability to develop and utilise new knowledge and skill when it is needed and to combine and adapt existing knowledge and skills in order to improvise in new and unfamiliar situations.

The fourth component of capability is *self-awareness* the ability to recognise and evaluate the effects we are having and adjust what we are doing if necessary. Our ability to sense and observe situations and make sense of what is happening (our ability to create meaning) feeds into our self-regulatory action-oriented mechanism to help us refine our actions and intentions. Our preparedness and ability to reflect on a situation enables us to learn from our experience so that we can have more immediate effect and more impact in the future. Reflection is the key sense and meaning making process in our life and it ultimately feeds into what we value and our sense of satisfaction and fulfillment.

When we participate in a formal learning situation we are conscious that the purpose of what we are doing is to learn. But much of what we do in life is not directly concerned with learning, rather it is to accomplish a task where learning, or may not be, learning is a bi-product of the process of trying to accomplish something. Rogers (2003) uses this distinction to argue there might be two basic contexts for learning namely, task-conscious learning and learning-conscious learning.

Task-conscious learning goes on all the time. It is 'concrete, immediate and confined to a specific activity; it is not concerned with general principles' (Rogers 2003: 18). Examples include much of the learning involved in parenting or with running a home. In this situation whilst the parental learner may not be conscious of learning, they are aware of the specific task they are engaged in and what they want to achieve by accomplishing the task.

Learning-conscious learning arises through processes (directed or self-directed) that facilitate learning. There is a consciousness of learning - people are aware that the task they are engaged in entails learning and the job of facilitation whether it is through a teacher directing a class, a coach or mentor guiding someone in a work situation or a parent guiding a child, is to make people more aware of their learning or what they need to learn.

At one extreme lie those unintentional and usually accidental learning events which occur continuously as we walk through life. Next comes incidental learning - unconscious learning through acquisition methods which occurs in the course of some other activity... Then there are various activities in which we are somewhat more conscious of learning, experiential activities arising from immediate life-related concerns, though even here the focus is still on the task... Then come more purposeful activities - occasions where we set out to learn something in a more systematic way, using whatever comes to hand for that purpose, but often deliberately disregarding engagement with teachers and formal institutions of learning... Further along the continuum lie the self-directed learning projects on which there is so much literature... More formalized and generalized (and consequently less contextualized) forms of learning are the distance and open education programmes, where some elements of acquisition learning are often built into the designed learning programme. Towards the further extreme lie more formalized learning programmes of highly decontextualized learning, using material common to all the learners without paying any regard to their individual preferences, agendas or needs. There are of course no clear boundaries between each of these categories. (Rogers 2003: 41-2).

This synthesis by Rogers effectively embraces all the conditions and catalysts for learning that an ecology for learning might embrace. We participate in ecologies for accomplishing a task all the time and we may or may not be aware that we are learning in the process. But when we deliberately set out to learn something we are conscious of what we have to do in order to learn and what we have learnt in the process. Our ecologies for learning depend on this awareness.

Learning trajectories

Learning is often a byproduct of trying to achieve something rather than the explicit goal of what is being done: the net effect of a person creating a learning ecology to resolve a problem, overcome a challenge or exploit an opportunity is learning regardless of whether the person was successful or unsuccessful in achieving their goal. Learning is often not simple to define and we may only know we have learnt something when we suddenly realise that we can do something that we could not do a few weeks or months before.

Eraut and Hirsch (2008:11) used the term 'learning trajectory' to embrace the 'progress in a person's performance' and the learning and development that was associated with the progress. Examples of making progress in a developmental and performance sense involves doing things better, doing them differently and doing different things, and might include (ibid:12).

- Doing things faster
- Improving the quality of the process
- Improving communications around the task
- Becoming more independent and needing less supervision Helping others learn to do the task
- Combining tasks more effectively
- Quicker recognition of possible problems
- Expanding the range of situations in which one can perform competently
- Increases in task difficulty/ taking on tasks of greater complexity
- Dealing with more difficult or more important cases, clients, customers, suppliers or colleagues.

Eraut and Hirsch (ibid) viewed performance as complex and multidimensional, and the development of one set of performances (and related capabilities) along a trajectory does not necessarily mean that other capabilities are being developed at the same time. Indeed, some capabilities and related performances might regress if there are no opportunities to practice and perform them (ibid:12). Eight learning trajectory categories and 53 learning trajectories were identified to cover complex performance in the professional work environment (Table 2.1 and chapter 4).

Any significant experience that a person participates in will afford them the opportunity to accomplish d particular goals and also learn and develop along one or more trajectories simultaneously. Figure 2.8 provides a graphical representation of the complete learning trajectory model containing all 53 learning trajectories.

Table 2.1 Learning trajectories and categories defined by Eraut and Hirsch (2007)

Task Performance	Role Performance
1. Speed and fluency	1. Prioritisation
2. Complexity of tasks and problems	2. Range of responsibility
3. Range of skills required	3. Supporting other people's learning
4. Communication with a wide range of people	4. Leadership
5. Collaborative work	5. Accountability
Awareness and Understanding	6. Supervisory role
1. Other people: colleagues, customers, managers,	7. Delegation
2. Contexts and situations	8. Handling ethical issues
3. One's own organization	9. Coping with unexpected problems
4. Problems and risks	10. Crisis management
5. Priorities and strategic issues	11. Keeping up-to-date
6. Value issues	**Academic Knowledge and Skills**
Personal Development	1. Use of evidence and argument
1. Self-evaluation	2. Accessing formal knowledge
2. Self-management	3. Research-based practice
3. Handling emotions	4. Theoretical thinking
4. Building and sustaining relationships	5. Knowing what you might need to know
5. Disposition to attend to other perspectives	6. Using knowledge resources (human, paper-based, electronic)
6. Disposition to consult and work with others	7. Learning how to use relevant theory (in a rang of practical situations)
7. Disposition to learn and improve one's practice	**Decision Making and Problem Solving**
8. Accessing relevant knowledge and expertise	1. When to seek expert help
9. Ability to learn from experience	2. Dealing with complexity
Teamwork	3. Group decision making
1. Collaborative work	4. Problem analysis
2. Facilitating social relations	5. Formulating and evaluating options
3. Joint planning and problem solving	6. Managing the process within an appropriate timescale
4. Ability to engage in and promote mutual learning	7. Decision making under pressure
	Judgement
	1. Quality of performance, output and outcomes
	2. Priorities
	3. Value issues
	4. Levels of risk

We might speculate that any significant new project an individual undertakes will require them to create an ecology to achieve the goals of their project. All the components of the learning ecology will be involved and learning and performance will emerge through the implementation of the ecology. This way of viewing development as improved or new knowledge, skill or capability demonstrated through performances along one, several or many trajectories simultaneously provides a useful and holistic way of viewing the developmental outcomes from an ecology of practice.

Figure 2.8 Graphical representation of the learning trajectory model developed by Eraut and Hirsch (2007).

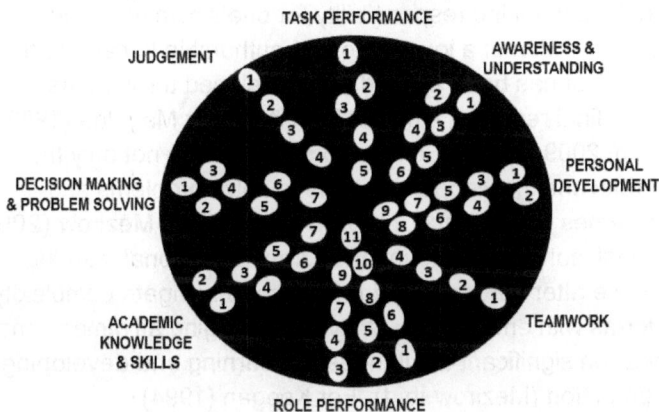

Self-authorship and transformative learning

The idea of learning ecologies is consistent with the constructive-developmental tradition of human development (Piaget 1950, Keegan 1982). Constructivism refers to humans' tendency to construct meaning by interpreting their experiences. Developmentalism suggests that these constructions evolve over time through periods of stability and transition to become more complex.

Piaget describes three interconnected dimensions of human development that are central to our meaning making. The cognitive dimension refers to our assumptions about the nature and certainty of knowledge and how we come to know. The intrapersonal dimension consists of our assumptions about our sense of self and identities. The interpersonal dimension addresses our assumptions about the nature of social relations. We construct these sets of assumptions by making sense of our experiences (Baxter Magolda 2014:8)

Kegan (1982) elaborated further the epistemological, intrapersonal and interpersonal dimensions in this evolving process describing a series of meaning-making structures that evolved from relying on external others for meaning making to taking responsibility for one's own meaning making. He used the idea of a journey to self-authorship to capture this process: an idea that has been applied and developed through the extensive longitudinal research study of Marcia Baxter Magolda (1999, 2001, 2004a & b, 2009, 2011). Self-authorship involves not only the acquisition of relevant knowledge and skills to solve problems and extending our frames of reference into new areas, what Mezirow (2000) calls informational learning, it also involves transformational learning, through which we alter our frames of reference to navigate complexity and come to terms with emergence. It involves bringing all dimensions of a person to bear on significant challenges for learning and developing, not just their cognition (Mezirow ibid). For Keegan (1994) transformational learning involves the growth of the mind, or the remaking of one's meaning making about knowledge, identity and social relations.

For Baxter Magolda, learning to deal with the complexities of adult life and play an active role in society requires learning to extend beyond the traditional acquisition of knowledge and skills gained in the classroom in order to achieve a level of maturity to think with complexity on the three dimensions of development (Baxter Magolda 2014).

Epistemological maturity is required to analyse and judge the validity of multiple perspectives to make wise decisions. Personal maturity is necessary to enable acting autonomously yet collaboratively and acting with integrity. Relational maturity is required for effective collaboration that integrates multiple perspectives in an uncertain and complex world. Kegan (1994) portrayed these three dimensions of development as integrated throughout the lifespan and defined self-authorship as the point at which adults take internal responsibility for their belief systems, their identity and the nature of their social relations (Baxter Magolda 2014:77-8).

Baxter Magolda (2011, 2014) recognises that the development of epistemological, personal and relational maturity is a lifelong and lifewide project and involves learning, developing, achieving and sometimes failing, in many different contexts and circumstances. It cannot be achieved in the classroom alone using methods that avoid risk and uncertainty, and only seek 'the right answer'.

The idea of learning ecologies might usefully be added to the conceptual toolkit for explaining the ways and means by which learners develop these maturities to think and work with complexity, uncertainty and risk. The learning ecology model developed in this chapter enables learning and development to be understood from the perspective of the whole person immersed in their situations dealing with complex relational and emergent problems and opportunities that require epistemological, personal and relational maturity. Many of the narratives in subsequent chapters that are analysed through the lens of a personal learning ecology, reveal the person in a state of transformation. They are transformed as they search for, find and utilise affordances for accomplishing what they value, create activities, processes and experiences to achieve goals which they determine for themselves, inhabit and create their own spaces for learning, use and develop their relationships with people who can help them, find, create and use the resources they need to accomplish their goals and progressively change their perspectives of and perceptions of the situations they encounter.

One of the key transformations to occur in the journey to authoring our own lives is the recognition that we cannot control reality but we can control our responses to it. I believe that the conscious and deliberate act and process of developing an ecology to learn, develop and achieve something significant, is the way that we respond to exploring our perceived affordances in the reality of the situation or circumstances. We change our understandings of reality as our perceptions change as we immerse ourselves in the situation.

Trust

To reach maturity in the manner outlined above, we have to learn to trust ourselves. We have to trust that the decisions we make for ourselves, in particular situations, are the most appropriate decisions weighing up the complexity of the situation and the effects our decisions will have. Trusting ourselves lies at the heart of our learning ecologies (Staron 2013).

> We learn in relationship and in context - not in isolation......This is why our learning ecology is so important to us. It tells us about our learning environment and interrelationships - with others, with our culture, work and with our educational institutions. And most importantly, it tells us about our learning relationship with ourselves. We need to trust ourselves to establish a learning ecology that is meaningful, authentic and supportive of our growth and personal wellbeing.
> For many, trust is an issue. We defer to what others expect of us and to the social norms of the day. We feel confusion or doubt around the decisions that we make or goals that we set. We respond to what others demand of us rather than to what's most appropriate and authentic for ourselves... How does this relate to learning ecology? Without self-trust, it's hard to understand and to modify our learning ecology. Our learning ecology needs to takes us towards our lifewide learning goals, rather than away from them. I believe it's crucial to trust that still small voice within (our higher self), that part of us that knows what works best for us (Staron 2013: 7)

Ecology of Practice for Learning and Performance Heuristic

Having explored the most important parameters of an ecology of practice for learning we are now able to create a heuristic that embodies these dimensions. Heuristics are approximate strategies or 'rules of thumb' for problem solving that do not guarantee a correct solution but typically yield a reasonable solution, in this case to the problem of what is an ecology of practice for learning.

An individual's self-created learning ecology grows from the circumstances (contexts) of their life and is established for a purpose that is directed to accomplishing proximal goals connected to more distal goals. Their learning ecology comprises themselves, their environment, their interactions with their environment and the learning, development and achievement that emerges from these interactions. It includes the space they create for themselves, their processes, activities and practices, their relationships, networks, tools, other mediating artefacts and the technologies they use, and it provides them with affordances, information, knowledge and other resources for learning, developing and achieving something that they value. We might represent these defining statement symbolically in a diagram (Figure 2.9).

Our learning ecologies are the means by which we connect and integrate our past and current experiences and learning and they provide the foundation for future learning. They embrace all the physical and virtual places and spaces we inhabit and the learning and the meaning we gain from the contexts and situations that constitute our lives. Our learning ecologies are the product of both imagination and reason and they are the vehicle for our creative thoughts and actions. They are one of our most important sites for creativity and they enable us to develop ourselves personally and professionally in all aspects of our lives.

The conceptual tool is heuristic rather than hierarchic. It represents the integration and interdependence of the person living in their environment perceiving learning and achievement needs and the affordances to satisfy these needs and creating processes to utilise the affordances they perceive. In acting on the affordances available to them through their own agency and creativity they form relationships, find, create and utilise resources and tools to aid thinking and action. Such actions may be directed explicitly to learning or mastering something but more likely they will be primarily concerned with performing a task, solving a problem, or

Figure 2.9 Components of an individual's ecology of practice for learning. The heuristic can be used to reflect on and evaluate a learning project from an ecological perspective

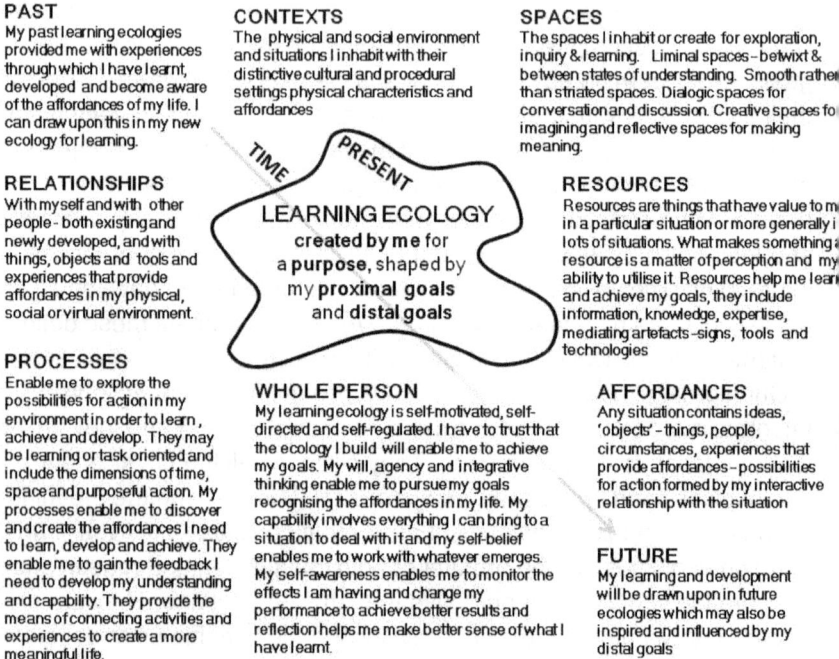

PAST
My past learning ecologies provided me with experiences through which I have learnt, developed and become aware of the affordances of my life. I can draw upon this in my new ecology for learning.

CONTEXTS
The physical and social environment and situations I inhabit with their distinctive cultural and procedural settings physical characteristics and affordances

SPACES
The spaces I inhabit or create for exploration, inquiry & learning. Liminal spaces – betwixt & between states of understanding. Smooth rather than striated spaces. Dialogic spaces for conversation and discussion. Creative spaces fo imagining and reflective spaces for making meaning.

RELATIONSHIPS
With myself and with other people - both existing and newly developed, and with things, objects and tools and experiences that provide affordances in my physical, social or virtual environment.

TIME PRESENT

LEARNING ECOLOGY
created by me for
a purpose, shaped by
my proximal goals
and distal goals

RESOURCES
Resources are things that have value to m in a particular situation or more generally i lots of situations. What makes something a resource is a matter of perception and my ability to utilise it. Resources help me lear and achieve my goals, they include information, knowledge, expertise, mediating artefacts – signs, tools and technologies

PROCESSES
Enable me to explore the possibilities for action in my environment in order to learn, achieve and develop. They may be learning or task oriented and include the dimensions of time, space and purposeful action. My processes enable me to discover and create the affordances I need to learn, develop and achieve. They enable me to gain the feedback I need to develop my understanding and capability. They provide the means of connecting activities and experiences to create a more meaningful life.

WHOLE PERSON
My learning ecology is self-motivated, self-directed and self-regulated. I have to trust that the ecology I build will enable me to achieve my goals. My will, agency and integrative thinking enable me to pursue my goals recognising the affordances in my life. My capability involves everything I can bring to a situation to deal with it and my self-belief enables me to work with whatever emerges. My self-awareness enables me to monitor the effects I am having and change my performance to achieve better results and reflection helps me make better sense of what I have learnt.

AFFORDANCES
Any situation contains ideas, 'objects' - things, people, circumstances, experiences that provide affordances – possibilities for action formed by my interactive relationship with the situation

FUTURE
My learning and development will be drawn upon in future ecologies which may also be inspired and influenced by my distal goals

making the most of a new opportunity. Furthermore, in the process of trying to achieve something new affordances for learning and achieving might be perceived.

The ecology we create to develop something, like a new educational course if you are a teacher, is the vehicle for our creativity. The ecologies we bring into existence for the purpose of learning and achieving are acts of creation using Rogers (1961) concept of creativity. Our learning ecology is our self-determined and self-expressed process for achieving tangible proximal goals, within which we create our novel relational products *[including our own development]* grown out of our individual uniqueness which has been shaped by our past histories and imaginings of a different and better future, and the materials, events, people and circumstances of our life. In this way our learning ecology becomes the means through which we seek and utilise the affordances for learning, development and achievement within the circumstances of our life and the environments we inhabit.

Figure 2.10 Graphical representation of an ecology of practice within which learning and performance are embedded. The complex developmental outcomes emerging from the ecology are shown as a family of learning trajectories (see Figure 2.7 for explanation)

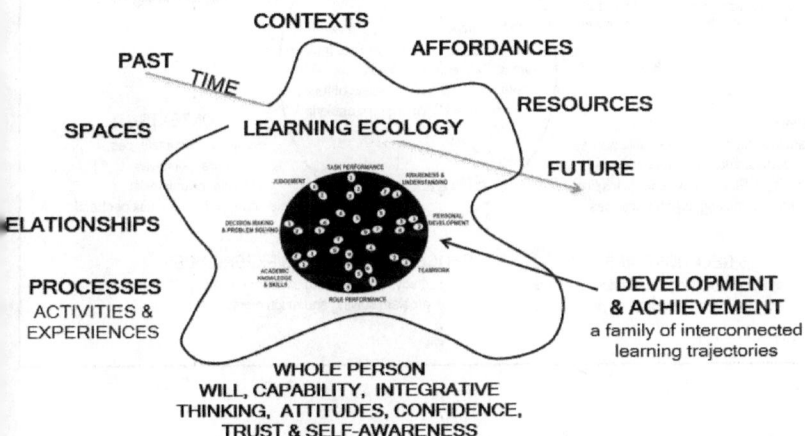

This example of an ecology for learning and achieving is hypothetical. Subsequent chapters draw upon real life narratives of people to bring to life the concept of a learning ecology.

Addendum

Figure 2.11 shows my most recent representation of an ecology for learning and practice (August 2019) (Jackson 2019).I simplified the shape and added the idea of places as some things can only be experienced and learnt in a particular place.

Figure 2.11 Ecology for learning and practice (Jackson 2019).

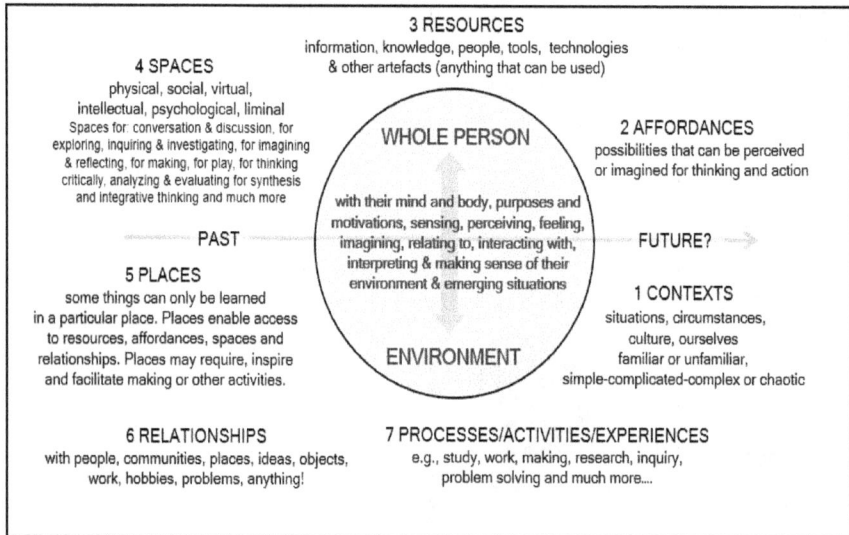

3 RESOURCES
information, knowledge, people, tools, technologies
& other artefacts (anything that can be used)

4 SPACES
physical, social, virtual, intellectual, psychological, liminal
Spaces for: conversation & discussion, for exploring, inquiring & investigating, for imagining & reflecting, for making, for play, for thinking critically, analyzing & evaluating for synthesis and integrative thinking and much more

2 AFFORDANCES
possibilities that can be perceived or imagined for thinking and action

WHOLE PERSON
with their mind and body, purposes and motivations, sensing, perceiving, feeling, imagining, relating to, interacting with, interpreting & making sense of their environment & emerging situations

ENVIRONMENT

PAST

FUTURE?

5 PLACES
some things can only be learned in a particular place. Places enable access to resources, affordances, spaces and relationships. Places may require, inspire and facilitate making or other activities.

1 CONTEXTS
situations, circumstances, culture, ourselves familiar or unfamiliar, simple-complicated-complex or chaotic

6 RELATIONSHIPS
with people, communities, places, ideas, objects, work, hobbies, problems, anything!

7 PROCESSES/ACTIVITIES/EXPERIENCES
e.g., study, work, making, research, inquiry, problem solving and much more....

CHAPTER 3
Learning Ecology Narratives

My Learning Life

There are two spatial-temporal dimensions to the narrative of my learning life. The first is a lifelong journey of personal change and development. If I thumb through a photograph album and pick a photo at a particular point in my life I might imagine myself as a particular sort of person with a particular set of skills, experiences and knowledge, perhaps performing a particular role. But if I take all my albums, that take in the scale of my life, it seems to me that, I have been in a perpetual state of transition from being one sort of person to becoming another.

Viewed in this way life is nothing more than being in a state of transition of moving into, through and out of - one stage of life into another, or one physical environment and its social - cultural contexts and relationships into another, one role with its particular contexts, problems, challenges and identities to another, and even one field of professional knowledge to another. Some of this change is self-determined out of necessity, obligation, interest or opportunity, but sometimes its forced upon us. Regardless of the cause we have to learn to adapt to the new set of circumstances. Looking back over my life I can create a narrative around my personal and professional development at each stage of my life so cumulatively my overall pattern of learning and development can be recognised and I can give an account of why I have come to be the person I am. Figure 3.1 shows the lifelong dimension of the pattern of my learning, development and achievement through my formal education and the various jobs and work roles I have had.

But there is another dimension to my lifelong narrative of development namely the lifewide journey I make every day by living and performing the roles I have in all the different contexts and spaces I inhabit simultaneously in my life (Jackson 2011a). While the lifelong dimension of my life makes sense after I have lived it, the lifewide dimension is the space in which the meanings of my life are created through every thought and activity I engage in. It is in this dimension of my life in which I think and perform, and engage in activity that enables me to move into, through and out of - one stage of life to another, and one physical environment and its social - cultural contexts and relationships to another, and one role with its particular contexts, problems, challenges and identities to another, and one knowledge field to another, which all give my life meaning and the sense of who I am.

Figure 3.1 Main educational and work domains in my life. The black jagged lines represent significant dislocations in my life which will be discussed in chapter 4.

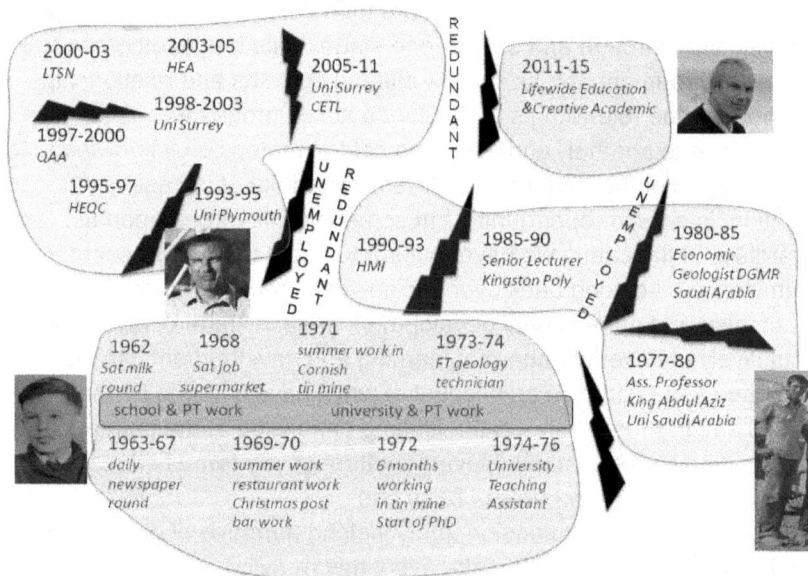

My every day journey is the one that really matters because it's the one I can influence and experience and that is why, from an educational perspective, it is far more important to recognise and work with than the more abstract idea of my lifelong journey. It is also important because it is this lifewide dimension of my life in which I grow my ecologies for learning, developing and achieving. Later in this chapter I will illustrate how these ecologies are grown from the personal interests, needs and circumstances of people's lives.

Learning Projects and Episodes

As adults much of our learning is incidental to our doings: the continuous flux of thinking, activity and being that make up the lifewide dimension of our life. It is worth reminding ourselves of what learning means in our adult life. The following passages written by Allan Tough capture well the variety and richness of our everyday learning (Tough 1971:3).

Men and women learn in many ways: by reading books, magazines and newspapers; by watching television and movies; by seeking subject matter and advice from friends, relatives, neighbours or fellow workers; by consulting a doctor or lawyer, a salesman or librarian, an extension agent or financial expert. They may also attend discussion groups, lectures and private lessons.

Sometimes the adult sets out to gain certain knowledge and skill because it will be highly useful in the very near future. At other times he simply wants to possess the knowledge and skill for its own sake, perhaps to have a broad understanding of the world around him. Occasionally the main reason for a learning project is the desire for credit toward some degree or certificate....

Adults learn a wide range of knowledge and skill. An individual may set out to increase his own understanding and self-acceptance, or he may simply want to learn how to refinish a coffee table. He may want to learn some area of history, philosophy, economics, current affairs, natural science or social science. He may want to gain more knowledge before making an important decision on the job, or about his own financial affairs. He may learn to play a musical instrument, or to play golf or bridge. He may want to increase his skill in teaching, raising children, supervising, or in some other major task. He may learn in order to plan a trip, buy an appliance, operate a ham radio, deal more effectively with people, or develop a philosophy of life.

Some efforts to learn are relatively brief or superficial...... Other learning efforts are aimed at changing one's self-concept, perception and understanding of others, deep feelings or creativity. Some efforts are aimed at modifying overt behaviour, such as a habit, or an addiction pattern.... Some learning projects are primarily cognitive or intellectual, some are aimed primarily at attitudinal and emotional change, some are designed to develop physical skills and many are a mixture...

But people generally don't talk about learning, unless they are situated in a context where learning is the overt activity, and they certainly don't talk about learning ecologies. Allen Tough used the idea of personal learning projects when discussing learning with adult learners. A learning project is simply a major, deliberate effort to gain certain knowledge and skill or to change in some way, according to the learner's interests and needs. His surveys of

A learning project is a series of related episodes, adding up to at least seven hours*. In each episode, more than half of the person's motivation is to gain and retain certain... knowledge and skill, or to produce some other lasting change in himself (Tough 1971:7)

An episode is a period of time devoted to a cluster or sequence of similar or related activities - including all the persons experiences, (everything he does, thinks, feels, hears and sees) during that period of time. (Tough 1971:7)

A learning episode is an accumulation of activities in which the primary objective is to learn, 'more than half of the person's motivation is to gain and retain certain definite knowledge and skill (Tough 1971:8)

adults suggested that almost everyone participates in one or two major learning efforts each year and some individuals undertake as many as 15-20 and it is common for individuals to spend 700 hours or more on their significant learning projects.

Learning projects are made up of episodes during which the individual engages in a cluster of related activities in order to learn and or accomplish something. A minimum time period of 7 hours was chosen in the definition of an episode: equivalent to a working day. Almost all projects contain several and sometimes many episodes. Our learning ecologies may be formed around a single learning project or many connected projects.

Narratives of Learning

Learning narratives are the vehicles for describing the substance and dynamics of a learning ecology. In the following section a number of learning narratives give meaning to the ideas of personal learning projects, learning ecologies and learning trajectories. To help appreciate and map the dimensions of the learning ecology the simple conceptual aid developed in chapter 2 will be used as a reference point.

1 How did I learn to play Pokemon?

Trying to master something that interests us provides the intrinsic motivation to create a learning project, and a process and new relationships (ecology) through which we might learn. In this narrative 12 year old Andrew describes his process for learning to play Pokemon.

> When I started playing it was around spring last year and I had pretty much no idea of how to play the game. My friends had played it for many years before me and I felt I should join in too. First I bought myself a "theme deck" which comes with a complete deck and a very rough and uninformative rulebook. I read this and still had hardly any idea of how to play the game so I went to a games shop and got

taught by a very experienced player. She taught me how to play the game but not the complex aspects such as deck building and

strategies. When I noticed that I still was lacking in many areas of playing I started listening to a podcast that was released every week. This was very valuable. I knew the person who ran it and frequently asked them for tips which helped me play with more strategy. I also watched tutorials and deck reviews on YouTube and read articles on the internet. This has all been very successful because, earlier this year I competed in the National Championships. I would have not got in if it wasn't for these things and they have been an invaluable resource.

This narrative reveals how the building of personal learning ecologies can occur at an early age if the *desire* to learn and master something is strong enough. Andrew's project grew from his desire to participate in

what seemed to him like an enjoyable social activity by playing the game with his friends (the social - cultural context). This was his proximal goal but through the *process* he developed a more distal goal - to become an expert player in the sense of competing with other experienced players. This ensured he persisted over a significant period of time. He realised that he couldn't learn much from the instructions so he sought help from an experienced player (*new relationship*) before accessing other learning *resources* available through a podcast (and interactions with the person who produced the podcast), YouTube tutorials and articles. Eventually he put himself into an entirely *new context* competing with other players at tournaments in order to see how well he has mastered the game and to learn from the experience of playing against others. His *learning trajectory* shows that he began this process with no knowledge and skill and ended up with sufficient knowledge and skill to compete with other experienced players.

2 Inspired to play the piano

Personal learning ecologies often emerge from the everyday doings of life as illustrated in this story told by 15 year old Nadia.

we have a music block and sometimes we go in there at lunchtime because it's warm and no teachers kick you out especially if you've got someone actually playing an instrument. One of my friends, Ellie she's amazing at playing the piano. She is grade seven. She was playing the piano. I was sitting there feeling slightly bored, because I couldn't play the piano and even if I could she was hogging it. So I thought, "Well I might as well do something with this time," and so I went and I sat next to her, and when she finished the piece I was like, "Can you teach me something on the piano?" Just because I wanted to be able to play the piano just so I could come home [and play it], because we've got a piano just sitting there. Even if I just sat there and played a scale over and over again, at least I had something to play.

She was like, "I don't know what to teach you," and so for about ten minutes she went through her own pieces and did a couple of things and I was saying "I don't mind what you teach me, just something easy so I can learn it." Eventually I said, "Okay, well why don't you just teach me a scale?" because I had done the flute before so I know what scales are. She was like, "Oh, okay." So she taught me the C major scale, which is just going from C to C. So yes I learned that and then I came home and I wasn't really in the mood to do any work because I'd spent the whole day in, like, this zombie state waiting to go home. So when I came home I had my break and because my internet wasn't working that well I came into the sitting room and just sat down at the piano and I started practising the scale. I saw my sister's [piano] book just sitting there on its own, looking all lonely. So I was like, "Well if that's got any instructions, I might as well see if I can do anything else because I know where C is now on the keyboard. Even if I just press that over and over again, maybe there is a song for that." I read the book and I just started teaching myself how to play the piano, just for fun, which is probably the weirdest thing I've ever done, especially for fun.

Although I was familiar with music notation from years ago when I started learning the flute, it was different for piano and then you've got the right and the left hand, which I'm just starting to teach myself five notes on the left hand. I'm very proud of myself, I can do both hands, just. Yes, so they are all different and my sister whose book it was before had written on the notes, but I wanted to learn the notes for themselves, like to recognise them on the page. I didn't want to read it off. So I'd rubbed it out. So I'm trying to learn it, where they are on the page so I can just look at it and be like, "Oh, that's this note. That is this note," because then it's much easier to learn other pieces.... I just learned a piece, which has five notes in it and I was insanely proud of myself because I'd done something I've never done before. I had done it on my own. No one was expecting me to do it.

My friend is such a nice person. She is always willing to help me and everything. So I think if I learned a bit and I went and I talked to her and I was like, "Well, could you help me with this?" or "Do you have any of your simple books on grade one that I could borrow?" if I didn't want to buy any, she would be like, "Yes, sure. That's fine." She wouldn't laugh at me. She wouldn't make fun of the fact that even though I'm her age I only I know five notes and I'm just doing it for fun... she is someone I feel would really help me.

In this narrative of learning we see Nadia in two different contexts (school and home). She has encountered the same situation before but this time she decided to try and learn something. She was both inspired by her friend and also felt that her friend would help her without making her feel stupid. But the motivations for her decision were complex.

I've got to say it's a bit out of jealousy that everyone else can play a musical instrument so well and I didn't, although I've only got myself to blame. Also, partly out of a bit of boredom, to be honest, because I wanted to do something different and the piano was something different that I had access to at home. I suppose also because she inspired me to do it....

Nadia's learning project grew out of the circumstances of her life. It wasn't planned, and she didn't have a distal goal. Her proximal goal to learn a tune, emerged through social interaction with her friend and she saw affordance in the situation and then realised the opportunity through her actions. Her personal learning ecology comprises the *contexts* of school and home, the material *resources* of two piano's, one at school and one at home, a book of music at home, a significant *relationship* with her friend who provided the inspiration and essential knowledge/skill resource (her expertise). Learning occurred when Nadia recognised the potential in the situation to achieve something worthwhile and she created a *process* to

CONTEXTS

PAST
PRESENT
SPACES
RESOURCES

LEARNING ECOLOGY
created by a person
for a purpose to achieve
proximal goals informed
by distal goals

FUTURE

RELATIONSHIPS

PROCESSES
ACTIVITIES &
EXPERIENCES

WHOLE PERSON
WILL, CAPABILITY, INTEGRATIVE
THINKING, EMOTIONS, ATTITUDES,
CONFIDENCE, TRUST & SELF-AWARENESS
DEVELOPMENT & ACHIEVEMENT

AFFORDANCES

make use of the resources that were readily to hand. She set aside the time to practise and master the musical notation and used the book of piano music that had been sitting on the piano ever since her sister gave up playing the piano. The personal learning ecology was created only when Nadia decided to use the situation to achieve something that she thought she could achieve that was valuable to her. One of the most interesting aspects of her story is the complexity of the motives that triggered her will to behave in this way - boredom, jealousy, the desire to do something different and being inspired by hearing her talented friend play, combined with the belief that she could achieve what she set out to do. Nadia's *learning trajectory,* her capability development, is manifest in the fact that she could play a tune that she couldn't play before. Interestingly, she did not continue to learn the piano - she lacked the distal goal that would have encouraged her to persist.

3 Mastering the mysteries of a Morris dance

The intrinsic desire to master something can infect people of all ages and in all circumstances and provide the motivation to commit time and energy to creating and sustaining an ecology for learning and personal development. In this illustration Paul, who was interested in Morris dancing (a form of English folk dance), wanted to develop his expertise and master a particular dance.

> I have taken it upon myself to develop an expert understanding of the Morris dancing and related folk music tradition.... I've committed myself to this journey and for me its about getting to mastery, not the rate in which I get to mastery. I purposefully put myself in positions to learn more..........I have been focused on learning a jig called "I'll go and enlist for a sailor". Some of the steps were eluding me. Over this last weekend I attended the Marlboro Morris Ale and was fortunate enough to meet John Dexter, who could teach me the jig. I was shown the steps in detail by a master of the dance, much of the mystery of the steps were demonstrated, they are no longer a mystery. All my reading of the dance and watching videos had prepared me well for this master / apprentice type session. I was ready to learn and the correct situation presented itself as I was on my learning journey, often it is important to hold the faith that the right learning is available at the right time. The Morris Ale became a part of my learning ecology

Paul had a distal goal - to develop his knowledge and expertise in a field that he was interested in. He also set himself a proximal goal to learn a particular dance. Paul makes the point that in order to learn you have to

put yourself into an environment (*context and situations*) in which you are more likely to find the *resources* and *opportunities* you need to learn. He saw the *affordance* for developing himself in the Morris dancing event. By reading about the dance and watching videos (*resources*) he prepared himself so that he was ready to learn. His most important opportunity for learning came about when he put himself into a situation where Morris dancers came together to perform and share their tradition. By building a *new relationship* with an expert he was able to gain access to the help he needed to enable him to complete his learning project. This example illustrates the importance in personal learning ecologies of particular spaces, places and times (contexts) in which specific social practices occur and the resources and relationships for learning are more likely to be available. It also illustrates the importance of creating a learning process that will increase the chance of accessing resources and relationships necessary for learning. His learning trajectory is demonstrated in the fact that he could perform a dance that he could not perform before.

4 Helping someone else

Sometimes our learning projects stem from a desire to help other people rather than being driven by our own interests and needs. Such learning may be quite modest in its scope but be of significance to the person we are helping. In this example James, who is now in his 80's, reveals an ecology for learning he created in order to help his wife.

This learning project began from my being an interested bystander of a complex situation. My wife is a member of the Business Committee of a charity. Recently they have been troubled by a very delayed claim of harassment, made by a former employee regarding his treatment by certain office bearers. This claim, which was being properly considered, was and is of no interest to me. However an intriguing side issue began to emerge when the former employee emailed a wider group of charity members. He sought to justify the case he was making. His source of addresses was from the "cc" section of an email which he had properly sent out from office equipment during his employment, and which he had presumably retained. Members of the Business Committee queried, and are still querying, what bearing the

Data Protection Act has on his activities after leaving the employment of the charity, using data to which he had access while employed. My wife described the Data Protection issue, but not the substance of the complaint, with me. I was intrigued.

What learning ecology came to bear? I consulted papers and notes I had retained from my training by a previous employer in Data Protection and Freedom of Information. I consulted the internet on several occasions, following several different though linked lines of enquiry. My wife reported to me at second hand, and discussed with me, the views and especially the questions and issues being raised in meetings of the Committee (of which I am an Emeritus member). I raised the matter in general terms with a friend who widely circulates "smileys" to those on her list, but always exhorts us to do as she does and only to copy them on under "bcc" which conceals addresses, of course. In a bizarre encounter, while waiting for a burly supermarket man to load a heavy parcel in our car, I discovered that the woman arranging this was a final year law student and was willing to offer me (free) advice on the question of culpability; but it was confusing advice, as too many options had emerged before the man returned having loaded our parcel.

I have now listed questions beyond the original one - and motivation to understand more about the implications of legislation regarding Data Protection. My list increased recently, when I sought to discover with what grade of second class degree one of my grand-daughters had graduated a few days previously. I spent ages on the university's websites, before being told that Data Protection legislation precluded them from making that information available, although the full graduation list had been published in the Times some days earlier. My new questions emerge from my desire to know if the Act does in fact preclude this publication and, if so, why? My learning ecology may expand to benefit from the eventual formal judgement by those to whom the case has been referred, further reading on the internet, and a discussion with a retired lawyer friend.

James' learning project grew out of the circumstances of his life. It wasn't planned, and he didn't have a distal goal, other than to support his wife. His proximal goal to answer the specific question about the use of privileged information after someone has left employment, grew out of a situation that he found 'intriguing'. His interest and motivation were driven by his innate curiosity. He describes and evaluates his own ecology for learning which included documentary and web-based resources, conversations with his wife, friends and chance interactions with a stranger and he illustrates well how new questions, for which he wants answers continues to drive his learning process. His learning trajectory reflects the knowledge he has acquired through this process.

CONTEXTS

PAST
PRESENT
RESOURCES
SPACES
LEARNING ECOLOGY
created by a person
FUTURE
for a purpose to achieve
RELATIONSHIPS
proximal goals informed
by distal goals
PROCESSES
ACTIVITIES &
EXPERIENCES
WHOLE PERSON
AFFORDANCES
WILL, CAPABILITY, INTEGRATIVE
THINKING, EMOTIONS, ATTITUDES,
CONFIDENCE, TRUST & SELF-AWARENESS
DEVELOPMENT & ACHIEVEMENT

5 Learning Italian

In this narrative Sophie a higher education teacher and educational developer, describes her attempts to learn Italian with her husband and draws attention to the emotional side of a learning ecology. The previous illustrations have all been about learning informally. This example of a personal learning project connects the formal and informal worlds of learning.

Italy has been our favourite family holiday destination for the past twenty years or more. For a long time we had said to one another that one day, when we had time, we would learn Italian - conversational Italian so that we could be more at ease, more engaged and in tune with the culture when on holiday.

The opportunity came with a short course at the local university comprising four taught sessions and access to the Rosetta Stone online learning software over six weeks. My husband and I both enrolled and were informed that this was to be a quite immersive learning environment of conversation and exercises in class, and computer-based exercises, quizzes, and pronunciation practice.

After the first couple of classroom lessons, I was taken aback to be so vividly reminded of the emotional elements of my own learning experiences. I have spent my career in facilitating the learning of others, as teacher, trainer, on-line tutor, coach, mentor etc., and managing my own continuing professional development. However, in this chosen learning experience I felt, by turns, nervous, shy and embarrassed, daunted, and uncomfortably competitive. I felt better when using the Rosetta Stone materials, even though I felt that I was making quite slow progress. I enjoyed the experience and the look and feel of the online materials and felt reassured by the repetition and revision built into the exercises. By contrast, I felt that the classroom lessons each added more new vocabulary and complex grammar to the unending list of what I still needed to learn. The fast pace of the group work in the classroom did not work well for me.

My husband seemed to be coping well with the course, whereas I started to feel that I was overwhelmed and at sea - truly "immersed". I found myself seeking out approaches to language learning that I had used in my school French: lists and rules, declined verbs, explanations of tenses and grammar etc. I reminded myself that I like to see patterns and linkages in my learning, and that I need to successfully master basics, before I move on to new learning. I tried to master some basics using resources such as books, web materials, and other language learning packages I had found and borrowed from friends. Meanwhile, my husband was progressing to reading Italian newspapers and browsing Italian dictionaries for new vocabulary. He started sending me texts written in Italian.....I started to panic and really felt like giving up.

I spoke to my sister who had learned Portuguese by simply moving to Portugal with her husband and very new baby, and just getting on with it. She was supportive and encouraging to me...

When we actually went to Italy, I found that although I was reticent to speak I was more ambitious in my decoding of menus, posters, radio and television commentaries, and overheard conversations........Several people we encountered on holiday: waiters, a café owner, people in shops, were remarkably warm to us, and seemed interested in our attempts to use our Italian (more my husband's than mine of course). I started to feel that I might be able to slowly learn enough Italian to feel confident to converse. The "list" challenge I had faced had morphed to the idea of more of a "map" to explore. I sent a couple of texts and instant messages home to family members, using a little Italian. I decided I might investigate Italian films this autumn.

There are lots of situations in life where, in order to learn something, we need to create a learning ecology that combines learning in a range of *contexts* both formally structured settings and informal unstructured settings. Sophie's narrative illustrates this type of learning ecology very well. Her implicit distal goal was to develop herself as a person but her proximal goal was to develop her language skills so that she 'could be more at ease, more engaged and in tune with the culture when on holiday'. With her husband, a co-learner in the process, she embarked on a structured course with tuition which she perceived as the key affordance for her learning together with holidays in Italy. She utilised a multitude of *resources* (books, language software, menus, posters, radio, TV, films) and a range of *relationships and social interactions* including a teacher, fellow learners, family members and people she encountered on holiday. The story also reveals how she felt about the process of learning - the emotional roller coaster that both inhibits and motivates us during such processes and her need for

encouragement and support to offset the feelings of incompetency. In engaging in this process Sophie realised something that was profoundly important to her professional role as a teacher and contributed to her distal goal of developing her professional self.

> I have been vividly reminded that my own learning ecology crucially includes other people, as sources of encouragement and inspiration. I guess this is also probably true for my approach to most life challenges. I have re-learned something immensely valuable for me as a teacher and mentor about the emotional environment in which learning occurs, an environment which extends far beyond a formal and managed learning situation and any support for learning that might be designed into it.

This story illustrates that by changing the context for her learning - holidaying in Italy, she created entirely new opportunities for learning. In this context she started to gain the confidence to practise what she had learnt. Her *learning trajectory*, though slow, is revealed in her attempts to interpret what she read, saw and heard and her willingness to text in Italian.

6 Learning to be an archaeologist

Turning to the higher education environment what can we learn about the way students create their ecologies for learning from their narratives? In this extended narrative Michael, an archaeology graduate, tries to make sense of his experience of trying to become an archaeologist using the idea of a learning ecology.

> [In going to university] my core aim was to develop my understanding of archaeology to the highest possible level I could achieve. I wanted to become an archaeologist and that ambition caused me to get involved in many things outside my course that I thought would help me become an archaeologist.

> The most obvious process and set of relationships I engaged with to learn and understand archaeology was the timetabled and structured

university course. This involved the reading of set course material much of it accessed through on-line journals and participation in lectures. This structure that was designed and taught by my teachers allowed me to follow a very clear process of learning, helping me to fully understand what information I had to know within the course. My degree course formed the backbone to my learning about archaeology. It provided me with contacts with people who were also interested in my subject and enabled me to develop a mind-set that encouraged me to engage with archaeology in many different ways.

The one experience in my course where I feel I had to create my own learning process was my final year dissertation which required me to create a learning project around something I found interesting and challenging. I had taken a module in my second year which involved a technique called ZooMS for analysing collagen in animal bones to identify animal genus. The academic responsible for developing the technique wanted someone to try the technique on erasure rubbings from bones. I thought this was interesting so I wrote my proposal and created a process that involved me sourcing samples, experimenting using different rubbing and collagen extraction techniques, analysing the collagen using a Mass Spectrometer, then processing the data and writing up the results. Although the process for achieving my goal was not particularly smooth it was one that I had largely created based on my past experiences of academic research gained throughout my three years at university. A lot of different people helped me including my supervisor, laboratory technician, two of my peers who were involved in similar work, a museum curator, and a PhD student within the department. I drew on a range of resources and facilities including collections of ancient animal bones, specialist laboratory, processing software, and articles. The research process was not straightforward and I was forced to modify my process as I realised that certain methods did not give me the results I was hoping for.

Some of the best opportunities for me to learn how to be an archaeologist lay outside my degree course. For example, in my second year I joined a group of students that acted as an editorial team for a monthly archaeology journal called The Posthole, which published articles by archaeology students. I acted as a coordinator and also tried to attract writers. Working within this team was an important learning curve, ensuring that the team operated together smoothly to achieve a goal while bringing together the priorities of different individuals within the team.

Being an archaeologist involves 'digging' to expose artefacts through which we can interpret the past. Unfortunately, my course only provided a four-week introductory fieldwork course so I joined a number of 'digs', six in total run by two different PhD students, a member of the academic staff, a commercial company, and an external public organisation. Overall I probably spent over three months on excavations which gave me valuable insights into how to organise and conduct a dig, how to conduct various types of surveys, how to prepare, identify and display artefacts and beyond this how to work as a member of a team. The commercial digs I undertook introduced me to the world of commercial archaeology and the different approaches and mindsets that are used in the commercial world.

One of these projects had a particular significance for me. Homeless Heritage was started in 2009 by a PhD student at the University of Bristol. It is dedicated to working with homeless communities in order to understand and value the spaces used by such communities using archaeological methods. But it is more than archaeologists just applying archaeological techniques to the study of spaces that a particular group of people use: it involves working *with* homeless people in order to understand the relevance of what is found. In this way I was able to form friendships with people I would never have come into contact with in my student life. I began to appreciate the problems of homeless people and to see the world through their eyes. The experience enabled me to understand the value of contemporary archaeology, but I also began to see a new relevance of what I was doing, through it I became interested in the ways archaeology can be used to engage communities. The excavation was only the first stage of our project, the next stage involved telling people what wehad learnt. After carefully cleaning, describing and cataloguing the artifacts we had discovered we organised a week- long exhibition, in which everyone was able to get involved and introduce the project to a wider audience.

Through the Homeless Heritage project I developed an interest in using archaeology as a means of involving people in a community project and I made this the subject of a seminar I had to give at the end of my course. In my final year I began to imagine myself working in the field of 'community archaeology' and I discovered that the Council for British Archaeology (CBA) offered a number of Community Archaeology Training Placements. I decided that I would apply for one of these and to give myself a better chance of securing this position I volunteered to help the local organiser of the Young Archaeologists Club (YAC) and was able to assist her with the running of a number of Saturday trips for school children which I really enjoyed. Unfortunately, because of illness, I was unable to apply for the Community Archaeology Training Placements but the experience provided me with a useful insight into archaeology as a possible career, outside the more traditional roles of archaeologists.

Throughout the three years of my course I was fortunate enough to attend a number of conferences organised by the Theoretical Archaeology Group. I had to pay for these and they were outside the academic term. I thoroughly enjoyed the experience and it was a great opportunity to be exposed to people working in the field who presented the results of their research. This experience gave me the idea that we could perhaps run a conference for archaeology students nationally . With two other students I spent a significant part of my final year organising and marketing the two day conference which we held in July 2013. It was a great success with over 60 participants. Throughout the months of organising the conference a whole range of problems and issues were raised from working out the live streaming of the conference through to booking rooms and organising payments. Each of these challenges required us as a team to find contacts and resources that would help us to overcome each challenge allowing us to fully develop the conference into the successful project it was.

Looking back over my higher education experience I can now see that my course provided me with the basic knowledge I needed but that my attempts to learn archaeology and become an archaeologist involved much more than turning up for lectures and studying the reading list. I believe that the choices I made in getting involved in these wider experiences personalised my experience and the learning I gained from it. Most of these experiences were connected not so much to my course but to the bigger context of being amongst, and putting myself amongst, like-minded people interested in archaeology. The relationships I formed with some members of staff and doctoral students in particular opened new opportunities for me and enabled me to find the help I needed when I needed it. Since finishing my course, circumstances have meant that I probably will not pursue archaeology, other than for my own interest, but what I will carry with me is the belief that there are always opportunities to learn and develop if you look for them and if you are willing to get involved.

The more complex and demanding the learning project the more complex is the journey to achieve the goal. This narrative summarises key features of a project for personal transformation. Michael's narrative demonstrates how the idea of learning ecologies can be applied to undergraduate higher education. It shows that the process of learning, being and becoming is not simply confined to the structure, content and assessment of a course. Rather we see how his intrinsic motivations, his desire to become the sort of archaeologist he wanted to be, form the central purpose around which he creates his learning ecology (actually a collection of learning ecologies for the purpose of learning the practices of an archaeologist) not only to gain a good degree but to develop himself beyond what his course alone could achieve.

CONTEXTS
PAST
PRESENT
SPACES
RESOURCES
LEARNING ECOLOGY
created by a person
FUTURE
RELATIONSHIPS
for a purpose to achieve
proximal goals informed
by distal goals
PROCESSES
ACTIVITIES &
EXPERIENCES
WHOLE PERSON
AFFORDANCES
WILL, CAPABILITY, INTEGRATIVE
THINKING, EMOTIONS, ATTITUDES,
CONFIDENCE, TRUST & SELF-AWARENESS
DEVELOPMENT & ACHIEVEMENT

Michael had a clear distal goal - to learn archaeology and become the best archaeologist he could be and gain a good degree. That goal sustained his motivation over the three years he was studying for his degree but it was the particular projects he embarked on that gave him his proximal goals through which he created his own understandings of what it meant to be an archaeologist.

Michael's story shows how he found *affordance* to be and become an archaeologist in many different contexts many of which grew from the immediate circumstances of his life but some of which he searched for and found beyond his everyday living. His story reveals an unfolding and sustained process to access and utilise these affordances. Figure 3.2 was constructed with his help. It attempts to capture the main features of his ecology for learning.

Figure 3.2 Michael's learning ecology to become the archaeologist he wanted to be

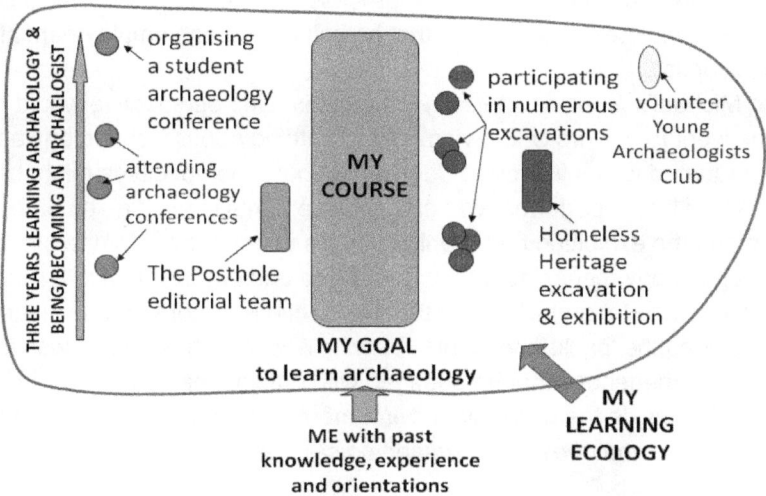

Within the boundaries defined by the three years of his course and the significant things he did that relate to his being and becoming an archaeologist, we see a multitude of *processes*, each with their own

purpose and proximal goals, connected by his overarching goal, a multitude of *relationships* involving people associated with the course and the university, and some people in the world outside the university, including people he met at conferences and on digs. He also experienced a multitude of *contexts* within which learning, development and achievement were accomplished. Through these different contexts he accessed and utilised an enormous range of *resources* eg codified and experiential knowledge and archaeological artefacts and tools such as specialist equipment.

We see his learning ecology being used not just to learn about archaeology, or even to be an archaeologist, but to become a certain type of archaeologist and beyond this we see Michael discovering that what he really enjoys doing is working with people. The narrative reveals how he discovered the particular aspects of being an archaeologist that he enjoyed and valued, and in that process how he found a possible way of continuing the ways of being that he valued through employment after university.

Michael's *learning trajectory* is complex. One perspective would be that he went to university knowing next to nothing about archaeology and he graduated with a first class degree. But other perspectives might be offered by his performances and achievements in the digs he participated in and the exhibition he organised, in his editorial work for the student-led archaeology magazine, or his leadership and organisation of a national conference for archaeology students. While Michael's course clearly provided the 'backbone' to his *'learning about'* archaeology it was the other experiences that he engaged with outside the course and in some cases outside the university environment, that enabled him to appreciate and learn what *'being an archaeologist'* meant to him.

7 Learning to be a radio news reader

Students use their time at university to explore possible careers in fields that are not related to their academic studies. They effectively build an ecology in order to gain experience and learn about a field they know little or nothing about. Natasha was in the second year of a politics degree when she realised that she had an interest in and a talent for radio broadcasting. She developed an ecology to explore whether radio might provide her with the basis for a career.

During the Easter vacation of my first year at university I got involved in the production of a play. It was through the play that I was first introduced to the university's radio station as a couple of us who were involved were given the opportunity to advertise the play on a news show. I enjoyed my role as guest on the radio show and after the show I talked to my friend about how I might get more involved and she recommended that I guest on her chat show, where students talked about topics that were of interest to them. In this way one opportunity led to another and opened up an entirely new interest for me.

I enjoyed the experience of live radio so much that when I returned home for the summer break I decided to look for a job in local radio. I called up lots of radio stations but no one was able to offer me any work experience. At this point my perseverance was tested as I could see no improvement therefore I lost motivation and thought about giving up..... Then my father spotted an advert for someone with media interests and skills for a local radio station. I ended up applying for a job at Susy Radio as a 'social media executive'. However, when I arrived for my interview I was informed that the role had already been filled. But I seemed to get on well with the presenter who interviewed me and when I told her about my work on the university newspaper and my interest in politics she told me that there was an opening within the news team as a news broadcaster. I bit her hand off! After a week of training, which was mainly observing how it was done, I took over as a news reporter, preparing a four-minute bulletin and reading it on air at 6pm and 7pm.

Working as a news reader has been a very steep learning curve. I observed news being read one day and the next I was reading it! I feel that one of my greatest assets in this field is my voice which because of past experience and coaching gained through drama and Lambda I can control and I am able to modulate, which makes it more interesting for the listener. Written communication has also been very important to the role. I had to write a script that is short, gets straight to the point and is factually correct.

Also, through working at Susy I met Geoff the radio station Director. Geoff has helped me improve in many aspects of my performance on the radio, he has offered me advice and helped me to analyse my own performance, helping me spot where I have done well and where there is room for improvement. From a practical point of view, having this experience in radio has greatly improved my employability as I have effectively started training for radio work through this job.

In this narrative we can see Natasha realising the affordance in her life to gain experience as a radio presenter. She is motivated by a number of distal goals, one of which was to develop herself so that she was employable when she graduated, so like many

CONTEXTS

PAST

PRESENT

SPACES

RESOURCES

LEARNING ECOLOGY
created by a person
for a purpose to achieve
proximal goals informed
by distal goals

FUTURE

RELATIONSHIPS

PROCESSES
ACTIVITIES &
EXPERIENCES

WHOLE PERSON
WILL, CAPABILITY, INTEGRATIVE
THINKING, EMOTIONS, ATTITUDES,
CONFIDENCE, TRUST & SELF-AWARENESS
DEVELOPMENT & ACHIEVEMENT

AFFORDANCES

students she is conscious that she needs to use all the opportunities available to her. The opportunity to get involved in live radio *(context)* emerged unexpectedly through being involved in a theatre production. She took the opportunity to be involved and found she had a natural aptitude and enjoyed the experience. She then went searching for other opportunities (local radio). The *relationships* she developed enabled her to gain the experience she wanted and also helped her develop the necessary skills for the role of news reader tapping into the *resources* - technical tools, information and the knowledge of the experienced broadcaster who became her mentor. Her *learning trajectory* was demonstrated through her live radio broadcasts which she had recorded and which sounded very professional.

Figure 3.3 Natasha's ecology for learning over 15 months while she was studying for her politics degree.

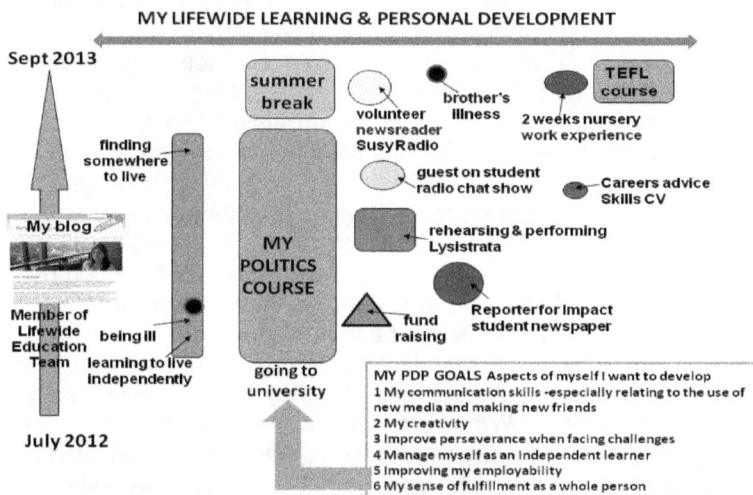

MY LIFEWIDE LEARNING & PERSONAL DEVELOPMENT

Sept 2013

summer break

brother's illness

volunteer newsreader Susy Radio

2 weeks nursery work experience

TEFL course

7

finding somewhere to live

My blog

MY POLITICS COURSE

guest on student radio chat show

Careers advice Skills CV

rehearsing & performing Lysistrata

Member of Lifewide Education Team

being ill

learning to live independently

going to university

fund raising

Reporter for Impact student newspaper

MY PDP GOALS Aspects of myself I want to develop
1 My communication skills -especially relating to the use of new media and making new friends
2 My creativity
3 Improve perseverance when facing challenges
4 Manage myself as an independent learner
5 Improving my employability
6 My sense of fulfillment as a whole person

July 2012

Exploring the unknown

We use our learning ecologies not only to explore our ability to cope with uncertainty but to challenge ourselves, test the skills we have developed and push ourselves to develop our capabilities further. For some students, physical activities like sport and outdoor pursuits provide an important context for skill development and the building of character. In this example Richard and Colin, two third year undergraduate students, describe the process of planning and then successfully participating in a kayaking expedition to Ethiopia to explore rivers that had not been kayaked before.

Richard: We originally intended to go to Pakistan, the northern area around Gilgut.....The only difficulty was that it was in Pakistan and Pakistan isn't very stable as a country....three weeks before we were due to go ten foreign trekkers were murdered by the Taliban in the area we were going to.... We decided it wouldn't be safe or sensible for us to go to Pakistan. So with three weeks to go we had to decide on another location for our expedition. We did in fact have a plan B. One of the team members (Peter) had proposed southern Ethiopia at the selection weekend....He had already done some ground work for an expedition to Ethiopia so we decided to go for that. He knew a lot about the rivers in Ethiopia but he didn't have contacts in the area we were going to, but he did have a contact in the rafting industry in Kenya who put him in touch with people in Ethiopia [which has been a great help]. One of the most difficult things has been trying to find a driver, a vehicle and a guide for when we are out there. We have tried to find contacts and people who can help us in a variety of ways. Some of it has been through internet searches and finding people who have kayaked in Ethiopia before and then trying to use their contacts. At a personal level my little sister is adopted from Ethiopia and when my mum was out there for just over a month she made connections in Addis, so I contacted these people and we're going to stay with them at their guest house initially and they said they would help put us in contact with a driver. .....We've got maps for the rivers but we will need a bit of a fixer. None of us speak Amharic, unfortunately, so we need someone who can fix things for us if we get stuck and if we're in trouble we need somebody who can talk to local people and if we're desperate we need to sort out food or water.

In this narrative we see a small group of people with similar distal goals of wanting to become great in their sport, and who were looking for adventure, coming together in the *context* of organising an expedition to a remote part of the world and pooling their *relationships and resources* to work out how to accomplish their goal. Each member of the team has his/her own ecology but they are woven together in a *co-created process* to achieve their collective goal. We see them identifying a number of logistical problems and the ways in which they were trying to solve them

CONTEXTS

PAST

PRESENT

SPACES

RESOURCES

LEARNING ECOLOGY
created by a person
for a purpose to achieve
proximal goals informed
by distal goals

RELATIONSHIPS

FUTURE

PROCESSES
ACTIVITIES &
EXPERIENCES

WHOLE PERSON
WILL, CAPABILITY, INTEGRATIVE
THINKING, EMOTIONS, ATTITUDES,
CONFIDENCE, TRUST & SELF-AWARENESS
DEVELOPMENT & ACHIEVEMENT

AFFORDANCES

under the pressure of a severe time constraint. We also see that they recognise that when they get to Ethiopia they will enter an entirely new and unfamiliar *context* and need to gain access to particular *resources* and develop a whole new set of *relationships* in order to complete the challenge they have set themselves. It is a continuous *process* of knowledge building and most of that knowledge will emerge through their experiences (process) and the relationships they make. Colin, another member of the team, continues the story of the expedition.

Colin: So the team were in high spirits after completing the first descent of a river called the Kola, first paddling a class three section followed by a lovely 10km bridge to bridge section of continuous class 3/4 and after some permit banter we decided to make a more ambitious plan... Our plan was to:
1 Wake up to find a lovely sunny day.
2 Drive to the Gidabo, a very promising river dropping an average of 20m/km for 25km through a big gorge, to find a perfect medium water level.
3 Paddle a 20km first descent gorge section of awesome class 4/5 whitewater.
4 Float leisurely down about 5km of flatwater meandering through vegetation to meet our driver and guide at the takeout in time for tea.

It was a lovely plan but it didn't happen like this. What actually happened was we were woken by thunderous tropical rain throughout the night, and crawled out of bed in the morning to find a day on the damper side of sunny. We drove to the river to find a promisingly not flood stage water level. Deciding it was good to go we jumped on and paddled 15km of awesome class 4/5 white water. Ear to ear grins were the order of the day as we proceeded smoothly and swiftly down what we all decided was some of the best paddling of its style we had ever done. The gorge was spectacular with untamed jungle and impressive cliffs towering above us. ....With beautiful black and white Colobus monkeys leaping overhead and only one straightforward portage round a scary 25ft waterfall our plan was developing well, the rapids were easing and we felt we must be getting close to the flat water at the end of the river.

The Google map terrain showed an ominous close packing of contour lines just before the flat section, whereas our Russian topographic maps from the 70's showed no indication of this. We had decided the Russians were right. [But] instead of petering out to flat water .....the river started picking up some significant gradient again. We found ourselves picking our way through some great class 4/4+ rapids characterised by huge boulders (and enough siphons to force concentration). Soon we found ourselves on the lip of a giant class 5+ boulder-jumble rapid and late in the day this was a clear portage for the team..... the gorge walls were [near vertical] and exactly how to portage was a lot less clear. Richard and Josh opted to gain a scary eddy above the lip of this beast and check whether access was possible along the left bank. Luckily it was and after one by one safely making the eddy some classic expedition jungle portaging ensued. A peek over the next horizon reluctantly concluded that the score was Google 1 : 0 Russia.

A few hours, lots of portaging, three swims (under trees and rocks), one paddle and some scary kayaking later we were running out of day in which to paddle. The *plan* was starting to go awry. We decided with limited daylight left and no sign of the borderline unrunnable whitewater relenting we had to call it a day and spend a night in the gorge. We found a decent footpath leading out of the gorge and pitched camp halfway up, with a troop of baboons surveying us from the opposite cliff face. Dinner was 375g of noodles and a tin of tuna shared between five of us and breakfast was a multipack snickers bar chopped into five pieces. Between these much enjoyed luxuries a bitterly cold night was endured, albeit in a stunning location.

Here we witness a small group of people working as a team *(collaborative relationships)* putting themselves into a totally unfamiliar and physically demanding *context* and relying on their *own resources and capability* as well as google and existing maps. Their passions and ambitions motivated them and they took calculated risks in order to challenge themselves and their own capabilities as expert kayakers. Their *process* for discovery was simply to engage with the river and try to read its behaviour according to their past experiences of kayaking. Through this process they discovered new knowledge about the river they were exploring: knowledge that could later be shared with other interested kayakers. The narrative also reveals that although we might make plans based on what we think might happen, the reality of the situation may be very different and we have to be prepared to improvise and adapt to the actual situations we encounter drawing on all of our past experience and capability. There is a strong element of learning from experience, much of it improvised in *their learning trajectory*. They had tackled and been successful with a challenge that had not been attempted before and developed their skills in the process.

8 Performing and recording a piano recital

There are many situations, particularly in the professional environment, where people work together in close collaboration to achieve a goal and in the process co-create an ecology through which they learn how to achieve their goal. In this narrative a concert pianist (Crapoulet 2008) describes how she worked with other university students to make a high quality classical recording of Chopin's 4th Ballade (for solo piano) to include in their respective professional portfolios to demonstrate their technical and professional skills.

The [recording] project was a true journey of discovery: it was a challenging undertaking that necessitated total engagement and concentration and the use of many skills - musical, technical, technological, creative and relational. It involved good preparation, good [technical] skills and an open enquiring mind..... We were plunged into a world in itself, with its own time-scale, its own space, and a complex problem to solve, which prompted us to respond with enthusiasm and dedication, revealing a rewarding and inspiring process of investigation, enquiry and revelation....

This project involved students from all years and backgrounds, thus cutting across the usual disciplinary boundaries. [The main people involved were] the pianist (myself) a PhD student (music) , Tonmeister, final year BMus student and a producer, MMus Production Module student. Others involved included an assistant to the Tonmeister (first-year BMus Tonmeister), observers (other MMus Production Module students) and a lecturer who was there to advise but who did not directly participate in the recording. Even though we each had specific technical knowledge and an individual role to play in the process, we were also very much aware of each other, constantly interacting with one another and learning new skills. Overall, the atmosphere of the whole project was particularly exciting because we felt that we were doing something worthwhile and meaningful.

Our objective was to produce and edit a high quality classical recording of Chopin's 4th Ballade (for solo piano), one which combined a good sound quality and a good performance. A good recording should make the listeners feel that they are sitting in a concert hall hearing a live performance, but without those distractions and potential flaws which can sometimes mar the concert experience (background noises, performer's mistakes, etc.).

The context was particularly conducive to good team-work and collaboration. We were all, in some way or another, seeking to achieve the best possible result, primarily because the whole process was not a purely academic exercise, but it was intimately linked to the world of recording classical music outside Higher Education. Not only was the recording to become part of our portfolios of recordings (which we shall be using as demonstration CDs for many years to come), but it was also conducted within a professional recording studio. It was particularly motivating, for instance, to have access to some of the most up-to-date technology in use at the moment in the recording industry. We thus discovered together the ins and outs of SADiE, for instance, the editing software we used at the postproduction stage. The Tonmeister student was very much familiar with this software as it was used in the (mainly classical) Chandos CD company with which he did his placement year. He was therefore able to show us how the programme worked in great detail as well as give us insights into his experience of his placement year.

Such a complex project, involving so many different skills and people, necessarily put us to the test and challenged our creativity. From this experience, we learnt first hand which qualities are fundamental to any form of enquiry which takes place within such a close-knit immersive experience: how to work together as a team, how to listen to each others' opinions in order to discuss the issues constructively, how to sometimes allow for compromise and how to always have an open, positive and dynamic attitude.

In order to achieve "perfection", the end result of a studio recording is in fact a *collage* of the best 'takes' we made during the recording session. A studio recording could best be described as a musical jigsaw puzzle - my performance is split up into sections during the recording session and then reassembled in step two, during the editing process. We aim to have at least two or three good 'takes' of each section from which we can choose when editing the piece.

Playing to a forest of microphones is not like playing to a live audience. In a recording studio, the musician relies exclusively on the producer and the sound engineer to achieve the best possible result. In order to be good, a classical recording must not only be note-perfect, it must also sound spontaneous and natural - something which is particularly difficult to achieve in what are often clinical studio conditions. At this stage, the producer's role is very important as [they have] the responsibility for noting down on the score all the errors and potential retakes. Throughout the session, the Tonmeister also keeps

106

a detailed record of all the takes we make (take numbers, bar numbers, sections played, quality of take, timing, etc.) so as to be able to locate them as fast as possible in the final editing phase of the project. In this way, at the editing stage, we will not have to listen through the whole 4 or 5 hours of recording in order to find the one we want each time. The producer and the Tonmeister's work at this point is crucial from my point of view, as I cannot remember all the mistakes I have made, nor can I judge certain aspects of phrasing, dynamics or tempo. It is indeed very important to keep the same tempi and dynamics throughout, in particular in multiple "takes", so that any potential cuts will not jar. It is not only my role but also the producer's role to judge whether my interpretation remains consistent throughout the session. The producer has to focus on listening to both the micro-level (specific mistakes which may require retakes) and the macro-level (the coherence of the takes in relation to each other).

The whole recording session is extremely tiring because I have to maintain my concentration and physical energy as well as the sense of spontaneity and freshness in my playing for the whole duration of the recording session. It is also a very exciting process as we try to solve problems of dynamics (the effects on tape are often achieved differently from those of a live performance, so I have to change my interpretation accordingly), discrepancies in tempo, technical difficulties, etc. within a short time-scale. We discuss various ways of interpreting passages and most importantly, the producer and the Tonmeister also support and encourage me when I get frustrated with certain passages which I sometimes cannot get "right" even after a dozen takes. Even in a sound-proofed recording studio, sometimes, a creaking piano stool, somebody banging a door outside or the ceiling cracking in a soft passage can spoil an otherwise perfect take, to our great dismay.

Once satisfied with all the takes, the producer, Tonmeister and myself will meet again in order to start the editing. The producer will prepare an editing plan which he works out from his notes. The idea is to have the fewest possible cuts in order to maintain continuity in the flow of the music. The tonmeister will use the producer's editing plan to make a "first" edit. The three of us will then listen to this first edit in one of the listening rooms, marking down on the score any spots which need re-editing. Very often, the first edit is a very rough cut and the editing will take several days to complete as we listen painstakingly to each and every note. The whole recording appears on the screen as a complex network of sound waves, which enables the Tonmeister to pinpoint the very start of each note with extreme precision. Sometimes it is very difficult to paste in certain sections where no silence occurs in the music and the Tonmeister will work on blending two takes together in order to smooth over the cut.

I have never had a more stimulating and rewarding time. If I were asked to briefly summarize what made this experience so valuable, I would emphasize the quality of the teamwork and the sheer excitement of having to deal constructively and creatively with the many problems and new challenges we faced at each and every stage of the project. All three of us - the Tonmeister, the producer and myself, worked in such close collaboration throughout and with such utter dedication to the task that we were able to produce a recording of Chopin's 4th Ballade whose quality we felt surpassed many commercial classical CDs. On the way, I also discovered many other things: the project involved not only sitting down at the piano and playing a piece of music, but also, in this case, listening to others' directives and opinions, deciding as a team how to proceed, and working out potential difficulties. To be allowed to try out our own ideas and proceed at times by trial and error was far more effective than to be simply told what to do. This was particularly valuable as in a non-academic or professional situation, we would not expect to be told how to solve the problems which we would be facing. [Rather] it involved making judicious decisions at every step throughout the process, working hand in hand and collaborating closely together at each stage of the project and always keeping an open enquiring mind as to the best ways to proceed and obtain the best result.

The narrative captures something of the intensity, energy and spirit of close collaborative working (*relationships*) under pressure and in an environment akin to a commercial recording situation. The *affordance* for professional development and achievement for all those who were involved, lay in the experience of musical performance and real-time recording of the performance in an environment that had been constructed for this purpose (*space*). It provides an excellent example of a group of highly skilled people working together to achieve a complex goal, striving for excellence in their achievement and learning and developing in the process. It reveals the complex interaction between people working together, with their specialist tools in a highly specialised environment (*relationships between people, tools and environment*) which provided the physical *context* for their collaborative learning ecology.

Complex performances and achievements, such as the one described cannot be accomplished by a single individual and the involvement of a group of people working as a team

and their *relationships* was core to the success of the project. Each participant contributed their talents and capabilities gained from past experiences, and together they created an inquiry-rich problem solving *process* which not only tested their own capability in performance but also provided an experience that was rich in opportunity and potential for their own learning and professional development. The process was authentic in the sense of mirroring the commercial world of recording with access to high quality *resources* - instruments, recording equipment and software that were all necessary for the performing and recording task. Their *proximal goal* - to create a recording of the highest technical and artistic quality was set within more *distal goals* concerned with both gaining the best marks for this aspect of their course and building a portfolio that would enable the students to gain employment in their chosen professional fields. Their *learning trajectory* is evidenced in the recording which was the tangible outcome from the learning ecology. The narrative also reflects the high degree of self-awareness of the narrator who was also the musical performer in the ecology.

Performance is one of the most difficult things to capture in a reflective narrative but this performer manages to convey a sense of her thoughts and feeling about the experience very well. She reveals something about her imaginings and planning for the moment of the performance, and her knowledge of the work, how she felt as she was waiting to perform and of her act of performing as she strives for musical perfection. She also reveals how she used her senses to access the information flows from her environment and use these in her performance. Such heightened self-awareness is a necessary part of the ecology of a performer and it enables her to convey what it is like to be immersed in your own ecology for achieving something you value and, through the reflective process, create deep meanings from the experience.

I sit motionless at the piano, my hands lying on my lap, my head bowed in intense and quiet concentration. I am about to perform one of my favourite pieces, a Ballade by Frederic Chopin. His fourth and last. Different from the others. Pervaded by mournful gypsy tunes reminiscent of Chopin's Polish roots, this work has always had an elusive, strange and mysterious quality. I remember walking alone in the hills, preparing this moment, playing the music in my head, over and over again, asking myself "what, why, how?", and linking tones with tones, phrases with phrases, chords with chords, trying to make sense of the music. As I searched for a meaning, a new world appeared, a world of abstract patterns and colours, relations and structures, a world which I would soon be bringing to life and communicating to my audience... A click. The black speaker in the corner of the studio suddenly comes to life, its little red light flashing urgently in the muted light, breaking the stillness. I look up towards the control room, vaguely seeing human shapes in the penumbra, separated from me by a thick tinted glass window. They wave and smile. I nod and wave back. 'All set, ready to go, take 1'. The disembodied voice of the producer breaks through the air. With another click, the sound engineer flips the microphone switch off. Again, I am alone.

A wave of silence washes over me. But it is not silent. Small sounds which would have otherwise gone unnoticed are suddenly magnified out of all proportion. The aeration vents are gently breathing in and out and the fluorescent lights are softly buzzing. The room feels alive, like some sleeping beast which will soon awaken to the sound and fury of Chopin's Ballade. I am not only to play the music. For a moment, I am to forget myself and be the music, and so doing draw my audience into the music so that they too forget themselves and become the music. But today, my audience is a forest of grey and black microphones. These are particularly difficult ears to please. Blind, unresponsive, unforgiving, silent, cold and calculating, they will remember and record every detail of my performance, the good moments, but also, the bad. It is difficult not to become self-conscious of one's technical limitations, to focus on the bad rather than the good. It is difficult not to give up in despair when two minutes into the music, something goes wrong and the whole section needs to be played again, and again, until every note has its correct place in the flow of the music. Every flaw, however minute, needs to be rectified until the piece is "perfect".

But what is perfection in performance? In a concert situation, many variables affect one's interpretation. The piano itself, sometimes bright, sometimes muted, its action heavy or light, greatly influences the way one plays a piece. The acoustics of the room - from a reverberant church to a dry, deadened hall - will affect its sound world. The audience, quiet or noisy, sullen or enthusiastic will change the whole atmosphere of the concert hall. Tempo, voicing, balance, phrasing or dynamic progressions are thus governed by such external variables, by a constant adjusting and readjusting of the interpretation to suit the moment, thus creating a two-way communication between the artist and the audience. That is why each and every live performance is never perfect as such because it is always different, but also always new and exciting, spontaneous and alive.

How different is the experience of the recording studio. Playing on one of the most beautifully toned and desirable pianos in the world, in one

111

of the most carefully gauged acoustics in the world, without the distractions that even the most well-behaved audience will provoke, my interpretation is stripped down to its most essential expression. Pencil poised above the score, the producer is waiting patiently, straining to hear the first notes of the piece, wishing me to play my best, ready to inspire me to new heights by taking on the role of an entire audience, responsive, enthusiastic and trustworthy. My lifeline.

The Tonmeister sits at the control panel, keeping an eye on the little screens, hands hovering over the buttons, ready to adjust volume and balance. He has already spent hours perfecting the sound, moving microphones here and there, until the recorded piano sounds as lifelike and natural as the piano itself. I reflect that they too are in a parallel world - a small box of a room dominated by two giant loudspeakers. Connected together by a thin network of wires, we are never so close as in those instants of silence before I play, when I can sense them holding their breaths, willing me to outdo myself. Lifting my hands to the keyboard, I close my eyes and feel the space around me receding, the walls of the studio falling away. The first three bell-like notes of the opening of the ballade seem to softly probe the surrounding air, an emerging melody as mellifluous and enticing as the call of a siren to lost sailors. Gradually, more voices are heard and the calm opening section gives way to an ever increasing crescendo of colours, textures and speed. Like fireworks, crisscrossing waves of sound build webs of lightning filaments, the chains of atoms dancing hand in hand to the sound of music. Sound is colour. Sound is texture. Sound is pattern. A revelation. I can see it, I can feel it, I can create it. Swaying slightly on the piano stool, I set my whole mind and body on building a living, ever changing architecture of sound from Chopin's masterpiece.

As the last notes of the piece die away, I feel the room heave a sigh, as if exhausted by such an onslaught of sound. The Tonmeister and producer are smiling and laughing, happy at the result. I too am elated, if slightly dazed by the intensity of the performance. Even so, for the next three hours, we painstakingly go through the piece line by line, page by page, over and over again as I try to recapture the spontaneity of the first take and improve each section so that the producer's final jigsaw of assembled takes will be as spontaneous, seamless and flowing as that first performance, so that it will be perfect not only in letter but in spirit. At the end of this experience, it seems to me that, together, we have transcended the emptiness and inhumanity of the recording studio, that I have been playing not to a blank wall of microphones but to a universal audience, the music thus reaching out far beyond the walls of the concert hall. Finally, we close the lid of the piano, disconnect the microphones and switch off the lights, locking the doors behind us.

CHAPTER 4
Ecology of Learning Through
a Higher Education

Introduction

The purpose of a higher education institution is to educate, to provide structured opportunities and experiences (modules and programmes) for learning and development. For some participants it is one of the most profound transformational experiences they will have in their whole life.

Michael's narrative in the previous chapter introduced the idea that we can examine the higher education experience from an ecological perspective. In this chapter I explore how we might develop the curriculum so that it provides greater affordance for learners to create their own ecologies for learning.

Learning Ecosystem

Higher education institutions are self-contained organisational ecosystems operating within a national tertiary education ecosystem (Jackson 2020). Since their mission is to educate and their primary task is to encourage and support learning we might view a university as a learning ecosystem rich in expertise, knowledge and other resources, tools, dedicated spaces and places designed for learning and social interaction, and many forms of professional support for learning. Together they create an environment that is rich in affordances for learning.

Environment denotes the totality of the surroundings, conditions and circumstances in which something or someone lives and functions. In human ecosocial systems the environment includes the cultures within which people live and work. A learning environment consists of a wide variety of things that affect learning. We might start with physical spaces such as classrooms, lecture theatres, computer rooms and specialist rooms where particular forms of social practice take place - like laboratories, workshops, dance studios and music rehearsal rooms, and then move to libraries and learning resource centres and into social spaces such as cafes, bars, and even the outside public spaces where people meet and talk. To these we must add the virtual spaces that provide spaces for people to interact. Learning environments are planned but how they are used can only be planned up to a point.

The idea of a learning environment implies a setting where intentions and design cannot account for everything that happens; some elements escape control or are at least unintended. Environment, then, is a mix of the deliberate and the accidental, the conjunction of planned and unanticipated events. To some extent, traditional teaching in conventional classrooms could support this dynamic—students could be given assignments to take in directions that show mastery but also imagination and creativity. Now, however, with minimally mediated access to large amounts of information and with a substantially enhanced social dimension available to students, the set of directions students can take in their learning is far larger and growing. Some of this change is sanctioned by faculty; other parts of it reflect the environmental changes brought by technology and a tipping of control in favour of students regardless of faculty intentions (Warger and Dobbin 2009).

The increasing use of information and communication technologies in teaching and learning is one of the primary drivers behind conversations about learning environments, though many of the fundamental principles involved are equally valid in settings with little or no technology. The idea of environment implies a multiplicity of participants, forces, resources and systems interacting. Environment is dynamic—changing in response to influences from outside or arising inside. It recognizes complexity in causes and effects (Warger and Dobbin 2009:6). Many authors have used the idea of ecology/ecosystem to represent the interaction of people in their learning environment. For example, Hannafin and Hannafin (1996) used the idea of ecology/ecosystem to embrace the complexity, interactivity and interdependency of the functions, activities, structures, resources and people that are involved in a university's learning enterprise and learning environment.

> Learning environments operate as ecosystems. Individual elements must function autonomously as well as interactively..... In learning environments, learners as well as facilitators observe, measure, test, listen and probe to assess the integrity and effectiveness of the environment [to support learning] and make needed changes. This may require the learner and facilitator to examine and adjust strategies, technologies or learning activities to achieve balance. It requires active teaching and learning to develop understandings of how each element, as well as the overall system is functioning.. Ecosystems are judged successful when they promote equilibrium among their components and interact in ways that support their functions (Hannafin and Hannafin 1996 52-3)

Ellis and Goodyear (2010) positioned their examination of students' experiences of e-learning in the context of 'the broader ecology of learning and teaching' that a university supports. They develop a compelling narrative for viewing the university as a large complex ecosystem involving the relationships and interactions of all the inhabitants - students, teachers, researchers, support and administrative staff, managers and leaders, and their connections with employers and society more generally, and the resources, physical spaces and virtual environments, processes and practices that are played out day to day. They used the term, 'ecology of learning' to represent the educational practices and learning activities that promote students' learning stating, 'we feel it best represents the nature of the phenomenon which has students at its centre, and includes all legitimate stakeholders including teachers, university service providers and university leaders.' (Ellis and Goodyear 2010:51). From a university ecosystem perspective the key aspects of an ecology of learning (ibid 20) are: maintenance of an ecological balance; the development of self-

116

awareness of how the parts of the ecology are related to the whole; the ongoing pursuit of feedback to inform self-awareness and the capacity of self-correction (agility) required to ensure (re)alignment in a rapidly changing world.

> Maintaining an ecological balance on learning requires all the parts of the university to act in ways that demonstrate self-awareness of their function and purpose in relation to the mission of the institution..... In order for the parts of the university to understand how they [its component parts] are functioning, in relation to the work and purpose of the whole, they need to engage in systematic processes of collecting feedback from stakeholders about the effectiveness of their operations..... Ellis and Goodyear (2010:30)

These perspectives on the university as a complex ecosystem for learning provide a useful foundation on which to develop and apply the concept of learning ecologies at the level of teachers and student learners.

Curriculum

Learning in higher education is traditionally formed around a curriculum that is determined by teachers who are organised into academic disciplines. In their book 'Engaging the Curriculum' (Barnett and Coate 2005:16) assert that 'curriculum goes to the heart of what we take higher education to be, of what might be and should be in the twenty first century'. This chapter and this book are trying to engage with the important question of what we take higher education to be, of what might be and should be in the decades to come, in the context of helping students develop themselves for their complex and unknowable future learning lives.

The word "curriculum" began as a Latin word meaning "the course of a race". By the nineteenth century, European universities routinely referred to their curriculum to describe both the complete course of study and particular courses and their content. How we define and perceive the curriculum has important consequences for how we approach the task of promoting students' learning and development, including the way they perceive their affordances for learning. From an ecological perspective, perhaps the most useful definition of a curriculum is that proposed by (Wiles 2008) and Kelly (2009) 'the totality of student experiences that occur in the educational process'.

It is all a matter of whether the educational process is defined narrowly or expansively. At one end of the continuum a learner's educational process might be limited to that which is taught and learnt within a programme. At the other end of the continuum it includes all a student's experiences while they are studying at university - since most experiences have some potential for learning (Jackson 2011a).

Smith (2000) considered the idea of curriculum from four perspectives:
- *Curriculum as content* - a syllabus or body of knowledge to be transmitted and learnt
- *Curriculum as product* - an attempt to achieve certain ends in students like the achievement of specified objectives. The outcomes model in higher education is a product-oriented curriculum
- *Curriculum as process* - curriculum results from the interaction of teachers, students and knowledge. It is what actually happens in the classroom and what people do to prepare and evaluate learning achieved.
- *Curriculum as praxis* - the process/activity by which a theory or skill is enacted, embodied or realised.

The last two conceptions have most relevance to the concept of a learning ecology. In higher education the term curriculum is often perceived as being synonymous with the subject or subjects taught within a student's academic programme. There is thus a relationship between curriculum and the disciplines that form the basis for the academic organisation of a university. In fact, Berger (1970) emphasised the idea of discipline as curriculum in his definition of a discipline as 'a specific body of

118

teachable knowledge with its own background of education, training, procedures, methods and content areas.'

Curriculum can also be visualised as an instrument or tool for delivering policy. Fotheringham et. al., (2012:2) visualised the *curriculum as vehicle* to recognise the curriculum as a fulcrum between high level policies and the students that these policies are intended to serve. Such a conception recognises the importance of curriculum, in the sense of both product and process, as the driving force supporting delivery of institutional policies and priorities. This concept would also be relevant to the idea of developing students' abilities to create self-determined learning ecologies if this became an institutional objective in the way personal development planning has for example.

Academics' conceptions of curriculum

In their study of curriculum in higher education Fraser and Bosanquet (2006:274) identified four ways in which academics think about curriculum:
1) the knowledge, learning and experience contained within a unit or module of study
2) the content and process of a programme of study comprising a variably prescribed set of study units or modules
3) the students' experience of learning: a process that is negotiated between learners and teachers and includes 'intended and unintended.....transactions' between a learner and a teacher'
4) a collaborative partnership between learners and teachers that results in changes for both learners and teachers.

All these conceptions are based on an assumption that learners learn a curriculum, whether it is designed for them or negotiated with them.

In their study of creativity and curricula Edwards et al (2006) derived a similar set of perspectives on what faculty thought curriculum meant but also detected something that was much more emergent.

Use [of the term curriculum] varied widely, ranging from 'syllabus' and programme plans, to notions of the hidden curriculum, in which the social, cultural and political context (what some participants described as the 'fuzzier bits') was counted as part of what was taught. ... However, one conception of the curriculum emerged for understanding the broader possibilities for understanding creativity. This was the idea of the lived curriculum as experienced in the classroom. ... The lived curriculum arose dynamically out of [the teachers] interactions with students. (Edwards *et al.* 2006:60)

Oliver's (2002) interview-based study confirms that these are the ways that academics think about curriculum and also recognised that individuals hold multiple conceptions' of curriculum which can be drawn upon in the same conversation. The following exemplify the variety of conceptions held:

- The absence of curriculum
- Curriculum as content map
- Curriculum as programme map
- Curriculum as process
- The hidden curriculum
- The lived curriculum

Whilst none of these should be viewed as *the 'right' definition* (they are all possible right answers depending on the way curriculum is being framed and used) it is interesting to note that some of the concepts presuppose others. With the exception of the absent and the lived curriculum, the definitions seem to become increasingly inclusive and holistic in terms of influences on teaching and learning.

The notion of the lived curriculum seems to represent a conceptual leap from conceptions that emphasise planning, designing, organising and instructing towards a conception of spontaneous performance, coping and being a part of a shared experience. It is a concept of emergence in which the experience of delivering changes what has been designed emerges dynamically out of interactions with students.

You've got to improvise - it's like a performance, in a way. One in which the audience can heckle and change the ending and stuff like that - you're not in complete control, and there's no road map, and you just have to prepare as best you can and then cope (Oliver 2002 faculty interviewee).

Curriculum as an ecology for learning

The idea that a curriculum is inhabited by people and brought to life through the interpretations and actions of the teacher and the responses of her students to those actions, in an environment that is structured and culturally attuned to encouraging and supporting learning is an ecological concept. It suggests also that learning itself is an emergent phenomenon: something that is only brought into being as a result of people participating and interacting in particular disciplinary and pedagogic contexts, working with the resources, tools and technologies that are available within the space it affords for

> Learning is 'the emergence in action of a *new* relational product growing out of the uniqueness of the individual on the one hand, and the materials, events, people, or circumstances of his life'. (adapted from Rogers 1961 - the word new has been substituted for novel)

learning, on the problems and inquiries that are relevant to the situation.

I have adapted Rogers' (1961) definition of creativity to capture the idea that learning emerges from the circumstances of a learner's life as a result of participating in a curriculum that has been brought to life by the teacher and enacted through their relationships with the teacher, their peers and the subject material and other resources in their learning environment. This way of thinking about a learner inhabiting their learning environment is entirely consistent with the notion of an ecology for learning and we can relate the idea of curriculum to the conceptual framework for a learning ecology developed in chapter 2 (Figure 4.1).

Barab and Roth (2010) discussed the idea of curriculum-based ecosystems and suggested that the curriculum could be 'usefully arranged' around problematic situations with accompanying resources and tools rather than disciplinary content alone. The problem frames the learning situation (context) and gives meaning to content and purpose to the learning with which it is associated.

> curriculum-based ecosystems begin by setting up the problem and then making available various resources and suggested activities through which students assemble the necessary networks for solving the problem (Barab and Roth 2006:9).

Figure 4.1 Visualisation of a learning ecology

Holistic curriculum paradigm

What if higher education whole heartedly embraced the idea of learning ecologies? What concept of curriculum would optimise the affordances for students to experience and be aware of their own ecologies for learning? As we saw earlier, there are many conceptions of curriculum and the way it is defined determines the nature and extent of affordances for student learners to create their own ecologies of practice for learning, developing and achieving.

For the purpose of exploring the what if question I will adopt the most expansive concept of a higher education curriculum that I can think of namely a lifewide curriculum (Jackson 2011b) which includes all a student's experiences while they are studying at university - since most experiences have some potential for learning. In fact, the recent expansion of co- and extra-curricular award schemes in UK higher education (Jackson 2014) means that many universities are implicitly adopting a lifewide curriculum although they do not use this term to represent what they are doing. Such schemes enable a learner to incorporate and integrate their learning from any aspect of their life into their higher education experience. The concrete expression of a lifewide curriculum is depicted in Figure 4.2.

Figure 4.2 A lifewide curriculum (Jackson 2011c, 2014)

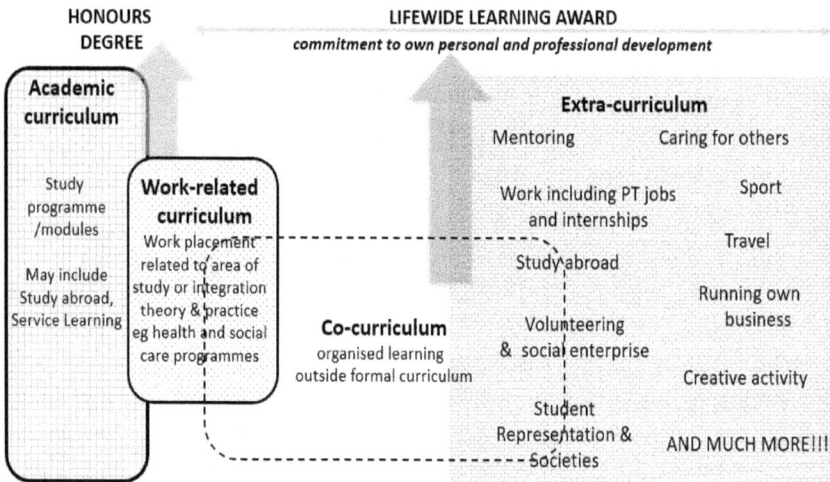

A lifewide curriculum contains four curricular domains:
1. academic curriculum, which may by design integrate real-world work or community-based experiences;
2. work-related curriculum which is linked to a programme but does not receive academic credit

3. co-curriculum: experiences provided by the university that may or may not be credit-bearing and for which learners may or may not receive formal recognition;
4 extra-curriculum: experiences that are determined by the learners themselves and constitute all the spaces that they inhabit outside the other domains.

The distinction between co- and extra-curricular has been deliberately blurred in some universities as experiences that would be considered to be extra-curricular in Figure 4.2 have been incorporated into the co-curriculum.

Academic curriculum
The academic curriculum is predominantly focused on *learning about a subject* with heavy reliance on explicit or codified knowledge mediated by teachers who embody an epistemology of practice that is appropriate to 'being an academic in a particular disciplinary field'. Experiences in the academic curriculum tend towards mastering theory-rich knowledge through transmission, self-study and sometimes small group study. Most subjects taught in universities adopt the lecture as the most efficient teaching vehicle for transmitting information but it is the poorest vehicle for enabling learners to develop their knowing. Barab and Roth (2006) are critical of pedagogies that do not permit learners to understand through situating their learning in a context of purposeful and relevant activity.

Fortunately, teachers in all disciplines employ a wide range of strategies to engage students in more active forms of learning. Approaches to learning that encourage learners to form personal or collaborative ecologies for learning include project-based, problem-based, inquiry-based, context-based - work / community / field -based, designing-making, enterprise-led, game-play/role-play, student-organised seminars, conferences and exhibitions, participation in competitions contract-based learning where goals and outcomes are negotiated. It is in the more active approaches to learning that the greatest affordance for students to create their own ecologies for learning.

Work/practice curriculum

In the work environment the emphasis is on tacit knowledge that is embodied in the conversations and relevant social practices of the people who are involved in work. In the work environment learning and development are a by-product of performing and accomplishing a task or project rather than being the focus for the task.

The practice-curriculum replaces the largely theoretical thinking experience of the classroom with the emotionally turbulent, real time, experiential and situational problem solving environment of work. It involves learning through doing in dynamic contexts, and sometimes not succeeding so that learning through mistakes is important. It involves working alongside and observing people who are already expert and tapping into their tacit embodied knowledge.

The role of the educator is to: a) prepare learners for their experience and support them through it, b) encourage reflection and support this process through tools and strategies that will enable learners to think deeply and systematically about their experience drawing maximum benefit from it and c) help learners recognise their complex learning and achievements, and value their self-evaluations of their informal learning.

Participating in the practice curriculum enables learners to learn and be inducted into an epistemology of social practice which is fundamental to being able to build ecologies for learning and achievement in a particular work environment. The epistemology of (professional) work practice (coming to know what to do through working in specific situations drawing on past experiences which includes learned theory) can only be learned through the experience of practising with other practitioners. The epistemology of practice pays particular attention to the idea of Legitimate Peripheral Participation (Lave and Wenger, 1991). It is situations of social practice that learners come to know what it means to be creative in the organisational and professional cultures of a particular work environment.

Eraut and Hirsch (2007 and chapter 4) notes that the basic epistemology of practice involves the professional actions of:

- *Assessing situations* (sometimes briefly, sometimes involving a long process of *investigation and enquiry*) and continuing to monitor the situation;
- *Deciding what, if any, action to take*, both immediately and over a longer period (either on one's own or as a leader or member of a team);
- *Pursuing an agreed course of action*, performing professional actions - modifying, consulting, evaluating and reassessing as and when necessary;
- *Metacognitive monitoring of oneself*, people needing attention and the general progress of the case, problem, project or situation; and sometimes also learning through reflection on the experience.

They are the essential processes that underlie self-regulation (chapter 5) and the key processes necessary to build and maintain an ecology for achieving and learning. Consequently, the work/social practice environment offers learners significant affordance for developing and applying their self-regulatory skills and behaviours, and developing and implementing their own ecologies for learning.

Co-curriculum

The co- (complementary) curriculum, is not part of the formal academic or practice curriculum. It contains experiences or opportunities provided by the university that may or may not be credit-bearing and for which learners may or may not receive formal recognition. The co-curriculum may contain opportunities for learning particular skills that are essentially taught and where a competent authority determines what will be learnt and how it will be learnt. But the co-curriculum is also likely to contain opportunities for learning in unstructured situations where learners participate in social practice in community organisations or employment settings outside the university, or perhaps involve themselves in an enterprise activity like creating a business, organising an event or entering a competition. In these situations learners, often working collaboratively, are more able to determine their own goals and purposes, knowledge and skill content, processes, resources, tools and technologies and outcomes/achievements.

A distinctive feature of co-curricular activities is their potential for incorporating diversity (learners from all levels, all disciplines and all cultural backgrounds) into the experience and for learners themselves to take a more direct role in shaping, co-creating and facilitating the experience. Such opportunities provide considerable opportunity for engaging in social practice and even creating such practice, and for creative self-expression. The role of the professional educator here is to ensure that learners are aware of these things and that self-evaluation processes designed into the experience draw attention to these forms of learning and creativity. The co-curricular environment offers learners significant affordance to develop and implement their own ecologies for learning often in partnership with their peers and facilitators.

Extra-curriculum

The extra-curriculum domain comprises all the experiences that are determined by the learner themselves and constitute all the spaces that they inhabit outside the other curricular domains. We don't normally consider this domain in higher education yet it is sometimes the largest and often the most creative part of a learners life. It is rich in experiences that involve complex relationships and social interactions with family and friends, sustained activities that are grown from need - like having to earn an income to support study, activities that are pursued for their intrinsic interest and challenges - like sport, hobbies, membership of societies, drama groups, religious affiliations, and looking after yourself as an independent adult. All these things need to be incorporated into a busy life. Space needs to be found and lives have to be organised to enable things to happen while retaining the ability to improvise when faced with the unexpected.

The extra-curricular domain is rich in novel experiences since this is where people experiment and try out entirely new experiences. For example, travel may put a learner into a culture very different to their own, or serious illness or loss of a close friend or relative may push people into emotional spaces that have never been encountered before and stand out as significant events in a learner's life. There is much informal and complex learning embedded in many of these situations which could be recognised as part of the personal growth of the individual.

In the extra-curricular domain learners choose their own contexts for participation and spending their time motivated by their own interests, purposes and beliefs. The unstructured and sometimes chaotic nature of experience provides great affordance for learners themselves to determine their own goals, plan and execute their own strategies, develop and apply their capability to deal with particular situations, identify, use and create resources, use their own tools and technologies, monitor and judge their own performance and what they have achieved. Because of these characteristics it offers the greatest affordance for students to build their own ecologies for learning, developing and achieving.

Teacher Ecologies for Students' Learning

Higher education teachers have the most wonderful opportunities to create ecologies to help and enable students to learn and they have abundant resources and infrastructures in the learning environment to support the ecologies they create. A teacher's ecology for learning involves the teacher and their students immersed in a curriculum (usually subject-based) which is brought alive by the teacher's pedagogic practices and expertise, enacted and supported within the university's learning environment which is rich in places, spaces, resources, tools, technologies and professional support for learners and learning. The teacher's ecology for learning is located in the present and emerging near future but it is connected to the past through the learning and capabilities gained in previous learning ecologies they have created. It will be connected to future learning ecologies when they are brought into existence. It is very much part of the 'flow' which Barab and Roth (2006) consider is so important to the creation of meaning.

When educators fail to engage students in meaningful relations and instead impart core ideas as isolated facts or abstract concepts, these facts and concepts are no longer connected to the situations that allow them to be powerful tools in the world. The core disciplinary formalisms (facts, concepts, practices, methods, principles) run the likely risk of becoming disembodied and effectively disconnected from any meaningful use in the world.........The irony is that we then wonder why [students] appear unmotivated to learn after we have disconnected meaning from the learning situation, assuming that the learner somehow will attribute the same functional value to the information as the teacher does. It is in response to this problem that we argue for an ecological view of learning and participation, one that allows content to live in its contextual richness with a focus on helping students attend to those underlying, invariant structures that also have cross-contextual value (Barab et al., 1999). In essence, we believe that "the place to look for meaningful content is not in the normal physical descriptors of individual particles [nor in the individual], but instead in the variables of the flow itself" (Swenson, 1999, p. 21). It is within this coupling of individual and environment, in the flow itself, that ecological psychologists locate meaning and intelligent action (Barab & Plucker, 2002) (Barab and Roth 2006:3-4)

Unfortunately, while teachers have huge affordances for the creation of ecologies for learning, learners themselves may not have the same opportunities to create their own ecologies for learning. Their affordances depend on the way their programme has been designed and the way the teacher interprets and brings alive these designs. Depending on the underlying educational philosophy learners' learning ecologies may be tightly controlled in terms of what is learned, how it is learned and when it is learned depending on whether the teacher adopts a transmission, guided discovery or self-directed learning strategy or any blend of these possibilities. A learner's experience has to be viewed comprehensively and holistically in order to understand the nature of the learning ecologies that are being deployed.

Pedagogy : bringing a curriculum to life

A curriculum without a teacher's pedagogy is a lifeless thing. It's no more than a specification that sets out the hopes and expectations of the curriculum designer, which may or may not be the teacher whose job it is to give it life. So what are the skilled social practices that breathes life into a curriculum specification? According to Smith (2000) the commonest view is that pedagogy is about teaching, and in the context of the academic curriculum it is about teaching a subject. In fact this view of pedagogy is essentially a didactic view, 'the concerns of didactics are: what should be taught and learnt (the content aspect); how to teach and learn (the aspects of transmitting and learning): to what purpose or intention something should he taught and learnt (the goal/aims aspect) (Künzli 1994 quoted in Gundem 2000: 236).

But there are, according to Smith (ibid), other dimensions of pedagogy that are more relevant to the idea of ecologies for learning, these include pedagogy as accompanying, caring for (and about), bringing learning to life and having a fundamental concern for enabling people to flourish. This moves us away from a transmission and acquisition model of learning towards a more social and relational view of a teacher facilitating students' learning and caring for them and their flourishing. This view of pedagogy is consistent with Thomson et al (2012:8) who locate pedagogy in the highly situated social practices of the individual teacher and their social-cultural setting. These authors capture well the relational and ecological nature of being a teacher in the most profound sense of the word.

> Pedagogy is more than teaching method, more than curriculum, more than assessment practice (Leach and Moon 2008). It is all these things, but it is also how they are made into patterns of actions, activities and interactions ..... by a particular teacher, with a particular group of students [in a particular context]. The concept of pedagogy encompasses relationships, conversations, learning environments, rules, norms and culture within the wider social context (Facer 2011).

Smith (2000) develops further the idea of pedagogy as *bringing learning to life* through the actions of : *Animation* - bringing 'life' into situations. This is often achieved through offering new experiences. *Reflection* - creating moments and spaces to explore lived experience and *Action* - working with people so that they are able to make changes in their lives.

Animation

In their book *Working with experience: Animating learning* (Miller and Boud 1997) link 'animating' to 'learning' because of the word's connotations: to give life to, to quicken, to vivify, to inspire. They see the job of animators (animateurs) to be that of 'acting with learners, or with others, in situations where learning is an aspect of what is occurring, to assist them to work with their experience' (ibid:7). They work with people on situations and relationships so that they are more stimulating and satisfying. However, they also look to what Dewey (1916) described as 'enlarging experience and to making it more vivid and inspiring'. They encourage people to try new things and provide opportunities that open up fresh experiences

Reflection

Conversation is central to the practice of informal educators and animators of community learning and development. With this has come a long tradition of working with the concerns and interests of those they are working with, while at the same time creating moments and spaces where people can come to know themselves, their situations and what is possible in their lives and communities.

Action

This isn't learning that stops at the classroom door but is focused around working with people so that they can make changes in their lives - and in communities. As Lindeman put it many years ago, this is education as life. Based in responding to 'situations, not subjects' (Lindeman 1926: 4-7), it involves a committed and action-oriented form of education. In short, this is

131

a process of joining in with people's lives and working with them to make informed and committed change.

McWilliam (2009) incorporates these ideas into her own *caricatures* of pedagogic practice suggesting that there are three basic pedagogic stances a teacher can adopt (Figure 4.3) which she calls, 'sage on the stage' (knowledge transmitter), 'guide on the side' (facilitator), and 'meddler-in-the-middle' (an involved co-learner/co-producer in the learning process).

Figure 4.3 Representations of teacher as 'sage on the stage', 'guide on the side' and 'meddler in the middle' (McWilliam 2009)

Each stance results in a different type of ecology for learning with different types and levels of affordance for student learners to form and pursue their own goals, define and create their own process for learning and involvement in assessment, create/co-create their own content, and give and receive feedback to peers and teacher. Transmission models of teaching have far fewer affordances for students to create their own ecologies for learning than more facilitative or meddling models of teacher as co-learner.

Active learning means that learners take more responsibility for and are actively engaged in their own learning rather than simply receiving and processing the information given to them by their teachers. Students must do more than just listen. They must read, inquire, question, discuss, write and be engaged in solving problems. In particular, students must engage in such higher-order thinking tasks as analysis, synthesis, and evaluation (Bonwell & Eison 1991). Of course, the reality is that even in a lecture-based course, students are, or should be doing all of these things alongside the lectures they are attending.

But purposeful active learning in which activities have been conceived and implemented to deliberately engage learners in particular forms of learning, engages students in two different ways - through doing things and thinking about the things they are doing and have done (ibid 1991). In this way active learning strategies can be aligned to the self-regulatory model of learning (Zimmerman 2000 and chapter 5) that embraces the motivations to do something and the thinking about what needs to be done (forethought), the doing (performance) and the thinking about what has been done and achieved (reflection).

In active learning less emphasis is placed on information transmission and more emphasis is placed on developing student thinking and communication skills and the exploration of attitudes, values and beliefs. Student motivation is increased because of their interest and involvement in what they are doing. Furthermore, in active learning, students are able to receive immediate feedback from their teacher.

All teaching and learning techniques that seek to encourage and develop students' as the creators of their own ecologies for learning must involve active learning and should embrace the triadic processes of forethought, performance and reflection of the self-regulatory model of learning (Zimmerman 2000 & chapter 5).

Pedagogy-andragogy-heutagogy continuum

Hase and Kenyon (2000) draw attention to the continuum of teaching practices used to encourage and support learning and development from instructional models at one end of the continuum, through teaching that is facilitative where learners have some autonomy over how and what they are learning (an andragogic approach) to educational environments where the learner is empowered and enabled to make their own decisions about their own learning (heutagogic approach). They argued that it was important for higher education to pay more attention to the latter.

> Education has traditionally been seen as a pedagogic relationship between the teacher and the learner. It was always the teacher who decided what the learner needed to know, and indeed, how the knowledge and skills should be taught....... It may be argued that the rapid rate of change in society, and the so-called information explosion, suggest that we should now be looking at an educational approach where it is the learner himself who determines what and how learning should take place. Heutagogy, the study of self-determined learning, may be viewed as a natural progression from earlier educational methodologies - in particular from capability development - and may well provide the optimal approach to learning in the twenty-first century (Hase and Kenyon 2000).

While most teachers in higher education are familiar with the idea of pedagogy, they are unlikely to be familiar with the terms andragogy and heutagogy which are more commonly used in adult education. Knowles (1975) suggests that andragogy is characterised by learner control and self-responsibility in learning, learner definition of learning objectives in relation to their relevance to the learner, a problem-solving approach to learning, self-directedness in how to learn, intrinsic learner motivation, and incorporation of the learner experience. In an andragogical approach to teaching and learning, learners are actively involved in identifying their needs and planning on how those needs will be met (Blaschke 2012). A key attribute of andragogy is *self-directed learning*, defined by Knowles (1975:18) as:

a process in which individuals take the initiative, with or without the help of others, in diagnosing their learning needs, formulating learning goals, identifying human and material resources for learning, choosing and implementing appropriate learning strategies, and evaluating learning outcomes

In adopting an andragogic approach, the educator acts as a tutor and mentor, with the instructor supporting the learner in developing their capacity to become more self-directed in their learning. Teachers establish objectives and construct the curriculum in response to the needs and inputs of learners and provide resources to support their learning. Their role is to guide learners along their chosen pathways while the responsibility for learning lies with the learner themselves (Blaschke 2012).

Heutagogy (based on the Greek for "self") views learning as an active and proactive process determined by learners themselves: learners are "the major agent in their own learning, which occurs as a result of personal experiences" (Hase & Kenyon, 2007:112). The teacher facilitates the learning process by providing affordance in their designs and practices, guidance and resources, but they empower the learner to create their own process (or ecology) for learning. Learners are able to negotiate learning intentions and the outcomes to be assessed. They are able to determine what will be learned, how it will be learned and how it will be assessed (Hase & Kenyon, 2000; Eberle, 2009). The heutagogical approach to learning is entirely consistent with the idea of self-determined learning ecologies, while the andragogic approach contains elements consistent with an ecological view of self-directed learning.

Signature pedagogies

Signature pedagogies (Schulman 2005) create ecologies for learning that are relevant in particular disciplines and curricular contexts. They are the modes of teaching and learning, used in the preparation of people for a particular profession such as law, medicine, teaching or being an architect, engineer or geologist. They provide the pathway to admission into the practices of the profession and involve not just learning to think academically within the disciplinary field but also to think and behave as a professional practitioner would.

> The educator in a profession is teaching someone to understand in order to act, to act in order to make a difference in the minds and lives of others-- to act in order to serve others responsibly and with integrity.....professional education is a synthesis of three apprenticeships–a cognitive apprenticeship wherein one learns to think like a professional, a practical apprenticeship where one learns to perform like a professional, and a moral apprenticeship where one learns to think and act in a responsible and ethical manner that integrates across all three domains (Schulman 2005).

Signature pedagogies are heavily routinised and systematic. There is little room for novelty in the approach to a case. Learning is undertaken in social practice contexts, for example - studios, laboratories, workshops, the field, hospital or other environment where people work. Such settings provide experiences that are more unstructured, informal and unpredictable and learners have to be able to assess situations, formulate strategies to deal with them and monitor and adjust their own performance in dealing with them ie engage in professional self-regulated learning.
  Signature pedagogies are crucial for enabling learners to develop their own ecologies of practice so that they can perform and learn in the relevant domains of practice.

Pedagogy for exploring the present

Facer (2016) argues that to develop a pedagogy that supports future learning we need to develop a pedagogy that develops people in ways that they can explore and understand the possibilities and affordances of the present: in other words a teacher pedagogy of the present that develops learners' heutagogic capabilities and orientations for exploring the present in order to understand its affordances and possibilities for learning and developing themselves into a different future (Facer 2016 58-9).

....an educational practice that wishes to take the future seriously might begin with the cognitive, affective and political task of becoming aware of *the potential for novelty in the future.* Stated simply, the future, from this perspective, would be understood as a source of rich possibility of *different* ways of being..........

As such, the future needs to be understood not as a known territory to be mapped and conquered and fought over, but as a source of abundant possibility for the present (Bloch, 1959/1986; Poli, 2011)....

From this perspective, the task of education is not a question of educating towards a pre-specified future that we know and have already imagined. Instead, the task is to explore how to create the spaces and practices that will continually enable the dynamic disclosure, imagination and creation of radically new possibilities in the present. Such an ontological assumption about the future as a site of radical novelty reframes the educational challenge, it constructs the present as a site in which as-yet unrealised possibilities are both latent and imagined....

Facer's representations of the 'task to explore how to create the spaces and practices that will continually enable the dynamic disclosure, imagination and creation of radically new possibilities in the present' is precisely the job of an individual's self-determined ecology of practice for learning in order to perceive, explore, and re-perceive the affordances in what (Poli 2001) calls the 'thick present' of their lifeworld.

To that end, the educational aim should be to enrich our own and our students' understanding of what Roberto Poli describes as the dynamism and emergent properties of the "thick present" (Poli 2011). This thick present is made up of the multiple layers of reality that are the materials for creating futures, from the physical attributes of the world, to the social and historical structures, to the anticipatory practices that work backwards from the possibilities we conceive about the future upon the present. (Facer ibid:59).

Ecology of Teaching Practice for Learning at University

A traditional face-to-face university course is designed, organised and implemented by one or more academic teachers who have both disciplinary and pedagogic expertise, within an institutional socio-cultural environment that is full of support and resources to aid learning. There is a structure (timetable/lecture schedule/credit structure) and procedural framework (rules and regulations) within which learning takes place. Programmes are organised into units or modules with explicit objectives, content, resources and processes that engage learners in activities through which they learn, and some of their learning is assessed using one or more methods determined by teachers. The institutional ecosystem for learning includes people - learners, teachers and other professionals who help learners, a physical environment including classroom spaces, social spaces, resources centre and virtual spaces where learners and teachers interact for the purpose of learning. Figure 4.4 identifies the components of a typical ecology for learning that is designed and taught by a teacher..

The *affordance* for learning is everywhere. It is contained in the course, programme or module content, in the activities that teachers organise and facilitate for learners, in the *physical and virtual spaces* that are provided which support particular activities (both academics and social) and in the *intellectual spaces* that the pedagogic activities promote. Affordance for learning and development is found in the *resources* including books, journals, computers, software and other tools and mediating artefacts that are used, and in the teaching and learning *processes* and practices that are used to engage learners and encourage them to form relationships for learning with these resources. Affordance for learning is found in the additional support and advisory services the university provides, and in the *relationships* and interactions between teacher and students, and student peers, and in learners own responses to all of these things.

But the university ecosystem sits within an even bigger ecosystem that is also full of affordance for learning in such social practices as work, volunteering and community-based activities. This larger ecosystem is available to students who have the will to learn and develop through their involvement in such activities. An ecological view of learning enables us to integrate all potential learning environments and activities into a students' developmental ecology in the manner demonstrated by Michael and Natasha in chapter 3.

Figure 4.4 Typical course-based learning ecology created by a teacher to encourage and support students' learning

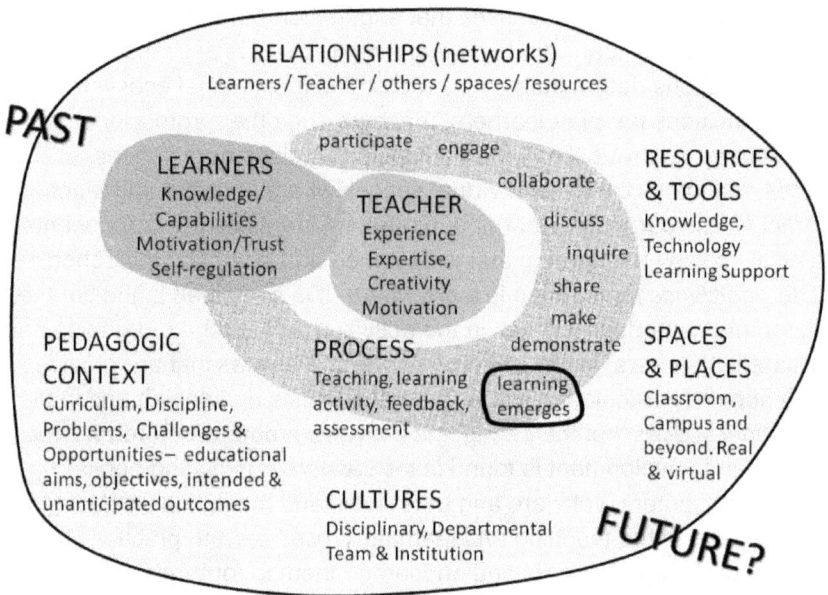

Ecologies for Learning Typology

Jackson (2014) provides a framework (Figure 4.5) to help visualise the relationship between individuals' learning ecologies and educational and other social practices that support and recognise the outcomes of learning from such ecologies. The conceptual tool was created to imagine the affordances for learning provided by a lifewide concept of curriculum (Figure 4.2).

Figure 4.5 Tool for evaluating the opportunities for higher education learners to create or co-create their own ecologies for learning in a lifewide curriculum. *Explanation:* The 'Learning Ecology' axis contains such things as the goals and purposes, intended learning, knowledge and skill content, process, resources including tools and technologies, spaces, relationships and what counts as learning.

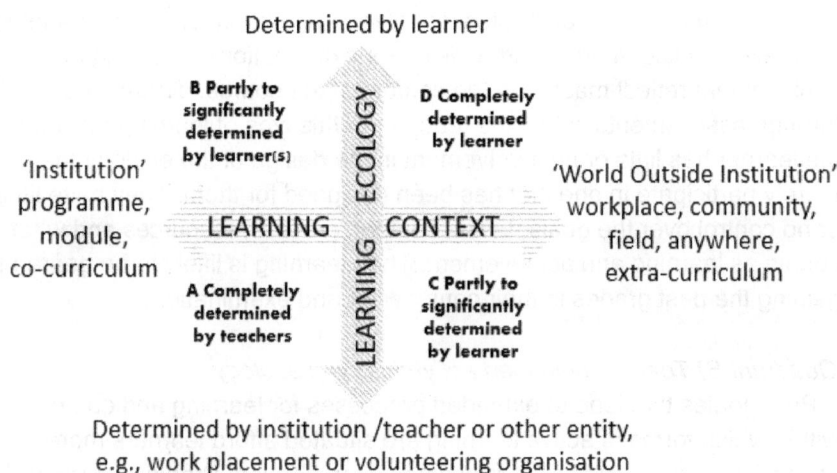

Determined by learner

B Partly to
significantly
determined
by learner(s)

D Completely
determined
by learner

'Institution'
programme,
module,
co-curriculum

LEARNING ECOLOGY

LEARNING

CONTEXT

'World Outside Institution'
workplace, community,
field, anywhere,
extra-curriculum

A Completely
determined
by teachers

C Partly to
significantly
determined
by learner

Determined by institution /teacher or other entity,
e.g., work placement or volunteering organisation

The 2x2 matrix is defined by the 1) *contexts for learning* i.e. whether the contexts are formally constituted and structured within an academic programme or whether they are informal and unstructured opportunities for learning and development, and 2) whether the *institution or the learner* determines the what and why, the how, where and the when of learning, and ultimately determines what counts as learning. The key question is who determines the goals and purposes, knowledge and skill content, processes, resources, tools and technologies outcomes and achievements. Four different scenarios represent the different conceptual spaces in Figure 4.5.

Quadrant A) Traditional lecture-based learning ecology
Teachers working with a pre-determined curriculum or syllabus containing specific knowledge and opportunities for skill development and supported by an appropriate set of resources, engage their students in a process for learning. The main activities undertaken by learners are attendance at lectures, perhaps supplemented by seminars, extensive reading from a course textbook or list of recommended texts, essay-based coursework assignments, and revision for examinations. Learning and achievement reflect mastering the content of the course, determined through assessments set by the teacher. In this type of learning ecology the learner has little or no involvement in the design of the ecology they merely participate in one that has been designed for them. They have little or no control over the goals, tasks, content, process, resources and what counts as learning and achievement. Their learning is likely to be geared to gaining the best grades in their coursework and examinations.

Quadrant B) Teacher designed active learning ecology
Pedagogies that lead to extended processes for learning and contexts within which forms of active learning are situated afford learners more scope for co-creating their own ecologies for learning. Problem-, project-, inquiry-, event-, design and make, and field-based learning all actively encourage learners to define and explore their own problems, build and utilise relationships for learning, be resourceful and discover for themselves the knowledge they need to produce possible solutions, sometimes in contexts that are unfamiliar. In these types of learning contexts teachers operate as facilitators, guides, supervisors and coaches rather than didactic transmitters. Such pedagogies and practices help learners develop the will, capability and confidence to create their own

learning ecologies for learning and achieving. Students will still want to gain good grades in their coursework and examinations, but in engaging in these sorts of processes they are gaining much more. They are learning through an experience that learning involves a process that has to be created. That involves assessing a situation, defining problems and seeing opportunities, setting goals, planning and executing tasks, discovering and applying relevant knowledge and other resources and forming new relationships. Although ultimately the teacher will determined what counts as learning and achievement and may give little or no recognition for learners' processes of learning, learners will still have learned important things about the ecology of learning.

Quadrant C) Self-directed but institutionally supported learning ecology
    There are some contexts in unstructured learning environments like for example work, volunteering in the community, independent fieldwork, co-curricular enterprise and event organising, which involve learners in activity in which they determine for themselves goals, tasks, content, process and resources. Such environments are not directly controlled by teachers and institutions. However, they may be controlled, to varying degrees, by other significant people like employers, supervisors, entrepreneurs, who may determine goals, tasks, content, process, relationships and resources, and ultimately the recognition of what counts as performance and achievement in which learning is embedded. Such environments are focused on performance but students may be given a degree of responsibility and autonomy to learn in what is a far less structured and supported environment than is encountered in formalised educational environments.
    Universities can capitalise on these contexts for students' development through frameworks and processes that enable learners to visualise, plan, record/evidence, reflect on, make claims and gain recognition for their own learning and development. These forms of support and recognition vary in the extent to which they focus learners' attention on specific goals and outcomes or they encourage learners to define their own goals and

achievements. Support may also be given to encourage and facilitate interaction between learners engaged in a similar process for example in providing a forum for students to exchange information and discuss situations.

Quadrant D) Independent self-directed learning ecology
This conceptual space is where people create their own learning ecologies for their own purposes typically for their own learning projects often associated with interests like sport, hobbies, travel, working in the community or for a charity, enterprise like setting up a business or organising an event, raising a child and countless more contexts. Involvement and learning are not driven by the need or desire for formal recognition but by the intrinsic desire to improve self, and the sense of doing something worthwhile to contribute and make a positive difference. In such self-motivated circumstances the learner determines for themselves and or with co-participants goals, tasks, content, process, resources and relationships and achievements. Although, learners do not seek recognition for learning and personal development gained through such experiences a university could provide the tools and mechanisms that enable learners to plan, record/evidence, reflect on, make claims and gain recognition for their own learning and development. From an educational perspective these contexts are particularly favourable for learners developing their own ecologies for learning and achievement in a way that a formally structured and controlled educational environment cannot.

Illustration of how this tool might be used
In chapter 3 (p 90-96) Michael told his story of the things he did to try and develop himself to become the archaeologist he wanted to become. Using the map of his ecology for learning and developing himself while he was at university we can appreciate the affordances he perceived and accessed to imagine and determine, sometimes with co-participants - goals, tasks and activities, content, process, resources, relationships and achievements Figure 4.6 provides a visual representation of the

experiences he used to become an archaeologist. His ecology for learning includes his BSc programme and many other activities that were outside his course. The letters ABCD relate to the conceptual fields in Figure 4.5. They show the affordances he recognised in a particular situation to determine his own goals, tasks and activities, content, process, resources, relationships and achievements. They reflect the degree to which he is able to create his own ecologies for learning, performing and achieving.

Figure 4.6 Mapping a student's ecology for learning and personal development based on Michael's narrative (chapter 3 p90-96).

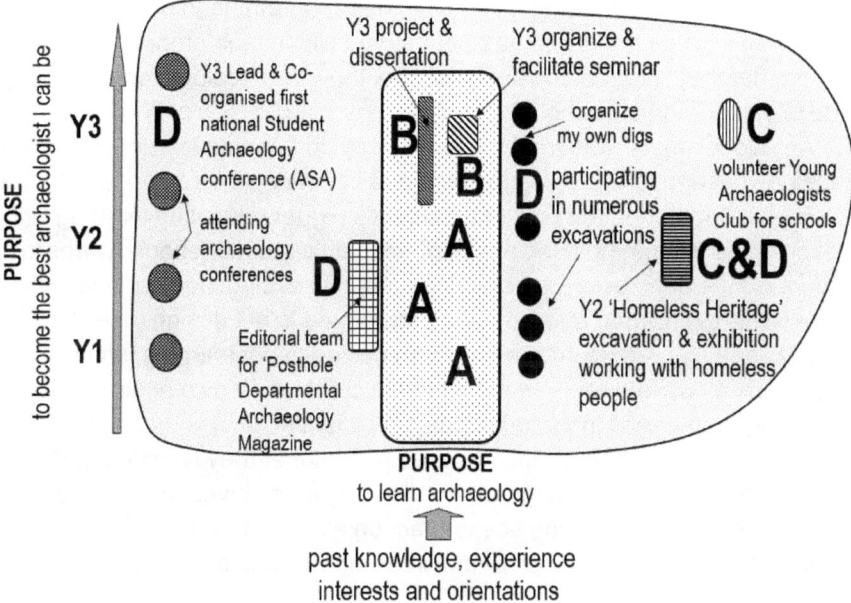

The outer boundary encloses the things he said contributed to his sense of being an archeologist and the way he developed his knowledge, skills, values, beliefs and confidence in being an archaeologist - his ecology for learning and personal development. The letters ABCD relate to the affordances he perceived in a particular context/activity to determine his own goals, tasks and activities, content, process, resources, relationships and achievements. It is clear that although his academic programme provided some affordances for him to determine his own ecologies for learning and performing, the projects he undertook or created for himself outside his course provided him with the greatest affordance for self-determined learning and development towards becoming the archaeologist he wanted to be.

This simple mapping device could be used to help learners reflect on, make sense of and appreciate their own learning and development. It shows them that what they do outside their programme to develop themselves is as important as what they do within their programme. It tells them that they, not the university, control their own ecology for learning, developing and achieving.

An educational institution may encourage and enable learners to create their own learning ecologies in some or all of the spaces outlined in figure 4.5. but all too often the bulk of a student's higher education learning experience is located in the space of academic routine (space A) where there is little or no scope for creating their own ecology for learning. However, even when an academic programme is not designed to encourage learners to create their own ecologies for learning, some (perhaps most) learners are motivated to create their own ecologies for learning that enable them to become the scientist, lawyer, geologist, engineer or any other discipline-based practitioner they want to be. We should be inspired to change our traditional perspectives on learning by the stories of students who see and act on all the affordances they discover for their own development in all dimensions of their life.

CHAPTER 5
Learning Ecologies: Habitats for Self-Directed, Self-Regulated, Learning and Performance

Ecology of Self-Regulated Practice for Learning & Performing

One of the espoused goals of a higher education is to develop autonomous learners who are self-motivated i.e. they can initiate and sustain their own learning projects, and self-regulating i.e. they can build their own learning processes and manage themselves. In the context of this book I am arguing that the concept of self-regulation might be broadened to embrace the self-determined and self-managed process of creating, implementing and sustaining an ecology of practice for learning and performance.

Naomi was a final year Biomedical Sciences undergraduate student when she wrote this reflective essay to explain how she challenged and transformed herself by organising and leading a small group of student volunteers to work in a village in Uganda.

The volunteer trip I organised was something I had thought about for years and finally had the means to do. I approached the Students' Union and asked whether there was a programme already set up. I was referred to a local non-government organisation called Experience Culture, which was set up by two ladies from Guildford. They informed me about the relationship the town had with its twin town in Uganda called Mukono. I had no idea of the extent of the connection until I attended a few council meetings and had conversations with the members. I was inspired by the idea of contributing to this ongoing project.

I emailed the entire university asking who wanted to come with me and soon realised just how much I had bitten off! The response was overwhelming and I tried to be as fair as possible while only being able to choose five other students. Once the group was assembled I started to organise the next steps and fundraising. I soon found that while students are generous to causes, it is difficult to stir up enthusiasm towards raising money without pitching the idea in an incendiary manner. It took a lot of planning and long hours, often through the night, to try and make our fundraisers enticing and fun, while maintaining the focus on the cause itself. We came up with ideas such as the sale of sweets at student events, a decorated bake sale, a pub quiz, a giant dodgeball tournament and a music concert at the university, all of which took place over six months. Any money raised was to be a donation towards the Mukono Children's Home and Medical Centre where we would be working.

This was all a huge challenge to me as I am not naturally outgoing, and I had to really pull myself out of my shell in order to achieve the results I needed. Being the organiser and leader of a group was new to me and extremely daunting; this proved to be one of the most marked times of my life, during which I grew immensely as a person, and developed my confidence through a comforting sense of achievement.

We started work immediately upon our arrival in Uganda, and soon became immersed in a life wholly separate and unique to our own back home. Working so closely with the students, teachers, hospital workers and volunteers was a wonderful experience, and we soon came to view the world through their eyes, with emotional and profound results. The humble and earnest attitude they brought to all aspects of their lives, and the courage they showed in the face of extreme hardships were true testaments to the strength of the human spirit. At the children's home we taught lessons in and out of the classroom, sports and games, and sex education. This was probably where I was most at peace while in Uganda, as the love and simple kindnesses the children bestowed upon us was almost magical. Their excitement towards learning was contagious and I looked forward to spending time with them every day. It was a sharp realisation to see the stark differences between the culture and attitudes in Uganda and those back home, where complacency and over-indulgence is rife.

At the Medical Centre we helped out at aids clinics, helped with filing, and went on 'field trips' out into rural communities to teach about HIV/Aids, sex education and health and nutrition. Our donations were spent on a library for the Children's Home, which we painted ourselves, shoes for the children, and mosquito nets for those in the communities. Seeing families actually living in conditions of extreme poverty and illness exposes a helplessness in a form so raw it takes your strength and composure away more swiftly than you could ever expect or prepare for. To shake the hands of someone who has lost their family, their health, and their independence, while knowing there is only so much you can do to change this changes you irrevocably. And yet, their strength, and their composure remain not only intact but more strikingly dignified than anyone you would meet under better circumstances.

One particularly draining day of work involved us going out into a community far away to try to obtain support for Sarah, an 11 year old girl abandoned by her family who was HIV-positive [because she had been raped]. She had walked 41km barefoot to the medical centre to ask for help. We negotiated with her family for four hours to try to get them to provide shelter and food for her in order for her to receive drug treatment from the Medical Centre. It was entirely surreal to be sitting under a tree in the African sun, fighting for someone's chance of survival, with the desperation and urgency of the conversation all too apparent. This drawn out and highly strung affair was absolutely worth it when they finally agreed, ultimately saving her life. I have since been co-sponsoring her schooling fees and trying to ensure her welfare from a distance, which requires careful budgeting and communication with our contacts. The knowledge that we can help at least one person in this way is something I cling to when it feels that we are just one drop in an ever-present ocean of suffering that often threatens to overwhelm us.

The experiences we had in Uganda spurred me on to try and make a bigger difference, and to sustain what we had started. I began compiling an education pack which would include information on sex education, HIV/Aids, health and nutrition, and simple translations from

English to Luganda as well as simple maths sums such as calculating monetary transactions. The idea was to make these packs durable and simple, so that one literate worker or volunteer from the Medical Centre could go out into the communities and teach it to large groups. I felt that one of the key targets to improving their quality of life was education. However, while this is often a daily component of life for most, it is painfully scarce in third world countries, where it is seen as a luxury rather than a necessity. The children in the communities we visited were unable to attend any schools as they could not afford it. Therefore, I hoped to bring a simple platform for education to them in the form of these packs.

Upon arriving back in England, we completed a video diary as a summary of our experiences. I also organised a book drive parallel to one being held by the Borough Council, to try and gather suitable children's books for the new library at the Children's Home. This required good advertising, such as printing and putting up posters around the campus, promoting it before lectures, arranging pick-ups and drop-offs and setting up boxes around the university. I plan to raise more money to send to trusted contacts at the school so that they will be able to buy local books for the children, but by sending books from England I hope to help introduce different perspectives and ideals to the children, and lend a new realm of imagination to their learning.

In my second year at university I set up a new volunteering society with my sister. Pioneering this society was daunting to say the least, with every step unpaved, and layers of bureaucracy to overcome. We held an AGM to elect a committee, and soon began planning events and ways to draw students in and promote volunteering. Our original goal was to keep raising money for different communities in and around Mukono, organise local volunteering opportunities for students, and send another group out to Uganda in addition to a volunteer trip to Thailand to work with children in slums and on an anti-trafficking project. This proved extremely trying, as university restrictions did not allow us to raise money for any charity or organisation ourselves, and also there were insurance restrictions on overseas university trips. As a result, we concentrated on local volunteering, and brought students together to participate in events such as 'Swim for the children', 'Tree

O'Clock', and various YMCA overnight events among others.

We planned the overseas trips on our own without the support other societies are able to lean on, and tried to prepare the students going on them as best we could by creating information booklets. These contained details on the respective languages and cultures of each destination, the projects they would be undertaking, helpful phrases and tips, and health and travel advice. I had not anticipated the immense amount of time required to run a society and plan events on this scale, and it is a credit to key members of the committee whose hard work and encouragement are really appreciated. Getting students involved in events that are purely voluntary is no easy task, and the skills I learnt through attempting this are truly invaluable. It took perseverance and optimism to make many of the events happen, and an incredible amount of committed time.

There were numerous moments when I felt disheartened or burnt-out, but the knowledge that we have started something to benefit others, which will carry on even after we leave university honestly makes it completely worth the effort. In my final year at university, I will be continuing the planning and support of the trip to Uganda and its communities with a new group of students, as well as an acting mentor of the volunteer society, which we have handed on to a new committee.

I cannot fully explain the feeling of wholeness that accompanies helping someone in a significant way. Every new experience adds to my person and expands or alters my perspectives. I feel that it has helped me to grow in so many ways, especially in terms of confidence and my capabilities for dealing with unfamiliar situations and create new opportunities for myself and others. I feel spurred on to continue what we started and more, and truly believe that I am now much better equipped to achieve these goals. Through the various activities I have undertaken I have an improved understanding and insight into myself, and others. I have acquired skills such as time management, leadership and the ability to communicate ideas to other people, and very importantly, the outlook that while an idea may start as just an idea, or may seem like just a drop in a vast ocean, it can manifest itself as a wonderful accumulation of events; a tidal wave whose ripple effects extend continuously outwards.

An ecological perspective on Naomi's story

Naomi's ambition was to become a doctor and she was planning to apply to medical school after completing her biosciences degree. This was her *distal goal* that shaped her everyday experience of the world and drove her to create more immediate *proximal goals* towards achieving her ambition. She actively searched for something meaningful to do and in the process expanded the *affordances* in her life for situations that would enable her to help other people. She changed the circumstances of her life and in the process she discovered a new purpose - to help people in small town in Uganda. This became her *proximal goal* and she was willing to dedicate a significant part of her life to the project alongside her academic studies. In committing to this goal she had effectively created an inflection point in her life which had a significant impact on her development as a person, "this proved to be one of the most marked times of my life, during which I grew immensely as a person".

Naomi created a *process* and *numerous activities* to enable her to achieve her ambition. There was nothing in a book to tell her what to do, she had to invent and

CONTEXTS

PAST

PRESENT

RESOURCES

SPACES

LEARNING ECOLOGY
created by a person
for a purpose to achieve
proximal goals informed
by distal goals

FUTURE

RELATIONSHIPS

PROCESSES
ACTIVITIES &
EXPERIENCES

WHOLE PERSON
WILL, CAPABILITY, INTEGRATIVE
THINKING, EMOTIONS, ATTITUDES,
CONFIDENCE, TRUST & SELF-AWARENESS
DEVELOPMENT & ACHIEVEMENT

AFFORDANCES

improvise this process for herself in the *contexts* in which she was living. She appreciated the enormity of what she was doing and realised that she needed the help and support of others so she developed a strategy to search for and find a group of like-minded self-motivated people (*new relationships*). She then set about involving them in developing the *resources* they needed to make their contribution. Naomi and her co-volunteers restructured the environment by organising numerous fund-raising activities that not only required considerable effort but also their imagination and creativity. These funds were used to buy basic medical supplies to give to the village community.

The second part of her story relating to her experiences in Uganda, involves putting herself into an entirely *unfamiliar physical and cultural context with unfamiliar problems and challenges* through which she learnt and developed. The *place* she chose was the only place in which she could do the things she did and learn the things she learnt. Through her activities she developed a new set of *relationships.* Through her conversations and other interactions with village people she and her team of volunteers began to develop knowledge that was situated in this particular socio-cultural setting. She and her team encountered many challenges - culture, language, poverty, difficult social situations and disease: all contributed to the rich environment in which they had to learn to adapt in order to perform. The students were certainly stretched and out of their comfort zone. Through their efforts and willingness to learn they managed to accomplish some useful short-term goals in Uganda and feel that they had made a positive difference to the lives of people they had met.

> 'Working so closely with the students, teachers, hospital workers and volunteers was a wonderful experience, and we soon came to view the world through their eyes, with emotional and profound results'

In the third part of her story, Naomi describes what happened on her return to university. It reveals the emotional impact the experience had on her. This new and different Naomi created new strategies for sustaining the work she had begun while in her second and third years at university. In this way the ecology she created for one set of situations developed into another ecology for another set of situations involving different people.

> I cannot fully explain the feeling of wholeness that accompanies helping someone in a significant way.
>
> In my final year at university, I will be continuing the planning and support of the trip to Uganda and its communities with a new group of students, as well as an acting mentor of the volunteer society, which we have handed on to a new committee

152

A learning ecology is a 'person-in-environment', 'person-in-activity' concept. By this I mean that the person - their beliefs, attitudes, values, knowledge and capabilities, behaviours, actions, learning, development and achievements is influenced and shaped by the circumstances, situations and physical, social-cultural environments they inhabit. Naomi's involvement in her self-motivated, self-regulated project and the involvement of others she engaged and connected with in the different contexts she encountered, constituted her ecology for learning, performance and achievement. This ecology included: her own self-determined process to enable her to achieve her goals, and complex set of relationships, novel contexts, situated social action, personal and collaborative learning, and the structuring of the environment to create usable resources. Her self-determined project was driven by a desire to make a positive difference and also the desire to be a certain sort of person, and through her efforts and experiences she became a different person - she transformed herself.

The next part of this chapter will examine the idea and role of self-regulation in such self-determined processes before returning to Naomi's story to examine her experience through the lens of self-regulation.

Regulating our thoughts, actions and feelings

Donald Schön's valuable insights enable us to appreciate the complex ways in which our thinking, action and prior and current experience connect, interact and integrate to enable us to deal with uncertain and challenging situations. Somehow they collude to engage us in an iterative process of inquiry, decision making and action through which we learn to engage with, deal with and possibly exploit a situation.

the practitioner allows himself to experience surprise, puzzlement, or confusion in a situation which he finds uncertain or unique. He *reflects* on the phenomena before him, and on the prior understandings which have been implicit in his behaviour. He carries out an experiment which serves to generate both a new understanding of the phenomena and a change in the situation.... He does not keep means and ends separate but defines them interactively as he frames a problematic situation. He does not separate thinking from doing... Because his experimenting is a kind of action, implementation is built into his inquiry (Schön 1987:69)

By reflecting on and judging our experiences and the effects of our actions, we eventually make better sense of the uncertainties through which we have travelled and consolidate our changed perceptions of reality. The complex process through which we imagine and decide what to do, then do it and reflect on it, when dealing with a new situation is called *self-regulation* and this process and its significance to the process of creating and maintaining a learning ecology, constitutes the theme for this chapter.

Self-regulation is not a mental ability or an academic performance skill; rather it is the self-directive process by which learners transform their mental abilities into academic [and other sorts of] skills. Learning is viewed as an activity that students do for themselves in a proactive way rather than as a covert event that happens to them in reaction to teaching. Self-regulation refers to self-generated thoughts, feelings, and behaviours that are oriented to attaining goals....... These learners are proactive in their efforts to learn because they are aware of their strengths and limitations and because they are guided by personally set goals and task-related strategies.....These learners monitor their behaviour in terms of their goals and self-reflect on their increasing effectiveness. This enhances their self-satisfaction and motivation to continue to improve their methods of learning. Because of their superior motivation and adaptive learning methods, self-regulated students are not only more likely to succeed academically but to view their futures optimistically (Zimmerman 2002: 65-6).

Self-regulation and performance

Research has shown a link between the use of self-regulated learning strategies and academic achievement. Students who score highly on measures of self-regulated learning are more likely to achieve higher marks in examinations and assessments (Gettinger and Seibert 2002, Kitsantas et al 2008, Kornell and Metcalfe 2006). Self regulation is also important to the improvement of performance when moving from novice to more expert states in such diverse domains as sport (Cleary and Zimmerman 2001, Jonker et al 2011) musical performance (McPherson and Zimmerman

> 'results show that elite youth athletes possess well-developed self regulatory skills, especially reflection, ... elite youth athletes reflect more on their past performance in order to learn and are making more effort to accomplish their tasks successfully. Moreover, the elite youth athletes in the pre-vocational system outscored their pre-university non-athletic counterparts on their ability to learn efficiently by means of reflection' (Jonker et al 2011)

2002) and video gaming (Soylu 2014) suggesting that the theory of self-regulation can provide an overarching framework for explaining self-directed learning and development in many different contexts. Furthermore, there is some evidence, at least in sport, that high performing athletes with well developed self-regulatory skills are also more effective in their academic learning (Jonker et al 2011, Jonker 2011) inferring that self-regulation habits and skills are transferable between the domains of informal and formal learning.

Developing capability in self-regulation

Research also shows that self-regulatory processes are teachable and once learned can lead to increased motivation and achievement (Schunk and Zimmerman 1998). Learners who possess some self-regulatory habits can also practise and develop these orientations and capabilities through their own self-determined projects outside the academic environment, for example through hobbies and sport and these new understandings and capabilities might then be transferred back into the academic domain. However, according to Zimmerman (2002), few teachers effectively prepare students to learn on their own.

Students are seldom given choices regarding academic tasks to pursue, methods for carrying out complex assignments, or study partners. Few teachers encourage students to establish specific goals for their academic work or teach explicit study strategies. Also, students are rarely asked to self-evaluate their work or estimate their competence on new tasks. Teachers seldom assess students' beliefs about learning, such as self-efficacy perceptions or causal attributions, in order to identify cognitive or motivational difficulties before they become problematic. (Zimmerman 2002:69)

The challenge to formalised education is how to teach and encourage learners to develop the skills, attitudes and habits of self-regulation so that they can be more effective learners and achieve more of their potential. A number of approaches have been developed to encourage self-regulated learning in the academic environment. Examples are reported by Merino and Aucock (2014), who describe a series of enrichment tutorials in an accountancy degree course, Mahon and Crowley (2013) who describe a group-based training programme in a university study skills programme, and Nicol and Macfarlane-Dick (2005) who describe the use of formative feedback to improve self-regulated learning.

In considering curricular processes that help develop self-regulation Nicol (2010:4) argued the main characteristic of autonomy or self-regulation in learning in the academic context is that students take significant responsibility for setting their own learning goals and for evaluating progress in reaching these goals. Developing learners' self-regulatory skills requires that students have regular opportunities to:

1 critically evaluate the quality and impact of their own work during and after its production (for example, academic texts, problem solutions, designs)
2 critically evaluate the quality and impact of the work of their peers.

In the educational literature these two processes are often referred to as self and peer-assessment.... In fact, peer-assessment and self-

156

assessment should both be implemented for the development of learner self-regulation (Nicol 2010:4). Nicol described these practices as 'high-impact assessment and feedback activities (HIAFAs)' which involve students in:

• reflecting on and assessing the quality of their own work
• engaging in peer review of each other's work
• determining criteria to apply to their own work
• identifying their own learning needs and setting their own learning goals
• engaging in collaborative projects where they give each other feedback
• creating problems or issues that they go on to address
• reflecting on and evaluating their own learning to build a portfolio
• devising their own module (for example, in collaboration with academic staff).

Another approach used to develop self-regulation skills across UK higher education is known as Personal Development Planning (PDP). In fact, I first became aware of the idea of self-regulation while I was involved in developing the higher education policy for Personal Development Planning (PDP) in 1999, and subsequently in the systematic review of evidence for PDP efficacy undertaken by Gough et al

> (QAA 2002, 2009:5) defines PDP as, 'a structured and supported process undertaken by an individual to reflect upon their own learning, performance and / or achievement and to plan for their personal, educational and career development.'

(2003). I believed that self-regulation provided an underpinning theory of thinking, action and learning for PDP, and good PDP processes and practices provide a concrete way of encouraging the development of self-regulatory skills, attitudes and thinking. The role of PDP in enabling students to practise and develop the habits of self-regulated learning will be examined later in the chapter.

Beyond the academic curriculum, the case for students developing skills, dispositions and habits of self-regulation to sustain them throughout complex learning lives, is neatly summarised by Zimmerman.

Self-regulation is important because a major function of education is the development of lifelong learning skills. After graduation from high school or college, young adults must learn many important skills informally. For example, in business settings, they are often expected to learn a new position, such as selling a product, by observing proficient others and by practising on their own. Those who develop high levels of skill position themselves for bonuses, early promotion, or more attractive jobs. In self-employment settings, both young and old must constantly self-refine their skills in order to survive. Their capability to self-regulate is especially challenged when they undertake long-term creative projects, such as works of art, literary texts, or inventions. In recreational settings, learners spend much personally regulated time learning diverse skills for self-entertainment, ranging from hobbies to sports (Zimmerman 2002:66).

Self-regulation and informal learning

This brings us to the possible involvement of self-regulation in informal learning settings, a topic explored by Boekaerts and Minnaert (1999: 534) who drew attention to the fact that researchers 'have failed to explore self-regulatory processes in informal learning environments'. Through a literature review they identified ten attributes of informal learning which together produce a natural form of learning that gives a person the impression that they are learning spontaneously and without much conscious effort (Table 5.1). Informal learning settings in which people initiate and manage their own participation and learning contrast markedly in their capacity for self-regulation with formal learning environments. The latter are bounded by intended learning outcomes defined and assessed by the teacher, content that is controlled by a syllabus or curriculum, learning activity that is initiated, directed or guided by the teacher who determines the goals of the learning enterprise and what learning will be recognised through her assessment instruments.

Self-regulation, in the true sense of the word, will only emerge when students are allowed to learn in a context where they can weigh the feasibility and desirability of alternative actions and goals (Heckhausen & Gollwitzer, 1987), using their own criteria. The perception of freedom of action (an appraisal which informs students that they can act according to their own wishes, expectations and needs) in a supportive context (where they can borrow resources when needed) will help them to translate their own needs, expectations and wishes into clear intentions...... The main point to be made is that students have a better chance of developing their own goals in accordance with their need structure when they are allowed to learn in a realistic context that they perceive as free from inappropriate social or evaluation constraints. ....formal learning contexts are not primarily geared to help students develop their own criteria vis-a`-vis objects, materials, persons, settings, and skills. Rather students are prompted to abide by the rules that make social interactions and assessment procedures run smoothly. In other words, in formal learning contexts students are expected to pursue teacher-defined and teacher-initiated goals and this calls for goal-maintenance, prompted by external regulation, rather than self-maintenance based on internal regulation (Boekaerts and Minnaert 1999: 542)

On this last point, broad fluid goals also open up greater possibility for what might emerge and therefore encourage an opportunistic orientation to learning. We are often surprised at the consequences when we engage informally with something new and this element of surprise is another aspect of the psychology of informal learning that reinforces motivation. Building on these perspectives on the relationship between self-regulation and informal learning contexts, this chapter explores the role of self-regulated learning in personal learning ecologies that are developed outside the academic curriculum. The underlying proposition is that higher education can do much more to encourage student development in these forms of learning by developing strategies like PDP that encourage learners to be more conscious of themselves and their effects in the world through the self-regulatory processes they are engaged in.

Table 5.1 Attributes of Informal Learning (Boekaerts & Minnaert 1999:536)

1 The learning process is described as active, voluntary, self-discovering, self-determined, open-ended, non-threatening, enjoyable, and explorative.
2 Learners use a number of self-regulatory processes spontaneously, such as self initiating learning and self-monitoring their progress.
3 These self-regulatory processes make an explicit appeal to intrinsic motivation; conversely, intrinsic motivation facilitates self-regulatory processes.
4 Most informal learning is embedded in a social context, meaning that social cues are highly relevant and that students engage in cooperative learning activities. These socially situated learning activities are loosely structured, learner directed, and mediated by peers who often share the same values, attitudes, interests, and beliefs.
5 Informal learning situations utilize (realistic) objects, materials or settings that are highly contextualized.
6 The learning experience is more qualitative than quantitative, more process oriented than product oriented, more synthetic than analytic, and more flow-driven.
7 Time allocation in informal learning episodes is unhurried in nature, self-paced, and open-ended with relatively few time constraints.
8 Even when there is a kind of curriculum (e.g., a path in a museum to discover the life patterns of the ancient Greeks), it is a flexible one, signifying that the structure is non-linear and bottom-up.
9 There is no compulsory, individual testing or assessment procedure, but rather a collective, informal type of assessment or self-assessment based on feedback.
10 Set goals tend to be broader which may result in considerable variability in what gets learned.

Theory of Self-Regulation

Self-regulated learning is defined as self-generated thoughts, feelings and actions that are systematically oriented towards achievement of the learner's own goals (Zimmerman and Schunk 2008). Social cognitive researchers describe self-regulated learning in terms of self-processes and associated self-beliefs that initiate, change and sustain learning in specific contexts. These processes and beliefs are linked to three fundamental questions about learners' self-regulated approaches to learning (Zimmerman 2000).

How questions refer to students' use of metacognitive processes such as planning, organising, self-instruction, self-monitoring and self-evaluating ones efforts to learn. Where questions pertain to behavioural processes such as selecting, structuring and creating learning environments that optimize growth. Why questions refer to processes and beliefs that motivate self-regulated students to learn, such as beliefs about their capabilities to learn, intrinsic interest in the task and satisfaction with their efforts...High levels of motivation are necessary to self-regulate when short term goals must be subordinated to long term goals and ultimate gratification must be delayed. In summary, self-regulation refers to metacognitive, behavioural and motivational processes and beliefs used to attain personal learning goals in specific contexts (Zimmerman 2000:221)

Without the will to learn things that are difficult and complex, there can be no hope for learning (Barnett 2007). Learning and motivation are linked by a sense of personal agency: beliefs about possessing the requisite cognitive and behavioral processes (or means) to achieve desired environmental outcomes (or ends). Personal agency is connected to a belief in one's self-efficacy to learn or perform at certain designated levels

'Will is the most important concept in education. Without a will, nothing is possible. At any level of education, a pupil, a student cannot make serious progress unless she has the will to do so. Unless she has a will, a will to learn, she cannot carry herself forward, cannot press herself forward, cannot come successfully into new pedagogic situations' [including the situations she creates for herself] (Barnett 2007:15)

(Bandura, 1986a & b). Self-efficacy beliefs are distinctive because they refer to the process, rather than the outcomes, of learning. The distinction between process and outcome beliefs is central to a social cognitive perspective on learning and motivation (Zimmerman and Schunk 2008:323-4). A learner who adopts a self-regulating approach to their own learning will be involved in a continuous process involving 1) forethought 2) action/ performance 3) self-reflection operating within a context specific environment that is structured by the learner to provide resources for

Figure 5.1 A model of self-regulated learning (Zimmerman 2000:226) coupled to notions of reflection Ertmer and Newby (1996).

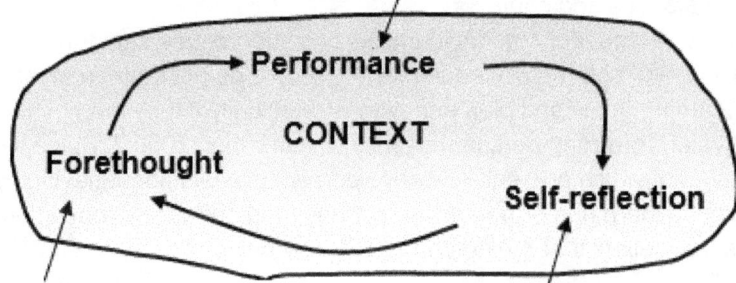

Self-control
- Self-instruction
- Time Management
- Task strategies
- Process creation
- Help seeking
- Environmental structuring
- **Self-observation**
- Cognitive monitoring
- Self-recording

Reflection in action – managing the process of learning and constantly adjusting and changing as new information is assimilated

Performance

CONTEXT

Forethought

Self-reflection

Task analysis
- Goal setting
- Strategic planning

Motivational beliefs
- Self-efficacy
- Outcome expectation
- Intrinsic interest
- Goal orientation

Reflection for action - employing reflective thinking skills to evaluate own thinking and strategies for learning

Self judgement
- Self-evaluation
- Causal attribution

Self-reaction
- Self-satisfaction
- Adaptive-defensive

Reflection on action - making sense of past experiences for the purposes of orienting oneself for current and or future thought or action.

learning and achieving specific goals (Schunk and Zimmerman 1994, 1997,1998, 2003, Zimmerman 2000, 2002, 2003, 2008). Figure 5.1 summarises the theoretical model.

Forethought

The thinking that occurs before decisions are taken about what to do involves thinking about the situation, context, problem, challenge or opportunity. Assessing the situation and imagining what might be done to deal with the situation (formulation of a goal or objective for action). Considering the sorts of actions or tasks that might be performed and the likely or possible effects and costs of such actions. Such thinking might involve 'assessing' an existing situation or 'imagining', based on past experiences or other knowledge, a situation that might unfold given the circumstances and contexts.

The self-regulatory model identifies two subordinate categories - task analysis and self-motivational beliefs. People do not engage in tasks or set learning goals and plan and work strategically if they are not motivated by strong personal agency (Zimmerman 2000:226) the key features of which are self-efficacy - personal beliefs about having the means to learn and or perform effectively, and outcome expectations - personal beliefs that the outcomes will be worthwhile .

Role of reflection and imagination

The role of reflection in the forethought stage is to enable us to think about past experiences or parts of experiences that might be related to the real or imagined situation we are encountering. This enables us to imagine mental models that help us make good decisions and plans about what to do. Reflection and imagination combined with our critical thinking helps us prepare mentally and practically for what lies ahead. As we begin to engage in the task of planning and making decisions about what we are going to do, reflective thinking can also help us test our planning against past experiences and enable us to refine our plans. Reflective thinking combined with our analysis of the situation can help us build confidence in our preparation for action: it can feed our belief that that we are likely to be successful by implementing the intended approach.

Figure 5.2 Representation of the model of self-regulation emphasising the ways in which reflection can be involved in the three parts of the self-regulation model - thinking prior to action & experience, thinking during action & experience, and thinking after-action & experience.

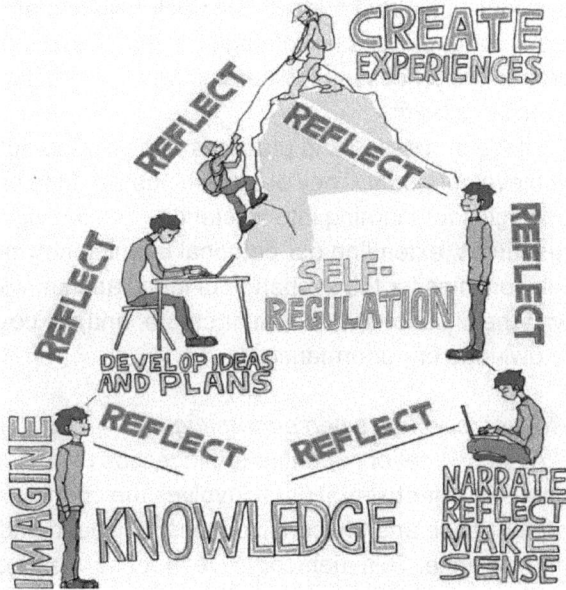

These processes for thinking enable us to imagine the possible ecologies we might create in order to learn, develop, perform and achieve. Forethought is the home of imagination (idea generation) and creative thinking (how our own or other people's ideas might be combined to create a new approach for the particular circumstances). It is our ability to make sense of the contextual particularities and nuances of complex situations that enables us to create responses that stand a chance of succeeding. By combining our creative thinking, reflective thinking and critical thinking we can develop new solutions to deal with situations we have not encountered before, test those solutions against past experiences and evaluate critically the ideas in the specific contexts that they will be applied. In this way we can see how reflective thinking is not a stand-alone process rather it is fully integrated with other thinking processes and heavily influenced by the social-cultural in which decisions and actions are located.

Performing

The second stage of the self-regulatory model is the action or performance through which we implement our plans to deal with, or create, new situations and experiences. It includes our capacities and attitudes to instruct our self and seek help to learn and accomplish our plan, our capacities for managing ourselves, our time and our tasks, the creation of processes for learning and the structuring of the environment in order to learn.

These processes and practices enable us to optimise our efforts to achieve our goals. They are the things we do in order to bring our ecologies for learning into existence - like finding, using and creating resources, extending our personal learning networks and creating new relationships for the exchange of ideas and knowledge, deal practically with the situations we are in or create, and the co-production of new knowledge or performance.

Role of reflection when performing

A second set of subordinate processes used during the performance phase is self-observation. It involves the cognitive monitoring of our own performance and the conditions that surround and influence our performance. This metacognitive process is also called reflection in action, and it enables us to adjust our actions and performance in response to our observations on the impact we are making and on our failures to achieve intended results. But, when we are fully engaged in a situation there is little time available for reflection and most of our responses, will be reactive and intuitive rather than derive from reflective deliberation (Eraut and Hirsh 2008:42-3). However, where spaces permit (eg during a break in activity) we may immediately begin to think about recent events as a way of learning and refining immediate plans for action when we resume activity.

Self-Reflection

After we have engaged with and performed in a situation we can create new space for thinking about our actions and their effects, and the social and physical dynamics of the situation we were in. In this part of the self-regulation process reflection becomes the dominant thinking process as we think about the whole experience and try to make more sense and draw deeper understandings and meanings from it. Our thinking involves both self-judgements and self-reactions to those judgements (Zimmerman 2000, 2002) .

Self-judgement

The two key self-judgement processes are self-evaluation and attributing causal significance to the results. Self-evaluation involves comparing our perception of our performance with a standard, criteria or goal - *did what we did work well or not so well in helping us achieve our objective? Could we have done what we did better?* It might also involve comparing own perceptions of performance with the feedback given from other people involved in the situation, or even people who were not part of the situation who offered us their perspectives on it. Attributional judgements are pivotal to self-reflection because attributions to a fixed ability prompt learners to react negatively and discourage efforts to improve. By contrast attributions of poor performance to inappropriate learning strategies sustains perceptions of efficacy and motivations to engage in different ways in similar situations in future.

Self-reaction

Self-reaction includes judgements on self-satisfaction and adaptive inferences. Self-satisfaction involves perceptions and associated effects regarding one's own performance. Courses of action that result in satisfaction and positive effect are pursued. Whereas actions that produce dissatisfaction and have negative effects are avoided. Self-regulated learners condition their satisfaction on reaching their goals, and these self-incentives motivate and direct their actions.

Role of Reflection:

Reflection - or thinking about the situation and the whole experience, is one of the three phases of the self-regulation model of learning. Reflection is an activity in which people mentally revisit and re-experience their experiences, think about them, feel some of the emotions they engendered, mull them over and evaluate and learn from them. They

- *Return to experience* - that is to say recalling or detailing salient events.
- *Attend to (or connecting with) feelings* - this has two aspects: using helpful feelings and removing or containing obstructive ones.
- *Evaluate experience* - this involves re-examining experience in the light of one's intent and existing knowledge etc. It also involves integrating this new knowledge into one's conceptual framework (Boud et al 1985:26-31).

Reflecting on and articulating the key lessons learned from experience, boosts our self-efficacy, which in turn has a positive effect on immediate learning and their motivations to deal with similar situations in future. Reflection also aids the process of making explicit what has been tacit ie knowledge that was embodied in dealing with the situation (Di Stefano et al 2014). By extracting deeper meaning from the situation individuals are able to create new personal knowledge to guide their future planning and actions and also refine or generate self-theories of why certain things happen in certain situations. Such high level abstraction helps us transfer what has been learnt from one context to another and one time to another. In this way lessons learnt during the implementation of one learning ecology can be brought to bear in a future learning ecology.

Reactive and proactive self-regulators.

Research into how people regulate themselves suggests that there are two forms of self-regulation (Zimmerman and Schunk 2008). Reactive learners avoid forethought and attempt to regulate functioning during and after performance whereas proactive learners engage in significant forethought, including reflecting-for-action, in order to improve the quality of their planning and performance.

Self-Regulation in an Emergent World

We might usefully add one further dimension to this explanation of how a person is actively engaged in learning and developing themselves through their self-determined life experiences. The model of the autodidactic (self-instructed) learner (Tremblay, 2000) incorporates the self-regulating model of learning but sets it in a context of emergence (Figure 5.3). A slightly modified version of Carl Rogers definition of personal creativity might be used to convey the idea.

Figure 5.3 The autodidactic model of learning (Tremblay 2000)

- The process develops without prior condition
- Knowledge emerges through action and the individual is open to recognising and exploiting its value
- The individual works with the process heuristically

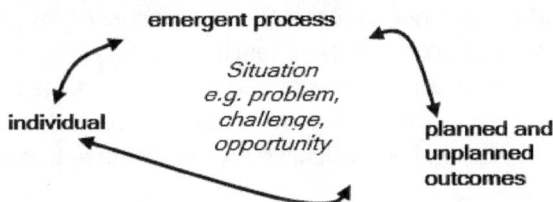

emergent process

individual

Situation
e.g. problem,
challenge,
opportunity

planned and
unplanned
outcomes

- The individual creates her own rules and vocabulary for learning
- The individual is strongly self-regulating

- The individual and the environment are reciprocal determinants
- The individual gains knowledge through a complex, diversified and expanding web of resources

An autodidactic process is heuristic, iterative and contextual. Situations may be orchestrated but they might equally be conditions of coincidence.

An individual's learning project does not develop in a linear way and the actions necessary for the realisation of a task are not presented in a sequential and predictable manner. Knowledge and knowing emerge through action. The process is a continuous experiment in which action and reflection share the same space. Theory (self-theory) develops from action and the knowing that emerges through action. This is an appropriate conception of the way that people approach learning as a sustained experiment in which action and reflection on action and the shaping of future actions share the same space. Autodidactic learners are dependent on the resources for learning that are available in their immediate environment and learning projects are shaped through taking this into account. Autodidactic learners often do not plan to use particular resources but see and exploit opportunities as they arise; they seize every opportunity that chance offers them to learn.

Social dimensions of self-regulation

The self-regulation model outlined above seems strangely individualistic given that we inhabit a social world. The Social Age (Stodd 2014) has added another dimension to our processes for reflection by enabling us to share our own experiences and our reactions and reflections on those experiences through websites, blogs and other forms of social media and receive feedback from people we do not know. In this way self-regulation and our reflective processes have become even more social.

Mobile technologies and Social Media enable us to record and share events and experiences in real time in ways that would not have been possible even five years ago and this creates a more dynamic and resource-rich and social environment which can be drawn upon for reflective purposes.

In January 2015 Tommy Caldwell and Kevin Jorgeson became the first people to climb the 1000m, sheer granite face known as the Dawn Wall of El Capitan in Yosemite National Park. The two climbers documented the entire endeavor in detail on Twitter, Facebook

Instagram so that people across the world could watch it unfold and share something of their experience.

The climbers used social media not only to chronicle the ups and downs of their journey (performance), but also to engage with their community of supporters and followers. They even held a question-and-answer session midway through the climb using Twitter. The Q&A covered everything from specifics about climbing techniques to choice of music and sleeping arrangements. This story simply illustrates how most experiences can be documented and shared in real time with others who are interested and that such acts can increase the social impact of an event and these shared resources can subsequently be used in the post event reflective process. The self-regulatory underpinnings to this pioneering ascent are revealed in the five years of planning, preparation, training and many failed attempts on parts of the climb and the whole climb for both men. Their story of planning, practice, self-monitoring and reflection, and perseverance and resilience is exemplary in illustrating the forces of self-regulation in a great achievement.

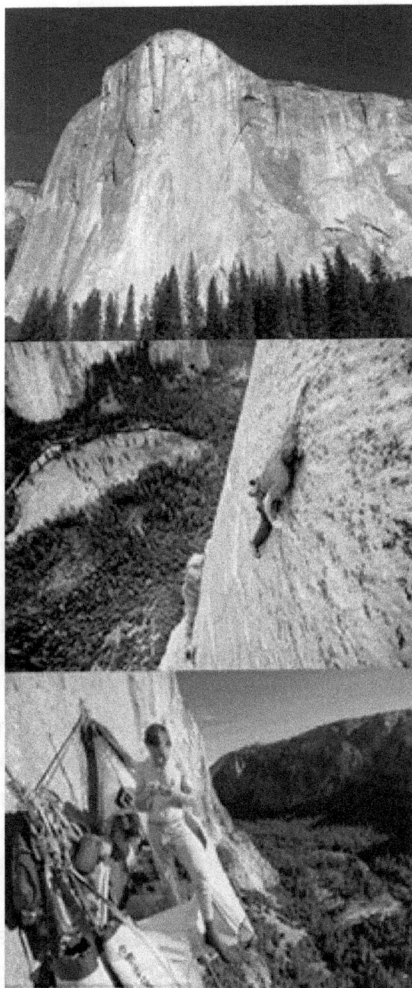

Self-Regulation and Learning Ecologies

Returning to Naomi's story, can we see evidence of self-regulation in the ecology she created to fulfill her ambition to make a difference to people living in a small town in Uganda? While her objective was not explicitly to learn and develop herself - significant learning and personal development were bi-products of the activities she determined and engaged in order to achieve her goal. Her interest in volunteering in the sort of situation she described, had been in her mind for a long time (*distal goal*) but it was only when she

CONTEXTS
PAST
PRESENT
SPACES
RESOURCES
LEARNING ECOLOGY
created by a person
FUTURE
RELATIONSHIPS
for a purpose to achieve
proximal goals informed
by distal goals
PROCESSES
ACTIVITIES &
EXPERIENCES
WHOLE PERSON
WILL, CAPABILITY, INTEGRATIVE
THINKING, EMOTIONS, ATTITUDES,
CONFIDENCE, TRUST & SELF-AWARENESS
DEVELOPMENT & ACHIEVEMENT
AFFORDANCES

became a university student that she realised she had the means to achieve her ambition and the confidence to begin the process of planning and organising herself.

When someone challenges themselves by putting themselves into entirely new places, contexts and situations. They know intuitively that their past experiences will not prepare them for what they encounter. They know they will be performing outside their comfort zone. But they also know that such spaces have the potential for personal transformation and achievement.

Naomi's *forethought* involved her in thinking about how to explore possibilities until she discovered and was inspired by a concrete idea around which she formed her personal project. In this way she appropriated an existing project and made it her own. Her attention then turned to involving others and she created a strategy to find and build relationships with like minded people so that they became part of the process of co-creating the ways and means of raising money to fund the experience and make donations to the medical centre. This task involved many different activities. It seems that she was in no doubt that with the help of others, she thought she could achieve her goal. Her significant commitment demonstrated that she believed what she was doing would make a difference to the lives of people and be worthwhile : a commitment that carried on after she had returned to the UK.

Her *performance* was demonstrated through the tasks she set herself in contexts that were both familiar and unfamiliar with problems, challenges and opportunities that she had not encountered before. She searched for and found like-minded people to help her accomplish the goal she had set herself and structured her environment to develop the resources she needed to accomplish her task. She invented, with the help of others, numerous activities aimed at improving the lives of the children and adults involved in her activities. These were connected within a coherent process for fund

> I feel that it has helped me to grow in so many ways, especially in terms of confidence and my capabilities for dealing with unfamiliar situations and to create new opportunities for myself and others. I feel spurred on to continue what we started and more, and truly believe that I am now much better equipped to achieve these goals. Through the various activities I have undertaken I have an improved understanding and insight into myself, and others. I have shown that I have acquired skills such as time management, leadership, the ability to communicate ideas to other people, and very importantly, the outlook that while an idea may start as just an idea, or may seem like just a drop in a vast ocean, it can manifest itself as a wonderful accumulation of events; a tidal wave whose ripple effects extend continuously outwards. (Naomi's reflective account)

raising. On her return she planned, organised and participated in activities to continue her project and involve other students and developed new resources to support the educational programme she had begun.

I felt that one of the
key targets to
improving their quality
of life was
education.....The
children in the
communities we visited
were unable to attend
any schools as they
could not afford it.
Therefore, I
to bring a simple hoped
platform for
education to them in the
form of these packs. Naomi

> Epistemological maturity is required to analyse and judge the validity of multiple perspectives to make wise decisions. Personal maturity is necessary to enable acting autonomously yet collaboratively and acting with integrity. Relational maturity is required for effective collaboration that integrates multiple perspectives in an uncertain and complex world. (Baxter Magolda 2014:77-8).

Naomi's commitment to *reflection* is evident in the time she committed to this activity during her experience through her hand-written diary, the film clips that recorded some of the events, people and the social-cultural and physical setting she worked in, and this reflective narrative. She evaluated her own performance by comparing who she used to be with who she was after being involved in these experiences. There is also a sense in her writing that when she looks back at what she did and accomplished she is satisfied with her performance. Here are some the ways in which she expresses judgements about herself and her performance and achievements.

Although there were numerous moments when I felt disheartened or burnt-out, but the knowledge that we have started something to benefit others, which will carry on even after we leave university honestly makes it completely worth the effort.
I grew immensely as a person and developed my confidence through a comforting sense of achievement.
I feel that it has helped me to grow in so many ways, especially in terms of confidence and my capabilities for dealing with unfamiliar situations and to create new opportunities for myself and others.

Naomi's inspiring story illustrates well the self-motivated, self-determined and self-regulated nature of a complex learning ecology which evolved over a significant period of time because she continually revisited and revised her goals as her understanding of the 'problem' and 'situation' changed. This continual refinement of proximal goals, framed within the distal goals of 'making a positive difference to the people of Mukono' and 'becoming a doctor', continually energised her to do more and drove the continuous development of her ecology for learning, developing and achieving.

In her account we see Naomi demonstrating epistemological, maturity (Baxter Magolda 2014) as she grappled with the complexities and uncertainties of the situations she encountered or created and took responsibility for her belief system, her identity and social relations as she authored her life (Kegan 1994, Baxter Magolda 2014)

Connecting Personal Development Planning (PDP) to Self-Regulated Learning and Learning Ecologies

Earlier in this chapter I drew attention to the use of Personal Development Planning (PDP) to support the development of self-regulatory skills and habits. PDP is particularly interesting phenomenon because it is the only approach to learning that has ever been mandated through policy in UK Higher Education. The purpose of the policy introduced in 2000, is to encourage approaches to learning that involve planning, action and reflection in all HE learning contexts and at all levels. The strength of PDP policy is that it permits and encourages diverse interpretations and practices: there is no prescribed way of doing PDP. Rather, teachers and institutions have the responsibility for creating practices that are meaningful and useful in specific learning and learner contexts. When expressed as a set of actions PDP processes contain a set of interconnected activities namely:

- *thinking and planning* - what to achieve and how to achieve it: setting goals

- *doing* - implementing plans with greater self-awareness so that more can be understood and learnt
- *recording* - thoughts, ideas, experiences and achievements both to understand better and to evidence the process and results of learning
- *reflecting* - thinking about what has happened, making more sense of it and creating deeper meaning
- *evaluating* - making judgements about self and own work and determining what needs to be done to develop/improve/move on
- *using the personal knowledge gained* to change thinking, beliefs, behaviours; learning from the experience

From this set of actions we can generate a process-based definition of PDP i.e. Approaches to learning that connect planning (specific goals for learning), doing (aligning actions to learning goals), recording (self-evidencing learning) and reflection (reviewing and evaluating learning and actions and their effects).

Planning and setting goals - The capacity to plan a strategy for learning and then align subsequent actions to personal plans is an

> PDP is 'a structured and supported process undertaken by a learner to reflect upon their own learning, performance and/or achievement and to plan for their personal, educational and career development.'
>
> The primary objectives of PDP are to enhance the capacity of learners to reflect, plan and take responsibility for their own learning and to understand what and how they learn.
>
> PDP helps learners articulate their learning and the achievements and outcomes of HE more explicitly, and supports the concept that learning is a lifelong and lifewide activity. (QAA 2009)

essential part of the process. However, life is very complicated and such plans should be seen as guides to be modified and refined rather than checklists that have to be adhered to. This requires people to be conscious of the effectiveness of their strategies in realising their goals and to plan in a way that enables changes to be made should this be necessary.

Doing - The idea of learning through reflection is meaningless unless it is rooted in the experiences of learning or past experiences of learning. Learning through the experience of doing enhances self-awareness and self-motivation. In the context of PDP the doing is connected to the action planning. To obtain benefit people have to be conscious of what they were doing

Recording - The extent to which recording is a feature of PDP varies according to the context. We naturally learn through reflection without recording anything but the discipline of recording helps us understand what we have learnt and provides us with evidence and a personal record of our own development. Developing the habit and skill of documenting one's own learning is a useful skill in a world that creates new explicit knowledge from the embodied tacit knowledge of people. But the requirement to keep records can become the driver for PDP and lead to a bureaucracy that impedes learning and stifles enthusiasm. Care must be taken to define the rationale for recording information and how this is integrated into learning processes and facilitative conversations with tutors.

Reflecting (Reviewing and Evaluating) - The idea of metacognition or self-awareness brought about by thinking about situations that have been experienced and trying to making sense of them, is central to the idea of learning in this way. PDP can be thought of as a way of building knowledge about self and through this a stronger sense of self-identity. The idea of evaluating requires people to make judgements about their own learning and performances. It requires people to develop the knowledge and skills in creating and using reference points and feedback mechanisms in order to enable themselves to make evaluations that are realistic and helpful. In fact PDP processes and practices are an important way of highlighting the central importance of feedback in self-regulatory processes.

Learning through reflection is central to developing self-awareness.

Reflection is a necessary part of the process of trying to assimilate and understand new knowledge and to relate it to what is already known modifying existing knowledge in the process and creating new meaningful learning. Reflective learning will already be incidental in the academic activities of most students but deliberate strategies for its use will make students more conscious of it so that it can become an integral part of their approach to learning. PDP tends to emphasise reflection on action and performance after the event or experience. In reality reflective deliberation occurs in the planning stage of the process (reflecting on similar situations in the past in order to plan for the future) and in the performance stage (I messed that up didn't I how can I avoid doing that in future?).

Using personal knowledge - The strength of PDP is that it is a method of creating knowledge about oneself. Ultimately the real benefit is to the individuals who create this knowledge and who are able to draw upon it and use in ways that are meaningful and useful to themselves. Such knowledge might be used in an instrumental way eg being able to relate personal knowledge and skills to the needs of en employer. Or it may be used in more profound ways to modify conceptions, attitudes, behaviours that lead to personal change. PDP therefore encourages people to learn about themselves and to act up on this learning by fostering and supporting the habit of personal change.

Learning through the processes that PDP promotes

A key question for PDP policy makers and those who support student PDP is whether the actions, attitudes and behaviours that PDP promotes actually result in positive learning outcomes and improved achievement. While there is an extensive anecdotal and self-reported literature to this effect, scientific evidence derived from researcher manipulated studies, is hard to come by. Gough et al (2003) conducted a systematic review and mapped the field of knowledge relevant to the research question - *what evidence is there that processes that connect reflection, recording, planning and action improve student learning?*

An initial trawl of the English language world literature since 1982 resulted in 14,271 potentially relevant studies being identified. The abstracts and titles of these documents were evaluated using a range of criteria developed by a 'PDP user group' in collaboration with the research team and 982 documents were identified as being worthy of further analysis. 813 of these documents were accessed and read and evaluated using the criteria developed and of these 158 documents were subject to more rigorous analysis and key wording to produce a map of the research field. Twenty five experimental researcher-manipulated studies, considered to provide the best research evidence on the impact of this type of learning, were subject to detailed analysis and data extraction. Nineteen of the experimental studies had a moderate or high quality rating using quality assessment criteria developed by the research team. Seventeen of these studies provided evidence of positive impact on students' learning.

PDP & self-regulation

From the descriptions above it is clear that there is a strong and positive connection between the self-regulation theory and PDP processes and practices. Indeed, many if not all the researcher manipulated studies identified in the systematic review were concerned with aspects of self-regulation in teaching and learning practices. The model of self-regulated learning provides a scientific explanation of the processes that underlie PDP and helps us understand how the actions, behaviours, attitudes and emotions of individuals engaging in PDP learning processes might be connected. There appears to be a good correlation between the key actions and behaviours in the PDP model of learning and those of self-regulated learning. But the model of self-regulated learning provides much greater detail of the thinking processes, motivations, values and belief systems that underlie PDP practices. As such it provides a useful analytical tool with which to evaluate different types of PDP practices. The following observations can be made.

PDP processes tend to focus on the instrumental features of action planning, record keeping and reflection on action and performance. The other important features of self-regulated learning are often implicit. There is often little consideration given to the richness of the forethought process and the underlying motivations, values and beliefs that underpin the sense of self-efficacy that drives the whole process. PDP offers a real opportunity to value the intrinsic motivations of learners yet we often see PDP being driven by the extrinsic motivation of teacher assessment which takes no account of the personal motivations that drive individuals. This runs counter to the ideal of preparing students for a world in which their personal motivations will be far more important in securing their own success in life than any external motivations.

Forethought is the home of imagination (idea generation) and creative thinking (how own or other people's ideas might be used). If we are to nurture imagination and creativity in students' learning this should be explicit in both PDP and self-regulation models of learning. Imagination is a source of personal energy that motivates us to do something in a particular way. The ability to imagine goals and impacts and then imagine interesting ways of achieving these things is important to sustaining the motivation to learn and do and fuels self-regulated behaviour.

The doing (performance) part of the self-regulation model identifies many sub-processes that are implicit in PDP practices - notions of self-instruction, help-seeking and using the environment to create resources for learning. These are all crucial in problem-working throughout life and they are rarely explicitly recognised in PDP models for learning. 'Doing' is the home of creativity in action (making use of own or other people's ideas). The process of engaging with emergent problems in real time, the structuring of the environment to create resources for learning, the adaptation and transfer of ideas to new contexts, the juggling of numerous tasks and the nurturing of relationships are all manifestations of creativity in action. These things all rely on self-efficacy and personal motivation to sustain them.

There is generally a strong emphasis on reflection in PDP practices but

179

the quality of reflection can be quite variable and it requires considerable practice and coaching to develop the critical thinking aspects of reflection. Comparing own performance and attributing causal significance to results - requires evaluation against criteria, standards or previous performance - what is good/poor performance attributed to? The extent to which we provide students with the knowledge and skills to do this, and the opportunities for practising self-evaluation are quite variable in PDP processes.

Emotions like *anger* (resentment, annoyance, hostility and even outrage), *sadness* (dejection/ depression, flatness, energyless, loneliness), *fear* (anxiety, misgiving, apprehension) and *enjoyment* (contentment, satisfaction, pride and even pleasure) are all part and parcel of everyday learning. But higher education, with its focus on the development of a rational/analytical/critical thinking and detached perspectives, tends to ignore the personal emotionally involved dimensions of learning. PDP provides an opportunity to put emotions back into learning within contexts that are meaningful to the learner and to acknowledge that learning is an emotional business.

How we feel about something has a major effect on whether we want to pursue something or abandon it. The interplay of emotions, beliefs, actions and contexts are complex and unpredictable but we need to be conscious of them as they will impact on our decision making processes. The self-regulatory model acknowledges these things in a way that PDP models often do not. Goleman's (1996) book on emotional intelligence depicts a world in which the capacity to cope with life is strongly dependent on attitudes of mind that have little to do with the thinking rational part of the brain and more to do with the emotional, non-rational and intuitive brain. The roots of self-efficacy, our senses of personal and professional satisfaction with what we have done and our willingness to adapt in the future, lie in these attitudes of mind. If we are to improve our ability to promote personal knowledge of these things through the higher education experience then we need to develop PDP strategies and evaluation criteria that clearly address and work with emotional intelligence.

PDP & learning ecologies

There is an opportunity for PDP practices, that accommodate the model of self-directed, self-regulated learning to support an approach in higher education that embraces the idea of learning ecologies. Naomi's narrative of the learning ecology she developed around her volunteering project was written while she was involved in the University of Surrey's Lifewide Learning Award which had within it a PDP process which invited her to record her thinking, activities and achievements. She used a diary and made film clips which were later assembled into a film. She produced a personal development plan which set out her goals and how she intended to achieve them and also provided a template for the reflective account she produced as she looked back on her experience. The framework and the award it supported, provided her with an incentive and a structure within which she could record her learning and achievements. In this way PDP could be a useful aid to the development of educational practices that encouraged and recognised learners' own ecologies for learning, development and achievement.

Concluding Thoughts

Self-regulation is a powerful theory that explains the relationship between a learner's willingness and desire to learn, their ability to set themselves a goal(s), create and implement strategies and activities to achieve their goals, monitor and evaluate their progress towards what they want to achieve and adjust their strategies if necessary, capitalise on new opportunities as they emerge, make judgements about their own performance and draw deeper meaning / learning from their experience through reflective processes. All these dispositions, ways of thinking, capability and behaviour are involved in the creation and maintenance of a complex ecology for learning, developing and achieving.

The fundamental difference between learning in an informal learning context compared to a formal learning setting is the learner's perception of choice - the freedom to choose between possible goals, activities, participants, resources, tools and technologies, when to start, when to change tack and when to stop, and to keep on choosing throughout a learning project, until the decision is made to stop. The creation of a self-determined, self-directed process for learning - an ecology for learning, developing and achieving, in an informal setting, provides the affordances to make use of these freedoms and choices, and experience the sense of learning spontaneously and without much conscious effort (Boekaerts and Minnaert 1999).

There are numerous ways of developing self-regulatory attitudes, skills and habits in formal educational settings. In the UK a policy has been developed to encourage Personal Development Planning (PDP) at all levels and in all higher education contexts. The attitudes, values, skills and habits PDP promotes can be related to the thinking and practice of a self-regulating learner. The policy emphasises that students' learning and development takes place in personal, educational and career (or work-related) contexts while they are studying at university and it encourages students to take responsibility for, plan and reflect on their own learning in these diverse learning contexts. PDP is ideally configured to support both the development of learners' self-regulatory skill, attitudes and habits and the skills, attitudes and habits necessary for creating their own ecologies of practice for learning.

CHAPTER 6
Ecology of Learning Through Work

Introduction

In higher education, students' efforts and performance are geared towards learning and understanding a prescribed curriculum and demonstrating through assessments that an amount and quality of learning, defined by a grade or mark, has been achieved. Teachers create and implement ecologies of practice for the purpose of engaging students in learning (curriculum content) and the learning practices of students are heavily influenced by the form of these ecologies. The environment is designed to support learning with abundant and accessible resources, spaces, tools, technologies and professional support.

The organisational work environment is different. In the work environment efforts are geared to the work of the organisation and performance is evaluated in terms of such things as doing a good job, meeting targets, delivering objectives, and maintaining standards.

Figure 6.1
Four very different work environments in which learning in order to perform is important.

In the work environment people whose role involves learning, create ecologies of practice but their priority is to perform with learning as an element of the performance. The environment is essentially designed for work but it may include resources and infrastructures that encourage and support learning.

This chapter begins by examining the nature of learning in and through work before considering and analysing the narratives of several people who were trying to change their practices and create new value through their innovations.

Learning in the Work Environment

In contrast to learning in structured educational environments, most workplace learning is informal and occurs as a by-product of engaging in work practices (Eraut 2010).

Newcomers often have to learn "How we do things here" without being given any specific objectives or advice. Thus a learning goal might be described by a vague phrase like "being able to do what X does". Even when more detailed advice is given, learning will still be evaluated by the extent to which you can do what X does, rather than by some indirect and less authentic type of assessment. You may be given sets of objectives or competencies, but the 'real' assessment will be whether your performance meets the expectations of significant others in your workplace.

Although the workplace appears to be primarily concerned with capability (what you do and how well you perform it), it is equally important to be able to do the right thing at the right time. In practice this means that you have to: (1) understand both the general context and the specific situation you are expected to deal with, (2) decide what needs to be done by yourself and possibly also by others, and (3) implement what you have decided, individually or as a group, through performing a series of actions. All three of these processes contribute to a person's perceived competency (Eraut 2010).

Improving/developing capability in the work environment can involve many things (Eraut 2010:2).

- Doing things faster
- Improving the quality of the process
- Improving communications around the task
- Becoming more independent and needing less supervision
- Combining tasks more effectively
- Quicker recognition of possible problems
- Expanding the range of situations in which one can perform competently
- Helping others learn to do the task or part of the task
- Increases in task difficulty/ taking on tasks of greater complexity
- Dealing with more difficult or more important cases, clients, customers, suppliers or colleagues
- Developing entirely new practice.

Some of these types of practice could be described as *doing things better*, some as *doing things differently* and some as *doing different things*. At the most inventive end of this spectrum is *trying to do things that have not been done before*: we call this innovation.

Progression often involves doing the same thing, or not quite the same thing, in more difficult conditions or across a wider range of cases. Although these types of progress seem fairly obvious, they are not necessarily conscious. People recognise that they have learned things through experience, but do not necessarily remember how or when. Often people simply realise that that they are doing things that they could not have done a few weeks or months earlier.

Learning is situated in the social practice and environment of work

Learning in the professional work environment is 'situated' in a particular social-cultural setting in which particular people perform certain sorts of roles and engage in certain types of social interaction. As a result people are exposed to, and learn from and with each other, the cultural knowledge of the organisation/department/team, as well as the field specific knowledge required for practice and production. These different types of knowledge are learnt and incorporated into the personal knowledge of an individual. Eraut (2010, 2011) identifies different sorts of knowledge that is used and developed in the professional work environment.

- *codified knowledge* necessary for the job in the form(s) in which the person uses it
- *know-how* in the form of *skills and practices*
- personal *understandings of people and situations*
- accumulated *memories of cases* and episodic *events*
- other aspects of personal *expertise*, *practical wisdom* and *tacit knowledge*
- *self-knowledge*, *attitudes*, *values* and *emotions*.

Work provides a context and a set of situations and circumstances within which things relating to work are learned and new capability to perform the job is developed.

Situated learning was first proposed by Lave and Wenger (1991) as a model of learning in a *community of practice* comprising people who share a craft and/or a profession such as a group of people performing similar roles in the same context. Situated learning is learning that takes place in the same context in which it is applied. Lave and Wenger (1991) argue that learning in a social setting like work is a social process whereby knowledge is co-constructed by the people who are directly involved in the work in the specific environment within which work takes place. From a situated cognition perspective, learning occurs in a social setting through dialogue with others in the community (Lave 1988). Learning emerges through a process of reflecting, interpreting and negotiating meaning among participants engaged in connected work practices.

Situated knowledge is obtained by the processes described by Lave (1997:21) as "way in" and "practice." Way in involves a period of observation in which a learner watches someone who is more expert and makes a first attempt at solving a problem. Practice is refining and perfecting the use of acquired knowledge in the same context (p. 21) and perhaps extending it to other contexts. Situated learning is not only reflecting upon and drawing meaning from previous experiences but is immersion in and with the experience. These ideas get to the heart of what an ecology of practice achieves in a situation where a person or persons has/acquired knowledge to work with i.e. they are performing in situations that are already quite well known. But an ecology of practice is able to expand learning beyond the situation by reaching out beyond what is known into entirely new situations and contexts, creating new understanding that can be brought back and acted upon in the original setting.

Situational understanding is 'a critical aspect of professional work, and probably the most difficult' (Eraut 2011). It tends to be taken for granted by all but newcomers in an organisation who often struggle to make sense of practice until they develop this understanding. Situational understanding is hard to develop because people who have it take it for granted and cannot imagine anyone else "not being aware of the obvious". Even more experienced members of an organisation may encounter this from time to time, for example if they take on a new role or move to a different part of the organisation or they embark on an innovation that involves them in interacting with parts of the organisation with which they are not familiar.

Modes of learning in work settings

Longitudinal studies of prospective chartered accountants, qualified engineers and nurses learning in the workplace during the first three years after graduating revealed that most learning was not a separate activity but a by-product of their ongoing work; and most of these events involved working with other people (Eraut 2007, Eraut and Hirsch 2007).

Eraut and his colleagues, developed a typology of learning modes (Table 6.1). Three modes are distinguished. In the left column learning is judged to be part of a *working processes*, from which *learning* was a *by-product*, while those in the right column are clearly recognizable as *learning processes in their own right,* several involving more experienced colleagues and more formal structured learning processes. *The middle column* contains comparatively *short activities*, such as asking questions, observing or reflecting. These activities can occur many times in a single process, and were found within almost every type of process, often several at a time.

Table 6.1 Modes of learning in work settings (Eraut and Hirsch 2007:25)

1 Work Processes with learning as a by-product	2 Learning Activities located within work or learning processes	3 Learning Processes at or near the workplace
Participation in group Processes - collaboration Working alongside others Consulting Tackling challenging tasks and roles Problem solving Trying things out Consolidating, extending /refining skills Working with clients	Asking questions Getting information Locating resource people Listening and observing Reflecting Learning from mistakes Giving and receiving feedback Using and creating mediating artefacts	Being supervised Being coached Being mentored Shadowing Visiting other sites Conferences Short courses Working for a qualification Independent study

Learning trajectories

In the early stages of a career trainees in most professions undertake a series of placements, through which they are expected, with suitable support, to acquire the specified level of competence. However, the learning affordances of each placement vary considerably according to

Table 6.2 Summary of learning trajectories organised into eight categories (Eraut and Hirsch 2007:16)

Learning trajectory	Details
Task performance	Speed and fluency; complexity of tasks and problems; range of skills required; communication with a wide range of people; collaborative work
Awareness and understanding	Other people: colleagues, customers, managers, etc Contexts and situations One's own organization Problems and risks Priorities and strategic issues Value issues
Personal development	Self evaluation; self-management; handling emotions; building and sustaining relationships; disposition to attend to other perspectives / to consult and work with others / to learn and improve one's practice; accessing relevant knowledge and expertise; ability to learn from experience
Academic knowledge and skills	Use of evidence and argument; accessing formal knowledge; research-based practice; theoretical thinking; knowing what you might need to know; using knowledge resources (human, paper, electronic); learning how to use relevant theory in a range of practical situations
Role performance	Prioritisation; range of responsibility; supporting other people's learning; leadership; accountability; supervisory role; delegation; handling ethical issues; coping with unexpected problems; crisis management; keeping up-to-date
Teamwork	Collaborative work; facilitating social relations; joint planning and problem solving; ability to engage in and promote mutual learning
Decision making and problem solving	When to seek expert help; dealing with complexity; group decision making; problem analysis; formulating and evaluating opinions; managing the process within an appropriate timescale; decision making under pressure
Judgement	Quality of performance, output and outcomes; priorities; value issues; levels of work

the local context, and these differences will affect what each trainee learns and ultimately, their profile of experience-based competence. The research undertaken by Eraut and his team indicates that a better way of monitoring progress across complex performances in the professional work environment is to think in terms of learning trajectories for describing or classifying what had been learned and the capability that had been developed (Eraut and Hirsch 2007 and Table 6.2).

The concept of learning trajectories takes account of the fact that at any point in time:

- Explicit progress is being made on several of the trajectories
- Implicit progress can be inferred and later acknowledged on some other trajectories
- Progress on other trajectories is stalling or even regressing through lack of use or because new practices have not yet been adopted.

Any significant work project that a person participates in, will afford them opportunity to develop along a number of trajectories simultaneously but will reflect development in a specific set of contexts. Indeed, a complex work project (such as the two cases described later in this chapter) may involve development along all the trajectories over a relatively short period of time eg 6-12 months. The experience and knowledge gained may, or may not, be transferable to other contexts. What is transferable is the ability to learn in these sorts of circumstances. Anyone wanting to develop themselves across all categories of learning trajectory needs to be involved in the range of work projects that will enable them to do so. Prolonged engagement in work situations that are very similar will not enable a person to develop along a full repertoire of trajectories as they will not be afforded the experiences to do so. This is why professional development is closely linked to affordance in the work environment. In cases where affordance is limited a person may need to seek affordances for development outside their immediate work environment (lifewide affordance) or seek work in another organisation.

Dynamics of working & learning in an organisation

Eraut and Hirsch (2007) draw attention to the complex dynamics of learning and developing through work in an organisation which they captured in a simple diagram (Figure 6.2). At the centre of the diagram is the individual, located in their particular contexts and situations, working on their particular projects some of which might be highly developmental. They have particular knowledges, skill sets and attitudes which together constitute their capability i.e. what persons bring to a situation that enables them to think, interact and perform. Performance embodies what the person actually does when they deal with a particular situation - how well they perform their role. Learning underpins performance which is context and situation dependent whereas capability is inferred from a series of performances and should not be judged on only one performance. Therefore, performances in different contexts spanning different levels of complexity, feed into the continuous development of capability i.e. it leads to progression along a range of learning trajectories.

Figure 6.2 Dynamics of learning and performing in an organisational setting (Eraut and Hirsch 2007:2)

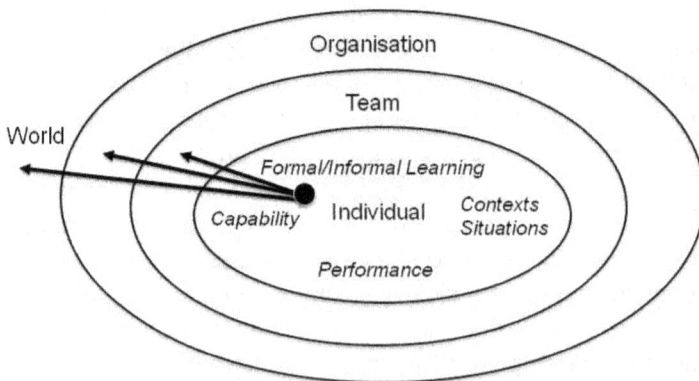

Learning in an organisational setting, can be gained through formal study - for example studying an on-line module offered by a university, training organisation or the organisation in which the individual works. However, much of the learning gained by individuals is through the process of work itself through their involvement in projects, often with colleagues, which introduce and involve them in situations that they have not previously encountered. Eraut and Hirsch (2007) estimated that between 80-90% of learning was gained through work itself rather than more structured learning situations.

Socio-cultural environment

Learning occurs as individuals interact with their own organisation as they try to work out what they need to do in order to perform and how what they do fits in and connects to existing ways of doing things. If it doesn't fit into existing practices, they need to work out what needs to be changed and how it needs to be changed. It is the organisational context with its people, culture and structures that introduces complexity and challenge into the learning process and demands attention to the situational knowledge required in order to perform.

Organisations, communities and teams big and small develop their own cultures 'the way we do things around here' (Deal and Kennedy 1982). Culture derives from many factors, eg purposes and values, traditions, styles of leadership and management, and structures, processes and practices enacted everyday by the members of the organisation as they interact in their work. Culture is conveyed in the conversations, actions and stories of every member of the organisation.

Culture affects the way people think and behave, the way people interact with each other and the way people want to belong to and be involved in the work of the organisation. The culture of an organisation helps or inhibits people as they perform their roles. An emotionally nourishing environment helps people deal with the challenges, stresses, anxieties and frustrations of trying to fulfil their role and helps them to remain positive in the face of setbacks. Such an environment recognises the efforts and celebrates the achievements of those who are involved in change (Amabile and Kramer 2012).

Stress, anxiety and frustration are often associated with work and are especially associated with times of instability and change - a frequent occurrence in organisations. They are particularly apparent when people take on new roles or engage in challenging and demanding projects that take people into unfamiliar territory. In such situations people are building new ecologies for learning and development and the ecology provides the affordance for not only learning to fulfill work objectives but also the means of coping with the stress associated with it.

Amabile and Kramer's (2012) study of the socio-cultural work environment identified two types of event or condition which they termed catalysts and nourishers, that support what they term a person's *'inner work life'* - the constant stream of emotions, perceptions and motivations that people experience as they go through their work days (Amabile and Kramer 2011: 29-39). Throughout the day, people react to events that happen in their work environment and try to make sense of them. These emotional reactions and perceptions affect their motivation for the work - all of which have a powerful influence on their performance. When people have a positive inner work life, they are more creative, productive, committed to the work, and co-operative toward the people they worked with. When they have poor inner work lives, the opposite is true - they are less creative, productive, committed and co-operative.

The catalyst factor includes events that directly enable a person to make progress in their work. Catalysts include such things as: having clear goals (self-determined goals are more motivating), having autonomy to determine how to work, having access to sufficient resources when you need them, having enough time to accomplish the tasks, being able to find help when you need it, knowing how to succeed, being encouraged to let your ideas to flow. The opposite of catalysts are inhibitors; these make progress difficult or impossible. They are the mirror image of the catalysts, and include giving unclear goals, micro-managing, and providing insufficient resources etc..

Amabile and Kramer (2012:131-33) identified four factors that *nourish* a work culture in which people felt supported and positively influenced their motivation, productivity and creativity namely:

1 Respect - managerial actions determine whether people feel respected or disrespected and recognition is the most important of these actions.

2 Encouragement - when managers or colleagues are enthusiastic about an individual's work and when managers express confidence in the capabilities of people doing the work it increases their sense of self-efficacy. Simply by sharing a belief that someone can do something challenging and trusting them to get on with it without interference, greatly increases the self-belief of those involved in the challenge.

3 Emotional support - people feel more connected to others at work when their emotions are validated. This goes for events at work, like frustrations when things are not going smoothly and little progress is being made, and for significant events in someone's personal life. Recognition of emotion and empathy can do much to alleviate negative and amplify positive feelings with beneficial results for all concerned.

4 Affiliation - people want to feel connected to their colleagues so actions that develop bonds of mutual trust, appreciation and affection are essential in nourishing the spirit of participation.

Tensions and conflicts

Amabile and Kramer (ibid) highlight the fact that work environments host a range of conditions that make them complex and often turbulent places for the intermingling of personal and social learning and development. This is particularly the case when we build ecologies for learning and development that extend beyond our immediate work environment and involve parts of the organisation with which we are unfamiliar and where our goals are at odds with the way things are done. Posing questions like, 'how can we do this?' challenges existing ways of doing things and the innovator initiates the struggle to resolve the issue. These areas of 'local contentious practice' (Holland and Lave 2009) are the 'pinch-points' where innovations can be thwarted and innovators can become demotivated if progress cannot be made towards resolving the problem. One of the really crucial factors in enabling 'local contentious practice to be resolved', is for the people who are trying to bring about change have the support of people who can help them overcome the procedural and decision making barriers between different parts of the organisation. These are the brokers and boundary spanners that silo'd organisations need in order to unblock things that seem to be frozen. They are important relationships in the ecologies of people who are developing changes in social practices within an organisation and they feature in the two case studies below.

Ecologies of Practice for Performing & Learning

In the second part of this chapter I try to show the relevance of the ecologies of practice model to performing and learning in and through work. The two case studies involve five experienced education professionals who share their stories of trying to innovate within a university's strategic change programme. For a comprehensive description and analysis of this programme see Baker, Jackson and Longmore (2014). The two case examples describe different sorts of learning ecology. Both involve turning conceptual thinking into practice but the first case is focused on exploration and design (learning through the process of designing for new social practice), while the second is more concerned with applying and implementing a design (learning through the process of implementing new social practice).

The people involved in these narratives are not the early career learners, that Michael Eraut and his co-researchers studied - they are experienced professionals involved in inventing entirely new organisational and administrative structures and social practices. Their learning and development is grown through the organisational developmental projects required by the strategic change programme and their experiences require the use of the conceptual framework developed by Eraut to show the way individuals interact with the complex socio-cultural environment in which they are situated in order to learn how to bring about change and all the messiness that entails.

Case 1

Linda is a senior lecturer, with experience and expertise in the fashion industry, works collaboratively with Mike, an instructional designer from the university's central e-Development Centre (EDC) in order to develop an innovative on-line course comprising 12 Professional Development Units (PDU's). The university wanted to expand its on-line offer of industry relevant learning opportunities and this project was in the vanguard or this development.

Linda's story

I obviously used the [market] research that we had done. Discussed with the head of school and the other school management what the outcomes of this research were and the headings that we would put together to begin to develop the short courses. Then I had to find external people to help with writing content. Obviously I had to start somewhere. My strongest feeling was that I needed to provide a framework for the people to work with. So I began to think about that before getting anyone external involved. I worked with Mike in the e-Development Centre quite extensively on trying to develop this effective way of delivering taught modules online and trying to put together a framework for the externals to use when putting together their teaching material. Basically I wrote most of the unit descriptors, the sort of bible for how these would be developed in terms of teaching material and then provided that usually to the external [person].

I found these [external] people [using] my own contacts and appealing to people's better nature because I think the payment that they were receiving wasn't necessarily equivalent to freelance pay that they would normally... But I worked very closely with them. They came into the university at certain strategic times throughout the development and a lot of email communication took place with them sending me materials and me checking it and going back to them with feedback. Really, really resource heavy actually. Really time consuming for me in terms of head space and having to pull myself out of my daily operation, job, my normal responsibilities and doing this on top of that.

I was getting six hours relief from my normal duties. Six hours doesn't reflect in any way, shape or form the amount of time that I put into developing these twelve short courses that were to be accredited by the university all at once with externals helping for some of them and not for others. I was doing a considerable amount of reading through materials and feeding back during my own time in the evenings and weekends. Without that, it would not have happened. But I felt very, very strongly at the time that these are winners. There is a market for them and if we can market them in the right way I always felt they would be successful. I believed in the framework that I developed and that it was an effective, clear and understandable way to go through a short course for anyone who is working and [wants learning] that is relevant to their industry.

It was a constant battle because I always felt as though I was having to push other departments and other areas of the university to give me answers to questions that I had. It always felt as though the answers didn't exist at that point in time, but I needed them. I needed to know answers to certain questions and I needed sometimes some kind of framework for me to be working within and none existed. I eventually got a hold of the guidelines for developing professional development units from our quality department, but I had no knowledge of that prior to poking and pushing and constantly asking for that information. I was actually quite aggrieved at the time that that existed and I hadn't been alerted to the fact that it existed before I began to develop the courses, because surely that would have helped. Some staff development for me would have been highly appreciated.

Once I had actually got past that initial stage of how do I put these first drafts of the units together, things began to roll and I began to discover who I could at least go and say 'Look I have this question, who can I ask? Who is going to answer it for me? I need answers.' I think I probably began perhaps to become a little bit annoying for some people because I kept saying 'I need an answer' and 'I need to know.'

Some of the most difficult issues, I would say, were managing the externals because some of them didn't have a huge experience of teaching.....it was very difficult to find people that could actually do this with me. I chose them based on their expertise in the areas that I wanted the content developed around. So I was having to sort of almost coach them in learning and teaching as we were going, plus trying to help them understand how their material was going to be used online and the amount of discussion on text that was required of them rather than just bullet point teaching. So that was another challenge that came later.

I was having to be a subject person - most of these [PDU's] are in an area that I can apply my expertise to. I was having to be a learning and teaching person and an online education person, working with Mike and others from the EDC. Initially it was a couple of conversations that I was going to be doing this and understanding that a really clear framework would need to be put in place and how online teaching and learning would be different to in-class teaching and learning. They, I guess, explained to me the most important aspects to consider in on-line leaning. Then I gradually spent more and more time with the people from EDC, particularly Mike, and asked for their feedback on what I was developing and what the externals were developing with me. They got more and more involved in it because they really believed in what I was doing once the momentum got going. They sort of started to understand what I was trying to achieve from my perspective and then they saw the potential in that and gave me more and more time. Their time was then really important to the success of the project because without them helping me so much, I wouldn't have achieved the outcomes. Basically, I felt like I had made some friends there and they were going to help me get through this if no one else was. So they were incredibly supportive. It wasn't uncommon for Mike and I to both be online at 11 o'clock at night talking back and forth and looking at the units online and discussing areas of the unit that were strong or not so strong, that needed a bit of work, a bit of development, changing things, 'What do you think of this?' It wasn't uncommon for us to be doing that in the evenings because of our own personal motivations.

[The development project] was a huge learning curve for me and because at certain times I was quite vocal about the fact that I wasn't getting answers and I was quite persistent and tenacious about sorting things out and getting through this project. I was just tenacious in the fact that I will get this done and I will find the help somewhere and someone will give me the answers I need because I have to do this... and there were I think two occasions when... and I am being really honest now. Two times in the year when I said 'I have had enough. No one else is as driven as I am about completing these PDUs so I give up.' You know, those moments of kind of this is just so frustrating and no one else seems to be as bothered as I am so why am I doing it. You know? Actually, this is only my own personal motivation that is making this happen, so why am I so worried? But the next day was a new day and I continued to work on it because I know I am not really going to give up on doing this. I was venting frustrations and trying to I guess not get attention but get people to respond to me and find a way through. But yeah, there were two occasions at which I got to that point.

Mike's story

Early in 2010 I took on the role of Instructional Developer in our Flexible Delivery team. One of our first activities as a team was to start developing a set of high-quality standards for our on-line provision. We undertook an informal survey of the existing provision for distance and online learning from other higher education institutions in the UK and overseas. Places like the Open University obviously, and then Stamford and MIT, a lot of places have got open educational resources now as well and looking at the manner in which they deliver their content and what we felt was effective and what was less so. Also looking at some of the private providers as well, places like Adobe TV and Lynda.com and again, people are doing quite high-quality online training or online education. And we started to distil from that survey components that we felt different providers were demonstrating. But we also noticed that nobody had the whole package as far as we were concerned, so we were consolidating a set of standards that we felt if we could work towards so we would be creating the whole package. So it was a sort of benchmarking process and it resulted in a new University Framework for Online Learning. So the work that we've done has become policy in regards to courses or online content for courses that are predominantly delivered online.

I worked with a number of academics to help them develop their on-line courses targeted at the professional market - the concept is for entirely distance and entirely online professional development units, short 12 week credit bearing units. One of the people I worked with was Linda in the Fashion Department. She had a fairly good idea of how she wanted to structure the units in terms of how the content would be delivered and also in terms of some of the learning activities that the students would participate in. Where I came in was then to look at how that actually translates into online content, how you get it online, how you guide the students through the materials, how you make it accessible, how you stage and present particular events. Because on-line units have events such as web conferences that happen two or three times during the duration of the twelve weeks, and there's points where the students are asked to then communicate with a peer partner and they might have a one-to-one tutorial with their tutor.

So I went into discussions with Linda particularly at first over the unit that she wrote herself. She was at the forefront of this area of development: she was the first person [in the university] to actually get a unit developed. I looked at what originally was a word document map of how she wanted the activities to occur, and sat down and discussed with her how that might be better structured in terms of the activity points that happen throughout it, where you might place the assessment tasks, like the formative and final assessment tasks. And then, because what we'd worked on as a team was getting a look and feel and format for how the content goes online, I worked with her word document plans and putting that up online, putting the content in the correct places. Together we created the detailed design and content Linda typing directly the stuff online or I took ideas of hers and put it up for her, putting the online tools into the correct place. And between us, moving things within her unit until it felt like there was a structure that would actually guide the students through structured study. And the work on Linda's unit kept going on for a long time because that was the one we were really trying to refine down as an exemplar. So it was a highly co-creative process and the work we did then helped us to establish a template and a guide for how other PDUs could be developed and written ...which has proved very useful.

Ecological perspectives on learning, performing & achieving

The first point to make is that the two people involved were experienced professionals working in an organisational environment that was familiar to them. Their ecologies of practice were firmly situated in the same institutional environment i.e. this is the only *place* on earth where these practices could be enacted and this learning could be acquired. But their practice was not simply aimed at 'refining and perfecting the use of acquired knowledge in the same context' (Lave 1997: 21) rather, the aim of their collaborative practice was to expand their learning well beyond the teaching and learning situations they understood into entirely new situations and contexts, with entirely new tools and content and ways of doing things some of which brought them into conflict with their own organisation. So an important part of their learning was aimed at changing the organisational situation (systems, policies and practices) in order that new practices could flourish. This dual purpose is typical of the more significant work projects that people undertake in organisations. Three visual aids (conceptual tools) are provided in Figures 6.3 - 6.5 to help make sense of these narratives from an ecological perspective.

The narratives of the main actors involved in this developmental project, reveal the wonderfully productive and supportive relationships between colleagues from different parts of an organisation who share the same vision. They formed a team of two although other colleagues from the EDC were also involved and both interacted in their own ways with the university and the world outside the university (Figure 6.3).

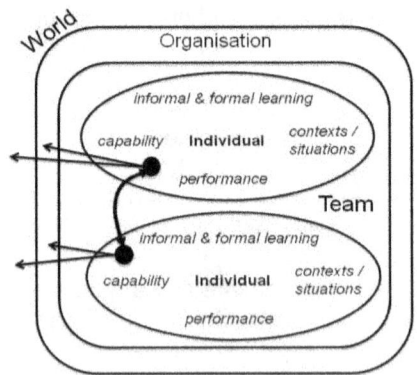

Figure 6.3 The dynamics of performing and learning through work in the contexts described above.

From each individual's description of the work they undertook we can see that it must have involved all of the modes of learning in columns 1 and 2 of Eraut's conceptual framework (Table 6.1) and included many other items (Table 6.3). Furthermore, because these are experienced professionals, the learning processes listed in column 3 of Table 6.1 are replaced by a self-motivated, self-managed and self-regulated process that engaged each participant in productive inquiry aimed at finding out what they needed to know in order to do what they needed to do.

Using Figure 6.4 as a descriptive framework we might elaborate the main features of Linda's learning ecology. The project lasted about 12 months. During this period of *time* Linda created *space* for herself, with the help of additional *resources* provided by the university (funding to buy out her teaching time), to engage in a developmental process. She had no prior experience in designing on-line courses so this space required her to explore, research, problem solve, design and experiment. It was clearly a space that was betwixt and between her past (non-existent knowledge and expertise) and her future capability in the area of on-line learning developed through the project.

Figure 6.4 Diagram summarising the essential features of a learning ecology.

The university provided the key *affordance* through its strategic development programme which set out a strategic vision for change and also provided funding for staff who wanted to contribute to this change. There were also other affordances in the environments of the two participants for example, Linda's network of professional expertise and the research that Mike and his team had undertaken to create a framework for the design of on-line learning.

While Linda had the vision and experience to see the value in developing a suite of on-line courses for professionals in her industrial sector, she lacked the expertise to be able to achieve this goal by herself. Mike's organisational role was to help staff who wanted to develop new forms of e-learning. By combining their expertise and interests both participants in this developmental project were able to contribute ideas, knowledge and expertise to the process that enabled the new on-line courses to be produced together with the knowledge and capabilities necessary to help other members of the organisation achieve similar goals in future. In other words, development gained through the project resulted in enhanced capability at the individual and organisational levels.

The narratives are grounded in the contexts of two people involved in the project: *Linda's work context* and her desire to bring about change in her professional field and *Mike's work context* and desire to help colleagues across the university to adapt and develop their practice in order to enable the organisation to change. Both of these contexts are situated within departmental and organisational contexts which at that time, were highly supportive of staff who were attempting to innovate in line with the organisation's strategic objectives.

Both Linda and Mike had clear proximal and distal goals. Both wanted to develop the best possible on-line course. In Linda's case her proximal goal was set in her distal goal of developing her professional skills as a higher education teacher. While Mike's distal goal was to develop himself as an e-learning professional. Both were intrinsically driven by the interests and beliefs in the value and potential of what they were trying to accomplish.

Table 6.3 Modes of learning inferred in the narratives above. Adapted from Eraut and Hirsch (2007)

1 Work processes with learning as a by-product	2 Learning activities located within work or learning processes	3 Learning processes at or near the workplace
• Participation in group • processes - collaboration TEAMWORK • Working alongside others • Relationship development • Consulting -checking • Market research • Meetings and discussions • Managing and contracting external contributors • Immersion in challenging tasks and roles • Creating new frameworks to guide others • Designing within existing frameworks • Learning to implement a service in real time • Problem solving • Coping and adapting to insufficient resource • Trying things out • Consolidating, extending /refining skills • Working with clients • Attempting to resolve local contentious practice • Creation of new on-line learning environments to support new social practices	• Asking questions • Getting information • Locating resources eg people • Listening and observing • Reflecting • Learning from mistakes • Giving and receiving feedback • Creation and use of mediating artefacts *Also* • Selling ideas • Persuading • Negotiating • Challenging existing practices • Designing new approaches	Very few of the activities listed by Eraut in Table 4.1 Learning is essentially a self-motivated, self-regulated and managed process. One of the people involved had a mentor but all used each other and other colleagues to learn.

Although the *process* was task-oriented significant new learning and personal development were gained in the process. Linda's *learning trajectory* shows that she knew little about designing for the on-line environment at the start, but with the help of Mike and other colleagues she designed and later facilitated an on-line course that became a model for best practice within the institution.

Linda's narrative reveals important *relationships* some of which enabled some of which hindered or mediated the innovation - but all had to be accommodated and worked with. The most important relationship was with her colleague Mike and his colleagues in the EDC. This provided her with access to the expertise she needed to learn how to develop a high-quality on-line course. Learning was a bi-product of a collaborative design process.

Figure 6.5 Summary of the process involved in bringing the new on-line course into existence

Table 6.4 Summary of learning trajectories organised into eight categories (after Eraut and Hirsch 2007)

Learning trajectory	Linda's Project
Task performance	Accomplishment of complex tasks and resolution of problems never encountered before; development of new skills in design and facilitation of on-line learning; communication with a wide range of people; collaborative work with people inside and outside the university
Awareness and understanding	Developed significant new situational knowledge and understanding about how the institution worked, her colleagues and people in roles she did not normally encounter.
Personal development	She encountered new situations which required her to engage with all the dimensions recognised by Eraut namely: Self-evaluation; self-management; handling emotions; building and sustaining relationships; disposition to attend to other perspectives / to consult and work with others / to learn and improve one's practice; accessing relevant knowledge and expertise. Through this experience she learnt much.
Academic knowledge and skills	In the writing of course units she applied her academic knowledge but mostly what she achieved was the codification of tacit knowledge in the heads of experts.
Role performance	Linda occupied many different roles in her innovation project - she was a leader, supported and supervised external contributors.
Teamwork	The narratives demonstrate considerable collaborative learning and problem solving; and providing support (eg the frameworks for course design) that promoted mutual learning
Decision making and problem solving	The narratives reveal that Linda involved other people in her problem solving including her manager and members of the senior management team, colleagues from the EDC and from other parts of the university. The project was completed on time and within budget.
Judgement	The judgement of colleagues and the university was that Linda delivered a high-quality product. She herself developed new expertise through her experience that enabled her to make new judgements about the quality and standards of on-line provision.

Her relationships included people in her professional network with knowledge and expertise *(resources)* who provided her with content for the on-line courses. She developed tools and frameworks (*mediating artefacts*) to enable other people to contribute to what she was trying to achieve. She in turn made use of the tools and frameworks *(mediating artefacts)* that the EDC had developed to support the design of on-line courses.

The narrative reveals something of the dynamics, messiness and emotion of developing new social practice that is significantly different to what has been before. Anyone who has to tried to bring about significant change in a university will recognise the elements of the story. Linda highlights a number of tensions as she encountered resistance or barriers to what she wanted to achieve. In some areas of organisational practice her innovation conflicted with current practice. Such areas of local contentious practice are common where bottom-up innovation encounters structures and procedures that were never designed for new practice emerging through innovation. These areas have to be resolved often with the aid of independent brokers who have the power and authority to overcome the barriers to change. Such people helped Linda to complete her work and without their help she might not have succeeded.

Their narratives reveal the wonderful effects of creative collaboration by talented people who trust, respect, support and understand each other. The relationship that grew as they co-created their ecology of practice did more than simply combine knowledge and expertise, it stimulated

Figure 6.6 Representation of Linda and Mike's overlapping learning ecologies

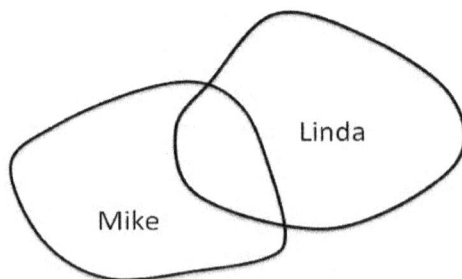

imaginative ideas and provided Linda with valuable emotional support that sustained her motivation and enthusiasm at difficult times. Engaging in innovation can be a very lonely business and its clear that Linda was on the point of giving up on more than one occasion but she didn't. With the support of her colleague she continued. The narrative reveals her will to succeed and her agency to imagine, implement and manage a strategy to achieve her goals with the help of people who were more knowledgeable than she was about some aspects of the project. In the process of achieving her goal she developed her capability and performance. For example, using

Eraut and Hirsch's typology of learning trajectories we can see that her development incorporated all 8 categories of the learning trajectory model. At the end of the process Linda could demonstrate that she could now design a high-quality on-line course, which she couldn't do at the start of her project.

CASE 2

In this second example of learning through work, Angela, Jane and Christine describe the challenges of implementing a Foundation Degree, which was radically different to anything the university had provided before. Although a course design had been approved the detail of the course, that enabled it to be delivered, had yet to be invented. Implementation involved a strategic and close working partnership between the university and a local hospital NHS Trust. The overarching theme of the narrative is people working collaboratively to develop new social practices that are significantly different to anything that had been before. An added complexity was that the two university education professionals involved (Jane and Christine) were newly appointed. They were working in an organisation that was unfamiliar, on a course that had not yet been implemented and was radically different to any previous course the university had provided. It involved organisational complexity of the highest order and posed significant learning and development challenges and risks to the people who were involved and to the university.

Angela's story

I work full time at the University Hospital NHS Trust, and I work a day a week, which [the] Uni ....fund to [help] develop a strategic alliance between the Trust and the University. What I've been trying to do is to look at opportunities between both organisations looking at what the university offers and looking at my organisation, the hospital, so I can say this is happening at the hospital, this is happening at the university, these two things might have a relationship and in a way mapping opportunities and connecting individuals together to say this is worth looking at.

[My role has] been about persuading people, it wasn't necessarily an issue at the hospital because for us we already knew we could deliver what we needed to deliver for the role because we had developed an internal training programme and tended not to use an awful lot of the Foundation Degree at Southampton University because it didn't fit what we needed. And so we had an internal programme and what we wanted to do was to review it and get it validated and then offer it as a Foundation Degree. So in that respect it was about influencing and negotiating here at the university is this something that you would be willing to do? It's not something you do already but does it fit, would you be willing to take the risk? And they were very happy to take the risk. But it was also influencing back at the Health Authority level to say this is a university you've never worked with before as a commissioning body, we want to develop this programme with them, would you fund it? Would you be prepared to take them as a preferred provider for this Foundation Degree if people want to go on it? And because we're a big enough organisation and because we said that we could get enough people together to make the course viable, 15 at least, it needs 20 students, the Health Authority suggested they'd fund it and the university said they wanted to do this very differently... So I think it has been about bringing expertise into the university and influencing people. A lot of it has just grown out of developing and understanding what's going on, working out where the opportunities might be, linking with different people, and it's grown in that way really. And I think one of the things that's been a benefit is me being here a day a week because I'm definitely here all day, people can generally find me and also that means that I get a better understanding of how the university works.

But it was an interesting thing to start with because apart from the general principle of 'what we'd like to do is look at how the two organisations can work better together', there was nothing set out like these are the objectives, this is what we want you to achieve, these are the areas we want you to work in, it was very much a go out and see what you can find sort of thing.

And I guess quite soon after I came in to this working relationship the Foundation Degree situation emerged.....I'd only been in post a few months and we needed to be in a position to offer it within the following financial year of the NHS.....so we had from a standing start... working with the likes of Jenny and the social worker team and Robert ....and my colleagues at the hospital, we literally spun together a foundation degree with a very unique structure.
.
One of the really good things to come out of all this is the way people from the two organisations is the way everybody's got to know one another and collaborating means so much more than it did..... in the last few weeks we've been planning the communication unit for the autumn, myself and my colleague and Christine, and somebody from [another] Trust, and one of our clinical skills team who does a lot of communication skills with simulated patients, members of the public who play act certain roles for us with staff as part of their training. All of us have sat down together and said what do we need in the communications unit because this is the first jointly delivered unit, what do we want in it? Who has the expertise to teach what part of it? How do we want to do this and how are we going to lay out the six week programme? So we have evolved from this very anxious position in January when our concern was about whose bit of the world does it fit into, to now where everyone sits down and says this is what we need, I could teach this bit, I could teach that bit, and those bits all fit and where will we get this from and how can we develop that.

I think the biggest challenge for us was probably understanding the way the university works, and I don't just mean this university but I think how education works. It feels at times quite laborious in terms of how things have got to be pulled together, the way you've got to go through the validation stuff, the due diligence is just unwieldy

So it's given me an insight into how a university works and another institution because I've always worked for the NHS my whole working life. I've worked with universities and colleges as part of my job role, but you're on the outside looking in. This has enabled me to be in and really get behind some of those things and understand how and why it works. What's been nice for me is being involved at the strategic level and being able to go between the strategic and the operational, learning more about things which are completely outside of my experience, I've come from a clinical background and then into an educational background in-house and now I've come out and doing stuff with a university, I've gained a lot in that respect, and it's given me confidence that I've got transferrable skills that will transfer into another organisation and that I have things to offer another organisation that they see as valuable

Jane's story

I arrived in November. ....I came from a health and social care background. I had been at the Subject Centre for health sciences...for years... I was delighted to be appointed overall manager of the programme

At the end of November this foundation degree in health and social care..... went for its validation.... It was literally the skeleton of a curriculum that was validated and then we had to work out the detail of the what and the how. A part time course leader had been appointed just before I came. But I had responsibility for the delivery of this programme that was due to start in January. The colleagues from the hospital who had been on that initial group, putting together the structure of the programme were all still very much involved. So it was about establishing relationships with them and just trying to get up to speed with what their vision was, what their intention was in having this kind of programme.

The fact that this was a programme that was not just written by the university and delivered to the hospital but it was actually to be developed jointly was a new approach [for the university]. The curriculum, the assessment, the delivery, were all to be developed in collaboration which the university and it hadn't been done before. I hadn't realized that at the time I started and it was only as I started to work with them that I realized we were doing something that there wasn't really a precedent for in the university.

To start with I did feel like I had jumped into a pool. I had to swim around, look around and find the right people and think "okay, so there is somebody that knows something about this and there is somebody that has got some expectations here." Identifying who those people were and trying to understand what it was that they were looking for and expecting to achieve was my initial priority. I think because of the world they work in, colleagues in health are used to responding quickly, making things happen, getting on with it. I really like that. So initially we had some very productive conversations about what we were trying to do.

I realized quite quickly there wasn't an articulated vision. I am not sure that what the hospital thought they were going to get was quite what the university thought they were going to deliver. I think as the year has gone on and we are delivering it for the first cohort of students, we are finding that out as we go along. Gradually, there is a coming together and we are developing a better collective understanding of the different roles, the different partners and whose responsibility it is to decide what is going to happen and how it is going to happen.

I think there was a lot of implicit.. Not expectations even, but sort of aspirations. I don't think it was necessarily clearly articulated. Because I was new and the course leader was new, we were trying to get a feel for finding our sort of position in it. For me a lot of that is about getting up to speed with what it is other people are expecting and how that might work.

Every single aspect of the programme has required something different from the university system than it is normally expected to do. So how the students are funded, how they register, what days they come into the university, who is responsible for writing the assessment, deciding who is going to assess it. None of that was the traditional format. So here we are, we've got a programme that is going to start in January to which students had to be recruited, but no precedent of how that was going to happen. So we made it up as we went along.

There was a lot of invention.... We didn't have the time to think everything through and try it out in advance. We had a start date for the programme and we had a hospital that knew it needed to get a particular group of employees onto it. So we worked on the assumption that we are going to have interviews. We need to meet. We have got a validation document which tells us what the entry requirements are. We have got a hospital team that need to have managers supporting them, releasing their students to this programme. So we need a joint application form which meets our requirements and meets their requirements. But we didn't quite do it in time. So we had joint interviews between the course leader and the hospital team did the interviews together and selected the students meeting two sets of quite distinct criteria really. Our education criteria and the hospital's management and professional development criteria. So next time we do it, we know what we are looking for. But we didn't know at that point.

The students actually started at the end of January. So during January we had to work very quickly to get a handbook ready for them with all the details of the course as it would look. So we had to work out the timetabling, the dates, how that would work in terms of when assessments were due in and when the exam boards would be scheduled and all those university processes in order for when the students started to say, 'This is the course you are coming on. These are the different units and when you are going to be doing them. These are the assignments you are going to write and this is when you are going to hand them in.'

we [also] had to work very quickly to identify who was going to deliver the units and be responsible for developing the detail of the curriculum content. That has been a huge learning journey for us as well because again, it is this combination between university expectations of what counts as a level four or level five qualification and the high level thinking and the academic skills that are needed for that combined with the hospital's need to develop specific competences so that the students could do a particular job. Again, we have had to be fairly reactive in getting the units ready to deliver in the short timescale. We have learned a lot by doing it the first time, about getting that balance right between a university-driven course and a hospital-driven course. And I think we will get to a point when we get the best of both worlds.

Because the time was so tight when we had to deliver the first unit... we just had to deliver it. That raised our awareness of the different expectations of the university and the hospital and who could say, 'Yes, we can include that' or 'No, we are not going to do that.' We have learnt that each unit has to have a unit leader which may not necessarily be the person who delivers it but who has overall responsibility for it. That person needs to be really clear about liaising with the clinicians who want a certain aspect in it and then to shape that into something that has got academic purpose and rigour as well. I think I am currently teaching an option unit on human growth. I think I have benefited from the learning that we have had in the other units that it is really important to seek that input to shape what it is you are going to deliver.

I think for the next time around it will have been a really good way of doing it because you know what went well and what didn't go well and what you need for the next time because it is a real situation and it is really happening. You don't just try to imagine what ifs, you actually know what they are.

One of the big challenges for the university has been around the pattern of delivery for this course.....the university traditionally has two semesters. We are not doing that. So we are still teaching now even now the university is sort of finished. So we are still teaching right up until the middle of July. The way we are delivering the units is in blocks. So they do one unit and then they do the next unit, whereas traditionally in university they are doing two or three at the same time. So that is very different. Another difference is that they can take a unit in this university called a Professional Development Unit. So the whole programme, every unit in the programme, is also validated to be studied as a standalone PDU, which is also unique in the university. So students can just register for a unit and then build up the units to complete the programme, or just take the units they want.

So we have a start date for the programme in January, but because of the way the hospital likes to get people, if they want some training they want to access it quite quickly. Students can join at any point in the year, do that unit, do any other units until January and then APEL those units into the programme and continue as registered in the programme. That has not been done in this university before. So it is a great model and I think we should do more of it because it is very responsive to employer's needs. It can be taken in bite-sized chunks if they want it that way.

...we thought originally that we would have different points of entry through the year to the whole programme. What have realized that this is actually very difficult to do in terms of how the university creates their records and how they monitor that... we are still working on that but it requires new systems to be created.

I do think [what we are doing] is very, very risky. I think for the university it is reputationally risky and in a difficult commercial environment in higher education and in the public sector, which is what health is, it is a risk to try and do something in that field and to do it in a different way, which is absolutely the most likely way to succeed but it also might all fall badly wrong and it is a reputational risk for the university. Trying to do this without a long lead-in time, makes that even more risky.

If you say to yourself 'What is the worst that could happen?' well that wouldn't be so bad, that would be alright. No one is going to die if the programme doesn't succeed so let's just give it a go. And there is always a chance of something quite good coming out of it, you know, even if it is not exactly what you expect some real good things might happen along the way. I suppose I am quite grateful I am not at the beginning of my working life and I feel 'Oh well, not the end of the world if it doesn't work.'

[So we have accomplished a great deal in the last 6 months] and that is all due to the quality of the people who are actually doing it and how much respect and trust they have in each other. It is totally, the people that make it happen. You know... we have got new partners we are now working with. You very quickly know who are the key people that you know you can work well with them, they will make things happen, that is where you are going to make your key point of contact. You get a feel for that very quickly. The challenge will be for us to make sure these things are embedded beyond those individual relationships. Because I think it is still at that level. ...I think that is a challenge for the sort of sustainability of the programme. Any of us could go and who would know what has happened and who would be able to keep it going.

people are willing to put their own time, their own energy and their own ideas in to it because they have got this trusting and valued relationship they go the extra mile. They do things well beyond their contractual obligation as long as we feel this is going to achieve the aim we want. You know I think because everyone is busy and it is not the only thing that any of us are doing, it is sort of...I want to make use of the good working relationships as long as we are moving towards getting what it is I need from my university or they need for their employees. And while we are moving in that direction we will definitely go the extra mile. There is a huge amount of extra activity. Not just activity, but commitment to it because we have all been through these kinds of things before and realized that is what gives you the energy to make something happen.

I think the key thing is you need to have people in both organizations who have the strategic positions to allow things to happen, to approve things so that they can happen. You need to have them with you and on board. They don't need to know the detail, but they need to trust you to be able to say 'I need this from....', and they will put their weight behind it to enable it to happen. Because otherwise... you just get caught up at this low operational level, 'the computer says no' sort of level of things. Actually, the computer doesn't have to say no but someone with influence has to realise and acknowledge this. So you need those people in all sorts of areas. You need them in the clinical area, you need the management of the hospital, you need the quality people here, the strategic leadership here, to say 'Actually if the computer is saying no it needs to say yes.' You need those people on board and you need them to trust you so that when you say you need something that they will use their power to support you. So these are a crucial set of relationships that you have to maintain and develop continuously?

It is not necessarily the obvious people. Yeah, it is people you think 'If I happen to bump into you at a workshop or a meeting or something we were at and you got what I was talking about. If I needed to run things by you, you would be somebody I would come to.' It is that sort of ad hoc stumbling across people that you see 'Yeah, you get where I am coming from and I can sound you out about something and I know you will help and encourage me.'

Being new to the institution and not being in a particularly influential position you know, I am only a PL. I am not really in a strategic position. So I am continually trying to find the people who get it and then going to them and saying, 'Who do I need to speak to? Who is going to help me with this?' and being a bit of a thorn in their side, really.

For example this morning.... we have the central university and we have got the faculty. Because this is collaborative provision it tends to sit in central services, and yet everything gets approved through the faculty. There has to be communication between the two. Things were getting sort of passed around between people. So I went to somebody who I respect and I said, 'How do I unblock this?' and she has kindly said she will go and see if she can. It is like a circle, I just need some way of breaking into the circle to make this happen. It is about finding the person who can bang heads together and say 'you got to find a way to make that work'.

I find the most effective way to get things accomplished is to constantly believe it is possible to have a sort of can-do attitude and to assume other people have also got a can-do attitude and to treat them as if they have. On the whole I find that I get more productive responses if I do that. But it involves huge amounts of diplomacy and of trying to establish and sustain relationships, really. We want the shared goal, don't we? How do we together make that happen? Sometimes you just want to say 'For goodness sake, get on with it and do it.' Yeah, I think its masses of flexibility, respect, grace and diplomacy.

We are still realizing the implications of the journey we have set out on. It is not just our expectations as a provider but it is actually melding together two lots of different expectations to create something which is quite new. So it seems to me there is a lot of originality in what we are doing.

Christine's story

I'm the course leader for the foundation degree. I'm a qualified social worker and I've worked for 22 years for Health and Social Care. I also worked for 11 years as a team manager.., prior to working here I worked in various fields of social work and in particular I've been integrating working with health staff and social work staff. When I saw this position advertised.......I felt I had a lot of experience working in building up relationships and so on. I've also been an associated lecturer between 2005 to 2007 so I knew the university....and I was quite keen that this course seemed to be just up my street really....And I felt it would be a really good opportunity to set something new up and use my skills and experience as well. So I applied for the job.

When I started my contract.....it was actually approaching validation... there were obviously some things needed doing before it could go to validation and that was the unit descriptors. So I came in and I had two weeks to get moving on writing some unit descriptors in time for the validation at the end of November..........I hadn't written unit descriptors before so obviously it was a fast learning curve for me.

I have a mentor .... who has been fantastic. So whenever I'm a bit stuck I go and see her and she's been able to help me and advise me and I have a good supporting manager as well.

The next step was to put the course handbook together...by January so that was quite a challenge to get that together. I needed to have all the information for students that they might need to refer to for the course and for the university. Things like understanding the way things are marked, understanding the credits, the units, core units, option units and so on and how that works. Also being aware of what they need to do as well in order to progress their studies. Obviously I was guided by other handbooks which helped and I obviously liaised with my mentor, and health staff .....to ensure that anything that they wanted included into the handbook was included. So there was a lot of talking to other people to make sure everything was there and also

218

checking "Does this sound okay? Are you happy with this?" And sharing just to make sure before we went to print. Obviously since then there's one or two things that we need to update or change but at the time it was complete..

The unit I was teaching was the first unit to go, so January was just mad. I did a lot more than 18.5 hours per week, it was impossible to complete the work... so I more or less worked full time throughout that period. Because it had to be done and I couldn't see any other way of completing it. Since then I've spoken to my manager and I've had some payment in respect of [the extra hours I worked], but at the time there was no other way of getting things done, and teaching on the course and so on, you know, on the unit that I was teaching.

Then we had to prepare for the students arrival, ensuring that registration and everybody else was aware of them coming and that they were prepared and had everything in place to enrol them. Making sure we had the rooms available, and I think all of those things as well has being prepared to teach was quite a challenge and obviously we had meetings to make sure things were in place so we could tick boxes, but there was a really difficult time. Because there were so many things that needed to be in place at that particular time, that January was really hectic.

[Once the students were registered] The main challenge was the preparation for teaching, because obviously I was developing a lot of content specific knowledge for this programme and I wanted to ensure that I was up to date on reading. I wanted to ensure that I could deliver in a way that the students found interesting and include various types of teaching so that it kept them interested and engaged so that they would go away and want to know more. So those were the areas that were a challenge for me.

I always feel you can do better, and I would want to do better next time. I'm not saying that I had negative response because the feedback was generally good... I mean obviously you get those who say "Oh that was a bit boring" or whatever, but I also had some very positive feedback too. But I do feel that I'd like to work on improving, or trying different things next time.

[Looking back I would say that] some of the challenges have been, because we've kind of run with this from the start is having the right people at the right time to teach on it. If people don't respond, because health want to be involved and sometimes you put something out "Is anybody able...?" and you don't hear anything. So perhaps that's been the challenge, you think "Oh right then I need to obviously address that one."
Other challenges have been to do with trying to do new things with university systems that were not designed to do these things. Because we are trying to fit it into the university's process and it doesn't fit in. So we have tried to be flexible in some of the areas and it's only when they arrived that we've realised we can't be so flexible... Well perhaps if I was someone who was a course leader before I might have thought about these things, but because I haven't been aware until it's actually happened and realised that "We need to do something here there's a problem."

one student who or extenuating circumstances was unable to take the exam. And this is quite interesting because our health partners felt that, "Oh well they can do it next week instead." They weren't aware of the kind of programmes we have at university, that there's only a certain week that you can resit exams. So we felt that she could resit in the resit week, but as it turns out she can't because of the unit boards and the Progress Boards and so on. So that's another problem we've now got to address because we hadn't got our Progress Board set up, not for this year certainly.

Recently I've been talking to people in registration about enrolment, because people have been saying, "Well you can't do this" or "You can't do that", they've been very good because they've looked for ways around things. Certainly we seem to be addressing some of these issues now but it's just that people have had the pain first, if you understand me students, you know, and it seems that's the way we have to do it because we're not always aware that there's a problem until there is some pain. But I have to say I've been quite impressed with the support that we've had in trying to address things and find ways round problems.

I suppose there have been times when I've felt concerned and worried about things. Because obviously I make mistakes, I'm not anything near perfect, and obviously I do worry that sometimes perhaps things are a risk and that's that. And I have to either take the risk or not. You just have to do it sometimes, and if I don't succeed then I don't feel that I would be shot down or anything like that, I do feel that I am well supported. And fortunately I haven't had to take too many serious risks as such..

But now the course is running well... And it's quite exciting actually that other Health Authorities are now getting more interested and wanting to send more students, so I think that's really quite something and it's quite fulfilling to see the course taking off as it is. So for me achieving that and seeing students are developing, I mean that's been amazing. And being involved with Health, I mean just recently they did presentations at the hospital for the unit that they'd just completed and it was just amazing to watch and listen to the students. The level of presentations, the standard was just very high. That alone in itself you think "Wow!" This makes it all worthwhile.

....initially it was quite difficult in looking at how we would work jointly with our colleagues in Health on this one and that I felt was a bit of a challenge to be quite honest at the beginning. Because obviously everyone's got their different ideas and perspectives on how things are going to develop and there were some underlying assumptions I think as well. ....but I think once everyone's role and processes and systems were made clear and put in place, things became much clearer and much better.

I have been spending half a day at the hospital with the idea that students can access me if they want to access me because I'm their tutor and also to build our relationship with Health and I get to know the people better and their systems and ways of doing things too. So that's been really, really good in developing our relationships and understanding as well, you know, their understanding in what the university processes must include and must have in terms of standards and so on and also our understanding theirs as well.

The thing that I found very difficult was learning everything at the same time as implementing the course that was a real challenge. I mean even yesterday I thought "Wow!" now I totally understand that, and that's how it's been all the way through. So it has been a steep learning curve. The biggest thing has been the hours more than anything else, I felt that 18.5 hours just doesn't even begin to address what's needed to implement a new course. So that's been a big problem.

Ecological perspectives on learning, performing & achieving

The first point to make is that the three people involved in these narratives were all experienced professionals. The situation described is more complex than the first case example because it involves three different organisations - a university, an NHS Hospital Trust and a Regional Health Authority.

As in the first case example, the set of situations is unique - this is the only *place* on earth where these practices could be enacted and this learning could be acquired. The practices of the three key actors were not simply aimed at 'refining and perfecting the use of acquired knowledge in the same context' (Lave 1997: 21) rather, the aim of their collaborative practices were to expand their learning well beyond the practices and systems they understood into entirely new situations and contexts, with entirely new tools, policies, procedures and systems and ways of doing things some of which brought them into conflict with their own organisations. As in many organisational innovation projects an important dimension of their learning was aimed at changing the organisational situations (systems, policies and practices) in order that new practices could flourish.

Figures 6.7 and 6.8 provide useful conceptual aids to help make sense of the dynamics of the work environment and the learning ecologies that were involved in these narratives of workplace learning.

The narratives of the three most important people involved in this substantial developmental project, reveal the complex dynamic of learning across and between organisations. They formed a cross-organisational core team although other colleagues from the university and NHS Trust were also involved.

From each individual's descriptions of the work they undertook we can see that it must have involved all of the modes of learning in columns 1 and 2 of Eraut's conceptual framework (Table 6.1) but included many other items (Table 6.5). Furthermore, the learning processes listed in column 3 of Table 6.1 are replaced by essentially a self-motivated, self-managed and regulated process that engaged in productive inquiry aimed at finding out what the person needed to know in order to do what they needed to do.

Learning, performance and organisational development were mainly *situated* within the work environment of the university and NHS Hospital Trust, although one of the participants was also actively involved in networking and negotiating with other organisations. At the time of the interviews the project from conception to implementation had lasted about 18 months, although for two of the interviewees (Jane and Christine) the project had lasted only six or seven months.

Figure 6.7 The dynamics of performing and learning through work in the contexts described above adapted from the model provided by Eraut and Hirsch (2007)

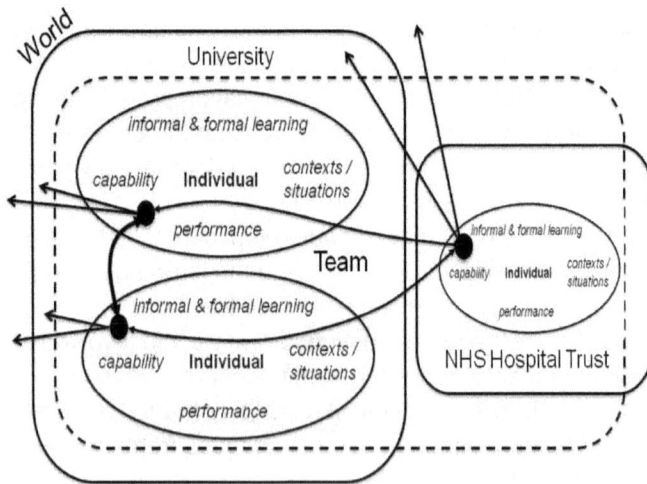

Table 6.5 Modes of learning inferred in the narratives above. Adapted from Eraut and Hirsch (2007)

1 Work processes with learning as a by-product	2 Learning activities located within work or learning processes	3 Learning processes at or near the workplace
• Participation in group processes - collaboration TEAMWORK • Working alongside others • Relationship development • Consulting -checking • Market research • Meetings and discussions • Immersion in challenging tasks and roles • Designing within existing frameworks • Learning to implement a service in real time • Problem solving / fire fighting • Coping and adapting to insufficient resource • Trying things out • Consolidating, extending /refining skills • Working with clients • Attempting to resolve local contentious practice • Coordinating contributions from many people. • Working across organisations with different cultures	• Asking questions • Getting information • Locating resources eg people • Listening and observing • Reflecting • Learning from mistakes • Giving and receiving feedback • Creation and use of mediating artefacts *Also* • Selling ideas • Persuading • Negotiating • Challenging existing practices • Designing new approaches	Very few of the activities listed by Eraut in Table 11.1 Learning is essentially a self-motivated, self-regulated and managed process. One of the people involved had a mentor but all used each other and other colleagues to learn.

One of the distinctive features of this set of learning ecologies was that they were developed in order to learn in real time. For the people involved, implementing the course for the first time was their vehicle for learning. There are particular pressures in such learning environments as entirely new social practices are invented and enacted they become an experiment with the possibility of failure. In such circumstances the learning space is more constrained and there is limited scope for exploration (unlike the first case study). Rather the focus for learning and achieving is on preparing for the next performance or deadline (immediate goals). In such circumstances learning occurs through the process of 1) preparation (eg preparing a timetable, finding content and preparing a handbook, sorting out classrooms and registration and developing resources to support the teaching) 2) implementation (eg preparation for teaching and teaching the course for the first time). The detail of the course was being developed and implemented in real time. This space was betwixt and between the knowledge and experience the participants had from the past and the new knowledge and understanding that was grown through implementation.

The university provided the key *affordance* through its strategic development programme which set out a strategic vision for change and also provided new resources (funding) for staff who wanted to contribute to this change. The NHS Hospital Trust also provided affordance in the form of its commitment to the development of its own workforce and its desire to form a strategic partnership with the university while the Health Authority provided the financial affordance that enabled new provision on this scale to be resourced.

By combining their expertise and interests all participants in this developmental project were able to contribute ideas, knowledge and expertise to the process that enabled the course to be designed, implemented and resourced and furthermore attract other potential users of the course. Through this process individuals developed new knowledge and capabilities and enabled the university to do something it had never done before..

All three participants had clear proximal and distal goals that all related to accomplishing the overarching tasks of getting the course up and running, recruiting students and providing them with a good educational experience. These were enacted within the university's strategic goal to bring about the sort of changes that the individuals were making. All participants were also see what they were doing in terms of their distal goal for career progression.

All the narratives reveal the importance of *relationships* in accomplishing the goals of the project for example - in working together as a team, in gaining support from colleagues, in finding things out, in overcoming the barriers of organisational structures and systems that were unhelpful, in redesigning new systems that were helpful, in securing the involvement of colleagues to teach on the course, in forming the strategic alliance and securing the resources to make it happen.

Financial resources to support the course were provided through the university and the Health Authority. The *resources* that the Programme Team were primarily concerned with were knowledge resources in the form of codified procedures, codified text book knowledge for the course and embodied knowledge in the practitioners who contributed to the course. They in turn developed new resources and *mediating artefacts* like the unit descriptors and course handbook.

The narratives reveal the complexity and messiness of bringing about significant change in a university. Problems arose during implementation and there were a significant number of areas where organisational structures and procedures would not permit what the innovators wanted to do. These problems often had to be resolved with the aid of independent brokers with the authority to intervene.

The learning and development of individuals through this developmental project was considerable. If we take Christine's involvement we can see that her development could be mapped across all 8 categories of Eraut and Hirsch's learning trajectory model (Table 6.6)

The scenario also shows how the learning ecologies of three individuals overlapped to varying degrees (Figure 6.9).

Figure 6.9 Representation of overlapping learning ecologies

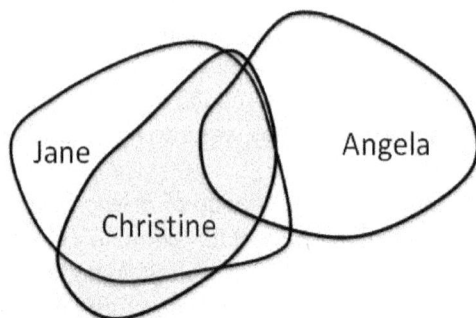

Learning by developing new practices and changing contexts

These narratives reveal how people working in a particular socio-cultural context bring about changes in their own practices and the practices and understandings of the organisation. In building and implementing their ecology for learning and interacting with the learning ecologies of others they change the context for others. For example, as a result of the educational developments described in the narratives the university has created entirely new learning environments and expanded affordance for learning to new social groups. It now has within its organisational capability new and different models of 'how we do things here'.

The stories describe the way people communicate and work with the intention to achieve particular goals which become clearer and more concrete with more detail as the work progresses. They are effectively moving ideas from one state to another previously unexplored state as they think about the problems of turning conceptual thinking into new and effective social practice. They can only accomplish what they set out to do because they are immersed in their context and they can appreciate the affordances and access the opportunities and identify and resolve issues and problems as they emerge. They are working with uncertainty as they try things out and recognising and exploiting what works as it emerges from the results of their actions in their situated context. It is

Table 6.6 Summary of Christine's learning trajectories organised into eight categories (Eraut and Hirsch 2007)

Learning trajectory	Christine
Task performance	Accomplishment of complex tasks and resolution of problems never encountered before; development of new skills in design and implementation of a novel course; communication with a wide range of people; collaborative work with people inside and outside the university
Awareness and understanding	Developed significant new situational knowledge and understanding about how the institution worked, its systems and practices and knowledge of colleagues and people in roles they had not encountered before. This was the main learning from this project.
Personal development	She encountered new situations which required her to engage with all the dimensions recognised by Eraut namely: Self evaluation; self-management; handling emotions; building and sustaining relationships; disposition to attend to other perspectives / to consult and work with others / to learn and improve one's practice; accessing relevant knowledge and expertise. Through this experience she learnt much.
Academic knowledge and skills	In preparing the handbook, writing the unit descriptors and preparing resources for teaching she applied and extended her academic knowledge.
Role performance	Performed the tasks requited of a programme leader/administrator and taught the first unit of the new course incorporating content that was new to her.
Teamwork	The narratives demonstrate considerable teamwork and coordination of colleagues including clinicians from NHS Hospital Trust.
Decision making and problem solving	The narratives reveal that problems arose as the course was implemented and these had to be solved in real time.
Judgement	The gathering of feedback, unit and programme reviews undertaken informed judgements that were made about the quality and standards of the education and training being provided. As Programme Leader she would be accountable to her manager and to the Programme Team.

possible to tell the story of what they did in a de-contextualised way and draw out certain principles that might be applied in other contexts. But the reality is that the 'devil is in the detail.' These new social practices have been brought into existence by particular people, with particular personalities, capabilities and orientations, developing particular situational understandings, solving particular problems as they emerge in real time in the ways that only they could. As such the recipe for change can never be precisely replicated because other people would have behaved and observed, interpreted and responded to their situation differently. This is what gives a person's learning ecology its unique characteristics.

The innovation of professional practice is a highly situated phenomenon. Only the people involved can see the possibilities and turn their imaginations into new practice that has meaning in and beyond their own interpretation of context. As part of the strategic change research study a questionnaire was developed to identify the factors that people who were involved in the change programme believed were important to accomplishing their innovation (Baker, Jackson and Longmore 2014:303).

The highest rated factors scoring 4.5 or higher (max = 5.0) were -
- My readiness and willingness to get involved in the opportunity provided by SDP
- My vision of what I wanted to achieve
- My will/motivation to succeed with something I cared about
- Having good communication with the people I needed to talk to
- The active involvement of others - good teamwork
- Feeling trusted and being allowed to get on with it without interference
- Feeling that I made good progress within the time available
- Feeling that what I was doing was valued by my colleagues

All but 1 of the 22 items in the questionnaire scored more than 4.0 and 19 factors scored 4.3 or more on a 5.0pt scale reflecting the level of importance in bringing about change, indicating that nearly all the factors have a significant influence.

Personal characteristics like will, vision and readiness to change feature prominently in what is important, together with the way people wanted to be trusted and feel that their contributions would be valued. High value is also placed on communication, the social-cultural dimension of the work environment - more specifically their particular context and the need to make progress within the time that was available. The large number of factors innovators believe are involved in enabling innovation to be accomplished is striking and accounts for some of the complexity involved bringing about innovative change. The factors also reveal the importance of how people feel about their environment and how supportive it is in enabling them to accomplish their tasks and implicitly to learn and develop. Taken together, perceptions of what is important in bringing about complex changes in social practices also provide an indication of what is important in the ecologies for learning, developing and achieving in the people who are trying to accomplish such change.

Returning to the perpetual challenge of how do we enable students to prepare for futures they do not know? These stories illustrate that one of the answers to this question is we are helping them to prepare for these sorts of collaborative learning and development projects that bring new social practices into existence and change the contexts in which they work.

CHAPTER 7

Mapping Ecologies of Practice for Learning and Performance

Introduction

In order to gain a footing in the landscape of learning ecologies we must dive in, experience the messiness of learning as we practice and perform in our work environments and pay attention to the details of ourselves as we interact with the world. We must become the mental cartographers of our own experiences mapping our processes and their effects, and the changes that happen to us as we perform and learn. The first stage in this developmental project is to develop self-awareness by making physical maps of our experiences and our engagements with a world in continuous formation.

In this chapter I present a slightly refined heuristic (Figure 7.1) to capture the essence of an *ecology of practice* as a way of representing the way we interact with our environment in order to perform, learn and create. The purpose of the chapter is explain how the heuristic can be used to map and evaluate our own ecologies of practice in order to reflect on how we learn, perform and create new value. It provides some simple methods for mapping an ecology of practice in order to perform, learn and create new value. In making these maps I draw on my own experiences as I prepared for an event I am helping to facilitate in October 2019.

Developing ecological awareness

Programmed into every human being is a need to understand themselves and the effects of their thinking and actions on the world. This type of

Figure 7.1 Refined heuristic to aid understanding of an ecology of practice for learning and performance . Learning can be the primary focus for practice or be a necessary or unimportant bi-product of performance. A set of questions to aid reflection is provided in Appendix 1.

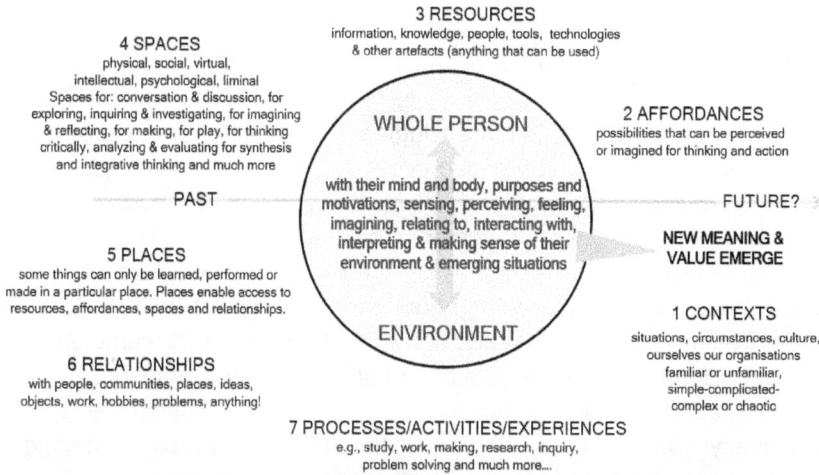

3 RESOURCES
information, knowledge, people, tools, technologies
& other artefacts (anything that can be used)

4 SPACES
physical, social, virtual, intellectual, psychological, liminal Spaces for: conversation & discussion, for exploring, inquiring & investigating, for imagining & reflecting, for making, for play, for thinking critically, analyzing & evaluating for synthesis and integrative thinking and much more

WHOLE PERSON

2 AFFORDANCES
possibilities that can be perceived or imagined for thinking and action

PAST

with their mind and body, purposes and motivations, sensing, perceiving, feeling, imagining, relating to, interacting with, interpreting & making sense of their environment & emerging situations

FUTURE?

NEW MEANING & VALUE EMERGE

5 PLACES
some things can only be learned, performed or made in a particular place. Places enable access to resources, affordances, spaces and relationships.

ENVIRONMENT

1 CONTEXTS
situations, circumstances, culture, ourselves our organisations familiar or unfamiliar, simple-complicated-complex or chaotic

6 RELATIONSHIPS
with people, communities, places, ideas, objects, work, hobbies, problems, anything!

7 PROCESSES/ACTIVITIES/EXPERIENCES
e.g., study, work, making, research, inquiry, problem solving and much more....

learning or self-awareness enables us to perform better and create better versions of ourselves and feel more fulfilled as we appreciate the way we can influence our own destiny. Self-awareness is key to understanding that we are all implicated and involved in an ecological world of practice and learning, and *to think and practice with such ecological awareness we must become cartographers and analyzers of our own experiences.* Experiences that become ever more complex. In the words of Jarche (2014):

- Our world is getting more complex as everything gets connected.
- Complex problems require more implicit knowledge.
- Implicit knowledge can only be shared through conversations & observation.
- Collaborative and distributed work is the norm.

- Knowledge-sharing and narration of work make implicit knowledge more visible.
- Transparent work processes foster innovation.
- Learning is part of work, not separate from it.

To which we might add:
- "We learn from reflecting on experience" (Dewey 1933 :78)

Mapping and interrogating our ecologies of practice for learning and performance contribute to an environment and culture in which 'narrating work to make implicit knowledge more visible' and making 'work processes more transparent to foster innovation,' are more likely. Mapping, analysing and visualising one's own multitudinous experiences is a learning process in its own right and there is research evidence that it is more beneficial to articulate and codify experience than accumulate similar additional experience (Stefano et al., 2016). What is learned through refection can lead to enhanced performance through increased self-efficacy((Stefano et al., 2016) i.e. " the belief in one's capabilities to organize and execute the course of action required to manage prospective situations"(Bandura 1995). The process of making a map becomes a powerful prompt for reflecting on our experiences enabling us to inquire into how, why, when, where we are learning and what we have learnt and created. A set of questions to aid reflection, based on the heuristic, is provided in Appendix 1.

An ecology of practice map is not only a checklist of the actions undertaken to achieve particular goals. Its purpose is to reveal the way the maker deliberately and imaginatively wove together and accessed the affordances in their environment, the ideas, resources, contexts, relationships, spaces and places to learn, perform and create new value. Once codified, we can mine our experience to learn from it and improve our own practices with questions like:

What have I discovered through assembling (or re-visiting) this ecology which should make more effective in the future that I have been in the past? Or, more metacognitively, how could I improve the assembling of an ecology like this one to make it more effective for me? (Professor John Cowan personal communication).

I have drawn on my own experiences at the time of writing this guide to reveal the ecologies of practice I developed in order to learn, perform and create new value. Four different approaches to making a map are described.

1. Narratives - a story using a timeline to structure events, situations, interactions and achievements
2. Diagrams - using a timeline to structure events, situations, interactions and achievements
3. Diagrams - using the ecological framework to identify the elements of an ecology of practice A) List & B) Narrative
4. Diagrams that seek to show the dynamics of an ecology of practice as a snapshot

1 Narrative mapping

As we have seen throughout this book, our ecologies of practice for learning and performance are revealed in the stories we tell about ourselves as we encounter and engage with new situations, problems, challenges and opportunities. Narratives can be constructed in such a way as to provide a map of our thinking, activities, relationships and interactions with people and the material world as we think, feel and try to accomplish things we value. Here is an example of a narrative that is based on work I undertook over about ten days in early September. Once the experience is codified we can reflect on and evaluate our ecology of practice.

Example 1 Using narrative to map an ecology of practice

1 Relaxing in front of the TV I happened to watch episode 6 of the Chefs' Brigade series televised on September 3rd and recognized that it provided insights into the nature of individual and collaborative ecologies of practice that I could draw on in the LILA project. My curiosity aroused I 'slept on it' so to speak and in the morning I was ready to develop the idea and got up early to make a start.

2 I watched several episodes of the series on iplayer (catch-up TV) and made notes on the structure of the story and the ecology of practice. I also did a bit of googling to find out more about the principle character - James Atherton and discovered he was one of the UK's top chefs with 18 restaurants and 4 Michelin stars. In my search I also came across a post made by the production team who talked about the challenges of organising and filming the programme. The more I learnt the more I felt I could use the material to make an interesting case study. By now I felt quite motivated to devote time and effort to this project.

3 I decided that I could form a case study around one of the episodes but I did not know how to make video clips from the streamed video so I Googled - How do I record streamed video from iplayer? I read several reviews and discovered many software tools to capture and edit streamed video. I tried to use some free software but the audio and video sound quality was very poor.

4 By now I had invested a whole morning in 'playing around' with the idea of making a video-based case study without making any significant progress, but this served to reinforce my beliefs that there was good potential (affordance) in the video materials to make an interesting and useful case study to illustrate my core theme of ecologies for learning and practice.

5 Having worked out that I needed to purchase some commercial software I read an on-line review https://zapier.com/blog/best-screen-recording-software/ to see which of the many tools would best suit my needs and pocket. I decided to buy the Movavi Screen Recorder and Video Editor software and started to experiment. Through trial and

error, and making quite a few mistakes, I learned to do basic editing which was sufficient for this project. I also realized that I can use the tool to do more sophisticated editing in future (new affordance).

6 I worked on the case study off and on over the next two days. I studied one episode and made 12 clips to tell the story that revealed the components of the ecologies of practice implemented by Jason Atherton and the brigade. I created a short narrative for each clip.

7 I decided I needed a website to host the case study so I build a password protected website. I have made many websites using the weebly website building so this was quite straight forward. I uploaded the clips and created some explanatory content and a set of questions to guide inquiry while watching the clips. Having built the site I realized it was a key part of my infrastructure for communicating with LILA participants so I added more pages and content (new affordance had emerged).

8 After uploading the clips as large files I realized that some users would have trouble viewing the clips if they did not have a fast broadband connection. Through a trial and error process I worked out the optimum file size for streaming, compressed the files and uploaded them to a hidden page on the website with a link from the page I had previously constructed. I was pleased with this solution as it provided users with two streaming formats to choose from and I had also learnt how to compress the video files.

9 A few days later I decided to add another page to the website to document the final episode as it reveals the brigade's highest level of performance and enables those who are using the case study to see the full extent of their transformative process. It felt more complete.

11 Ten days after I watched the TV programme that triggered this process, my ecology is still unfolding as I embark on an analysis of the case study in order to produce a Guide. Interestingly, as I develop new arguments and integrate new information these flow into this document. In other words, while my ecology for learning is active every artefact that is produced is provisional and is interdependent with other artefacts.

Using the heuristic to interpret and reflect on my ecology of practice

In this story we can see an unfolding ecology of practice that is firmly located in the situations of my unfolding life. It begins in an everyday incidental activity (watching TV), that triggers a thought that creates new affordance - the perceived possibility of creating new materials to support learning in the context of my contribution to the upcoming event I am facilitating.

At the start I had no idea that any of this was going to happen. Once the idea emerged I entered a liminal space - I didn't know how to achieve my goal

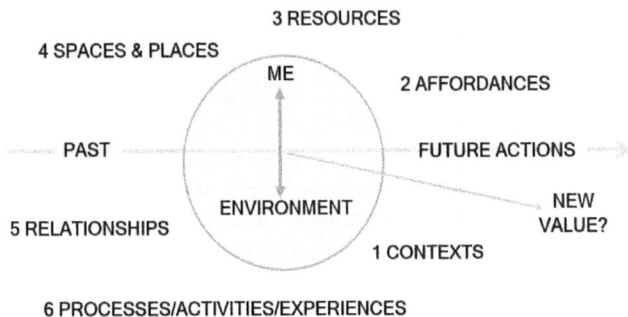

3 RESOURCES

4 SPACES & PLACES

ME

2 AFFORDANCES

PAST

FUTURE ACTIONS

ENVIRONMENT

NEW VALUE?

5 RELATIONSHIPS

1 CONTEXTS

6 PROCESSES/ACTIVITIES/EXPERIENCES

but I knew if I tried certain things I would find the way to realize the idea. My preliminary inquiries and fumbling's with the technology convinced me that it was worth committing time, effort and money to the project. My process unfolded over about 10 days. It involved a combination of inquiry, making video artefacts and the evaluation of those artefacts and the production of a guide to help others use them. It was quite a messy process with lots of trial and error. I searched for an appropriate tool and developed some basic proficiency in using it to download and edit streamed video which was my primary resource. I did not need a particular place to make this artefact but I did need a range of tools (computer and appropriate Apps) and access to the internet. My learning was driven by the video content and my inquiry into how it might be used. It bridged and connected my interests in the idea of ecologies and practice and my relationships with the LILA inquiry.

Using my narrative as the account of my ecology of practice, its purpose was clearly focused on performance - creating new value in the form of a video case study that can be used to support learning. There is no doubt that I needed to learn new things in respect of the content of the materials and the skills necessary to make use of the materials to create a new resource.

I can my narrative to reflect more critically on my practice. For example, what else might I have done to improve the quality of the outcome? At one point I did think that I might contact Jason Atherton with a view to seeking an interview to develop my understanding of the pedagogies he used. But I didn't act on this as I had other things to do and I considered it highly unlikely that such a busy person would respond. But the option is still there in the future. Also, I restricted myself to learning the basics of the Movavi Screen Recorder and Video Editor Apps so I don't know what their capabilities are. I could have perhaps added comments or questions onto the videos to enhance their value. Something That I can revisit in future.

Example 2 : A day in my learning life September 18th 2019
Here is an example of a micro-narrative covering a single day.
5.30am I woke up early because I had to catch a train to London to go for my visa interview at the US Embassy. I wanted to take something to read. My current need is to find out more about CLO's so I googled and found a couple of articles that I printed off.
7-8am - On the train. I re-read my draft Guide to mapping a learning ecology and made lots of edits. I identified several places that needed strengthening in the light of the recent conversation I had with the LILA team. I knew I needed feedback on the way I was presenting my ideas.
8.30- 11am It was my first visit to the new US Embassy.. lots of queuing outside and inside. Lots of time spent waiting for things to happen. It gave me time to read the two articles I'd downloaded. Both were interesting but the one by David Koehn 'The evolving role of CLO's' was really grabbed my attention. One passage in particular filled me with hope that my ideas might have some relevance and resonance to CLO's. I had the idea of

writing to him to share my ideas and hopefully gain some feedback from someone who knew the CLO's corporate world.

11.30am -12.30pm On the train home I searched for DK. It wasn't easy the address in his article was no longer relevant. Thanks to a photo in the article I eventually found him and sent a message via the contact form on his website. By the time I got home he had already responded saying send me the article and I will review it. I sent him the Guide that afternoon.

4pm I went for my daily walk around the field next to my house. It's a good space for pondering and the rhythm of walking helps me think. As I walked I thought about my experiences that day I also thought about the LILA event and how I might create an exercise to enable CLO's to understand the idea of mapping a learning ecology in a way that was meaningful within the limited time that was available. The idea of a micro-map of my learning ecology came into my consciousness (a map of one day).

5- 7.30pm After my walk I sat down and crafted this narrative to record the events of the day. A day in which I had to accomplish a particular task - attend an interview for my visa at the embassy and which therefore controlled my activities at least in the morning. A day in which my time and thinking about my problem (LILA) were distributed through lots of different physical spaces and places - office, train, car, London streets, US Embassy, field. A day in which I searched for and found new knowledge resources (articles) that I was able to read (thanks to the tools I have - laptop, smart phone, printer, internet, aps) which stimulated new ideas. Furthermore, as the day unfolded I discovered new affordance - the possibility of interacting with a knowledgeable CLO to gain feedback on my ideas and the potential to develop a new working relationship with someone who could help me with my problem.

It is often said that 'a picture is worth a thousand words' because a picture can convey an idea more quickly and effectively than the written word. We can create a map of the narrative above using time as the organising principle and identifying the key features of the ecology of practice in red and showing how different items in the ecology were

connected or woven together in order to create new value.

A visual map can be created for any scale of an ecology of practice - days, weeks, months, years. Figure 7.2 provides a visual map of my day in the life narrative. It uses a timeline as the main organising principle.

Figure 7.2 Map of my day-in-the-life learning ecology using a timeline to show how the ecology unfolds

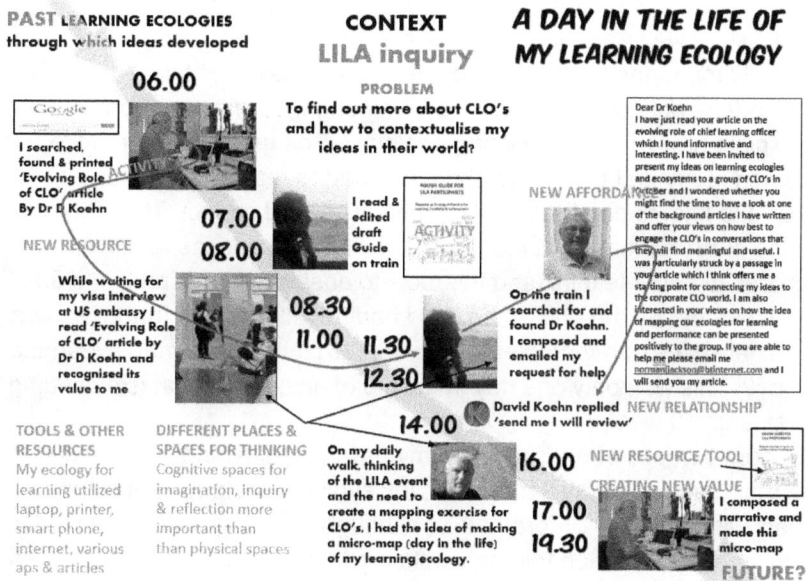

Although the diagram lacks some of the detail of the written narrative it is easy to assimilate the main events and dynamics of an unfolding day and appreciate the essential features of the ecology highlighted in red. As I produced the map of my unfolding day I could see more clearly how

different thoughts were connected to different actions and how ideas were turned into new resources and tools, and potentially a new relationship that holds the potential for enabling me to continue to progress my thinking. I can also see more clearly how I have created new value for myself by making my learning process more explicit and in the process codified it in this document for others to see. As mentioned in my account I sent my background article to Dr Koehn but three week later I have not received a reply. Not all of our efforts to create new relationships and information flows are successful.

Using the heuristic to interpret and reflect on my ecology of practice
In this story we can see an ecology of practice forming around the seemingly mundane task "going to the US embassy to obtain a visa". But this mundane act coincided with me being engaged with my problem 'how do I explain how to map a learning ecology?' So I used the affordance contained in the first project i.e. the time I had to read and think and search and find, to continue working on my second project. The place of learning didn't matter, what mattered was I had the spaces to think, the resources to help me think and the tools to enable me to search and find new resources. By the end of the day I had travelled a little further across the liminal space of my problem - 'how do I explain how to map a learning ecology?' This was only one day in the life of an ecology that is extending over at least 10 weeks.

It's now 4 weeks after I produced my day in the life map so I can see more of the effects of my actions i.e., my evolving ecology enables me to connect with my past. Unfortunately, although I sent my draft article to Dr Koehn in the expectation that he would provide me with feedback, he has not, so far replied. Perhaps, I should email him again but perhaps after reading my article he doesn't want to? Such is the messiness of the deliberation that goes on in an active learning ecology. But the positive outcome of this exercise is that it gave me the idea and confidence to form a task around the 'day in the life of an ecology' at the forthcoming event.

Using the heuristic to map any ecology of practice

The heuristic can be used to directly map an ecology of practice. Figure 7.3 uses the categories of the framework to identify and list the elements of my ecology of practice over about 6 weeks as I prepared materials to

Figure 7.3 Using the heuristic as a template to list/map the elements of my ecology of practice

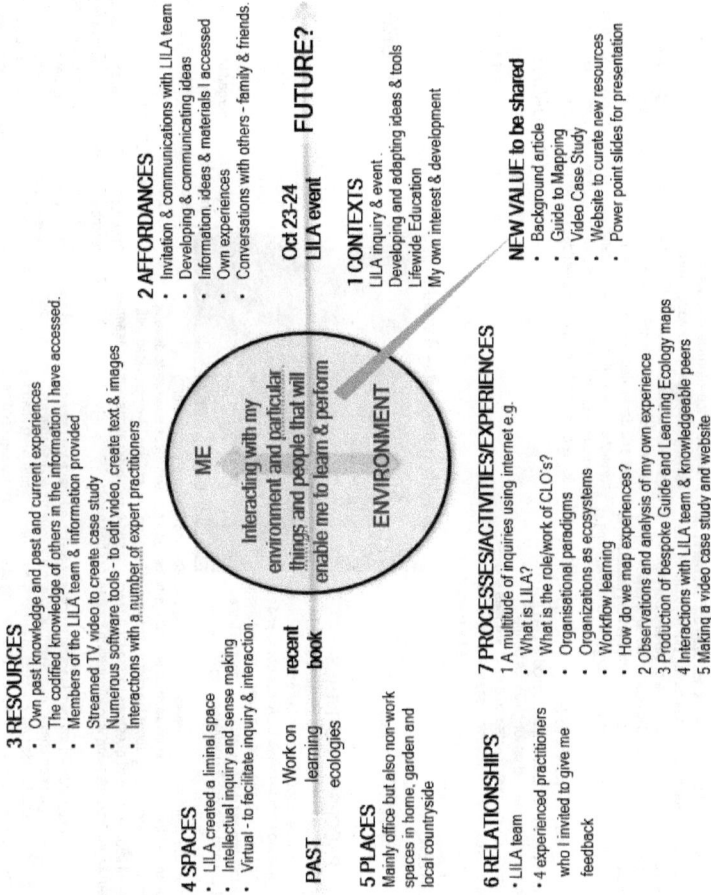

3 RESOURCES
- Own past knowledge and past and current experiences
- The codified knowledge of others in the information I have accessed.
- Members of the LILA team & information provided
- Streamed TV video to create case study
- Numerous software tools - to edit video, create text & images
- Interactions with a number of expert practitioners

2 AFFORDANCES
- Invitation & communications with LILA team
- Developing & communicating ideas
- Information, ideas & materials I accessed
- Own experiences
- Conversations with others - family & friends.

1 CONTEXTS
LILA inquiry & event.
Developing and adapting ideas & tools
Lifewide Education
My own interest & development

Oct 23-24
LILA event   **FUTURE?**

ME
Interacting with my environment and particular things and people that will enable me to learn & perform

ENVIRONMENT

NEW VALUE to be shared
- Background article
- Guide to Mapping
- Video Case Study
- Website to curate new resources
- Power point slides for presentation

4 SPACES
- LILA created a liminal space
- Intellectual inquiry and sense making
- Virtual - to facilitate inquiry & interaction.

PAST   Work on recent learning book ecologies

5 PLACES
Mainly office but also non-work spaces in home, garden and local countryside

6 RELATIONSHIPS
- LILA team
- 4 experienced practitioners who I invited to give me feedback

7 PROCESSES/ACTIVITIES/EXPERIENCES
1 A multitude of inquiries using internet e.g.
- What is LILA?
- What is the role/work of CLO's?
- Organisational paradigms
- Organizations as ecosystems
- Workflow learning
- How do we map experiences?
2 Observations and analysis of my own experience
3 Production of bespoke Guide and Learning Ecology maps
4 Interactions with LILA team & knowledgeable peers
5 Making a video case study and website

Figure 7.4 Using the heuristic as a template to list the elements of an ecology of practice adding a narrative to show how elements are related and woven to produce new value

PLACE & SPACES

This part of my ecology does not have to be based in a particular place. Most of my work has been undertaken in my office using a laptop/software /internet. But my thinking has been done in many other spaces e.g. garden, out walking, driving +++ LILA is a liminal space for me so to enable me to transit I needed to inquire, to find out things I did not know, to try to understand the new context of organisational learning.

RESOURCES

I have drawn on my accumulated knowledge and experiences and the codified knowledge of others in the information I have accessed. I am in the final stages of co-editing a book on learning ecologies which gave me access to lots of different perspectives. I drew on the members of the LILA team and my experiences in this ecology of practice to create new artefacts for the LILA inquiry to communicate what I have learnt. I drew on the mapping tools and developed new mapping tools and contextualized these in a bespoke Guide. I created a case study from video material that had been produced for other purposes. I communicated with a number of knowledgeable practitioners to gain feedback on the results of my work and used the feedback in my preparations.

AFFORDANCES

The possibilities for thinking & action are in the invitation and the performance of communicating my ideas. They are in the information I access, in my own experiences and in my conversations with LILA team members and others. They are in the artefacts I create to communicate my ideas.

FUTURE

Through my physical, intellectual, emotional and creative efforts I created new value. The background article, guide, website, video case study & learning ecology maps are domain specific artefacts, produced to facilitate learning (mine & participants) at the LILA event. They emerged through my purposeful interactions with my physical, intellectual, social, material and virtual environment.

CONTEXTS

CHALLENGE: The challenge of making a useful contribution to the LILA inquiry. Working with people/ organisations I have not worked with before.
ME : My long-term goal of developing and adapting my ideas and making them accessible to others.
MY ORGANISATION : Lifewide Education - fulfilling its purpose. In this way I connect my learning & performance to the purpose of LWE

RELATIONSHIPS

The key relationship during this period is the LILA team who I depended on for guidance on the process, on the participants and their challenges and the nature of my contribution. I shared drafts of my background paper and guide with four experienced and trusted practitioners in order to gain feedback. Their advice was very useful.

PAST

PROCESSES/ACTIVITIES

My interactions with my environment are not random. Over about 8 weeks I engaged in activities to discover what LILA was about and engage with the question 'how can I make a useful contribution to LILA?' How do I connect with the CLO world of organisational learning?

I created a number of processes for exploring and inquiring. Using my computer I searched for and found information in books, articles, posts. I used these sources to develop my own understanding about the corporate world of learning. In addition I was provided with useful information and questions by the LILA team and had two conversations with the team. In return I provided the team with information for their briefing paper.

I observed and recorded my own learning processes and used these to create new maps of my learning ecology. I had conversations with people in my network and shared my ideas in order to gain feedback. I made new artefacts to embody and communicate what I had learnt e.g. Notes, guide, website, power point slides, learning ecology maps, video-based case study. I sought feedback on some of these artefacts. Through this process and my activities I developed a better understanding of how to present my ideas in ways that are likely to be more relevant and useful to LILA participants and I have become more knowledgeable in the process.

unfolding present - 8 weeks

243

support my contribution to a forthcoming event. This is an efficient way of representing an ecology but it does not achieve the goal of showing how the different elements of the ecology are related or how they were woven together to create new value. This can be partly achieved by adding a narrative to the conceptual framework in the manner shown in Figure 7.4.

Snapshots of a dynamic ecology of practice

The third visual method is to use the features of the learning ecology framework to organize the design of the map and take a snap-shot of the ecology at a particular point in time (Figure 7.5).

Figure 7.5 Snapshot diagram of my ecology of practice for the 6 weeks prior to September 12th

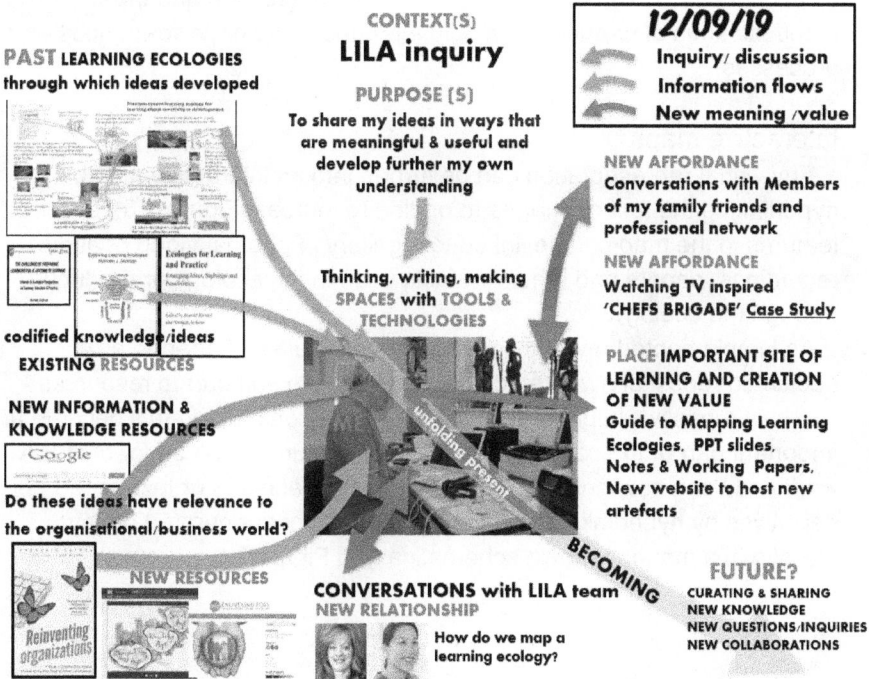

This map connects the theoretical model of a learning ecology to real practice and personal experiences. It attempts to show the way a person relates to and interacts with their environment and the things that matter within it, together with the spaces and places they inhabit, the affordances or opportunities they identify and work with, the resources they seek, find and utilise and the new resources (value) they create and share.

Such diagrams can show how the current ecology for practice and learning is connecting to past ecologies of practice within which learning that is relevant to this set of circumstances was developed. It can also show connections to other current ecologies of practice that are relevant. Annotations can be used to show the key problems, challenges and questions that are being addressed, and the important questions that are driving inquiry. They can also show the sites of creation and the manifestations of creativity in tangible products and or performances and processes.

Interactive maps

Any visual representation can be turned into an interactive map by hyperlinking the text or images to on-line resources (Figure 7.6). Different features in the map can be linked to a gallery of photos, video or audio recordings, papers and other artefacts used in the ecology or produced through the ecology.

As I implemented my ecology of practice I realized I needed a dedicated repository where I could contextualize and curate resources - so I built a password protected website. Once constructed this became an important part of the communication infrastructure I can use for my LILA work and I can now animate my two-dimensional maps or text-based narratives by hyperlinking them to resources that are curated on my website in a manner shown schematically in Figure 7.6.

Figure 7. 6 Interactive map of an ecology of practice. Hyperlinks (underlined text) can be used to reveal the nature of particular interactions or the products of work/learning

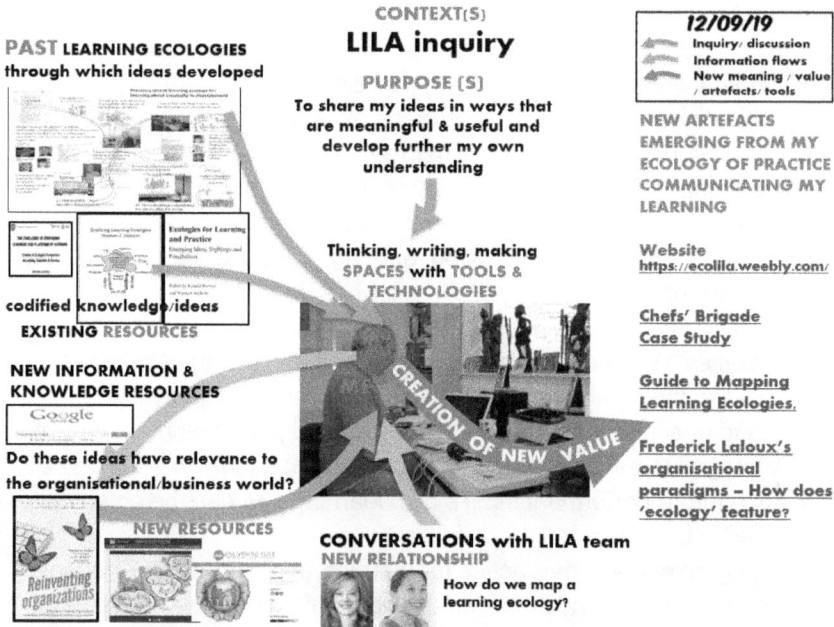

CONTEXT(S)
LILA inquiry
PURPOSE (S)
To share my ideas in ways that
are meaningful & useful and
develop further my own
understanding

PAST LEARNING ECOLOGIES
through which ideas developed

12/09/19
Inquiry/ discussion
Information flows
New meaning / value
/ artefacts/ tools

**NEW ARTEFACTS
EMERGING FROM MY
ECOLOGY OF PRACTICE
COMMUNICATING MY
LEARNING**

Thinking. writing. making
SPACES with TOOLS &
TECHNOLOGIES

codified knowledge/ideas
EXISTING RESOURCES

**NEW INFORMATION &
KNOWLEDGE RESOURCES**
Google

Do these ideas have relevance to
the organisational/business world?

NEW RESOURCES

Website
https://ecolila.weebly.com/

Chefs' Brigade
Case Study

Guide to Mapping
Learning Ecologies.

Frederick Laloux's
organisational
paradigms – How does
'ecology' feature?

CONVERSATIONS with LILA team
NEW RELATIONSHIP
How do we map a
learning ecology?

How might these ideas and maps be incorporated into the learning practices of organisations?

The ecologies of practice for learning and performance model described in this chapter provides a powerful heuristic with which to appreciate learning, performance and the creation of new value as ecological phenomena. A concept that reinforces the idea that organizations can be viewed as complex ecosocial systems (ecosystems) within which people learn as they perform. The argument advanced in this book is that by developing awareness and capacity to think about learning, performance and the creation of new value as ecological phenomena, individuals build their understanding of how they, as unique individuals, learn and perform in highly specific contexts, situations and circumstances.

The heuristic is a tool to aid reflection on how we learn, perform and create new value and supports the continued development of practitioners who are self-motivated, self-directed and self-regulating. The method outlined above is to create maps of selected practices to try to dig deep into the way we weave together the elements of our ecologies of practice to learn, perform and create value. Constructing a map and narrative of the unfolding story is a learning process in its own right with potential to develop new insights on learning, performance and how new value is created.

I am struck by the similarities of my ecological model to the thinking that underlies 'Workflow Learning.' (Pradnam 2017a & b). Workflow learning is a concept being used by some leaders of organisational learning to describe learning that is a necessary part of work. It's learning that is integral to performance and learning that has the potential to be utilized in future performances. It's also learning that has the potential to be shared with others.

Mapping an ecology of practice for learning and performance reveals the dynamics and nuances of learning during the flow of work. Such a map reveals the particular contexts for learning, it reveals what is being learned, how, when and where its being learned, and even why it's being learned. Such a map has the potential to reveal the questions that drive inquiry and how we access the information and knowledge we need, and the tools we use or make to help us solve our problems. It shows the relationships we make and the spaces and places we inhabit. The map celebrates the resourcefulness and inventiveness of individuals as they weave together ideas in order to come to know how to create novel solutions.

Pradnam (2017a & b) proposed a useful conceptual model (Figure 7.7) to show how 'workflow learning' can be supported by resources and infrastructures provided by the organisation and the world of infinite possibilities outside the organisation The learning support resources, tools and infrastructures of every organisation will be different as will the use of such support by individuals. The mapping of individuals' ecologies of practice could reveal exactly how such support mechanisms are used within an individual's workflow learning (Figure 7.7).

Figure 7.7 shows the conceptual model of workflow learning developed by Arun Pradnam (2017a)

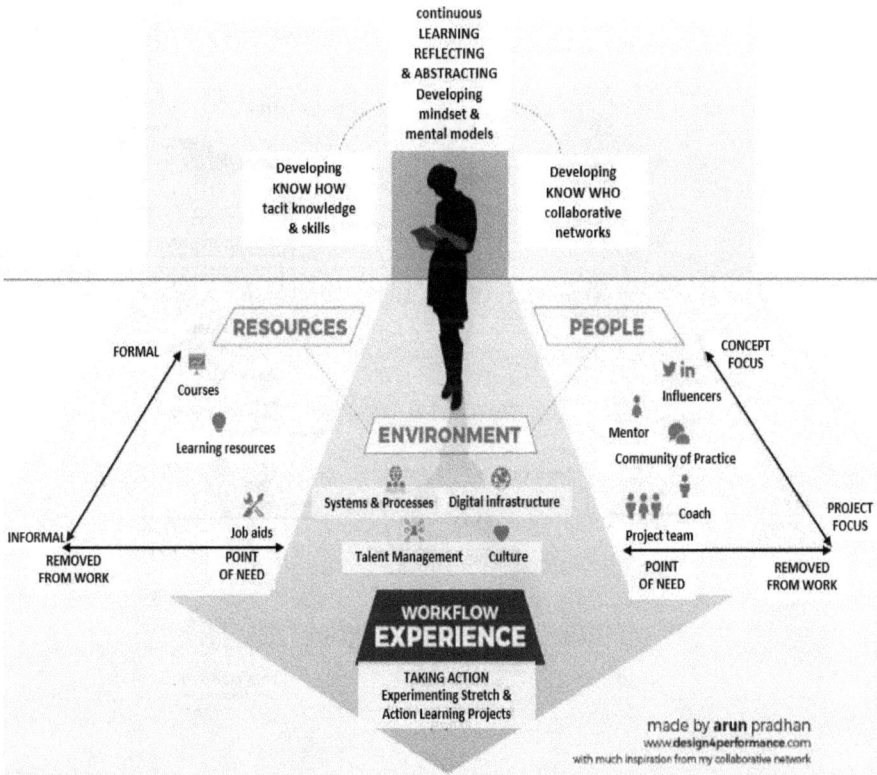

. Mapping ecologies of practice could become an integral element of workflow learning and viewed as a learning process in its own right. Such maps could be superimposed on an organisation's infrastructure for supporting learning in the manner suggested in Figure 7.8.

Figure 7.8 Hypothetical illustration to show how an individual's map of their ecology of practice for learning and performance might be connected to an organization's map of their support for workflow learning.

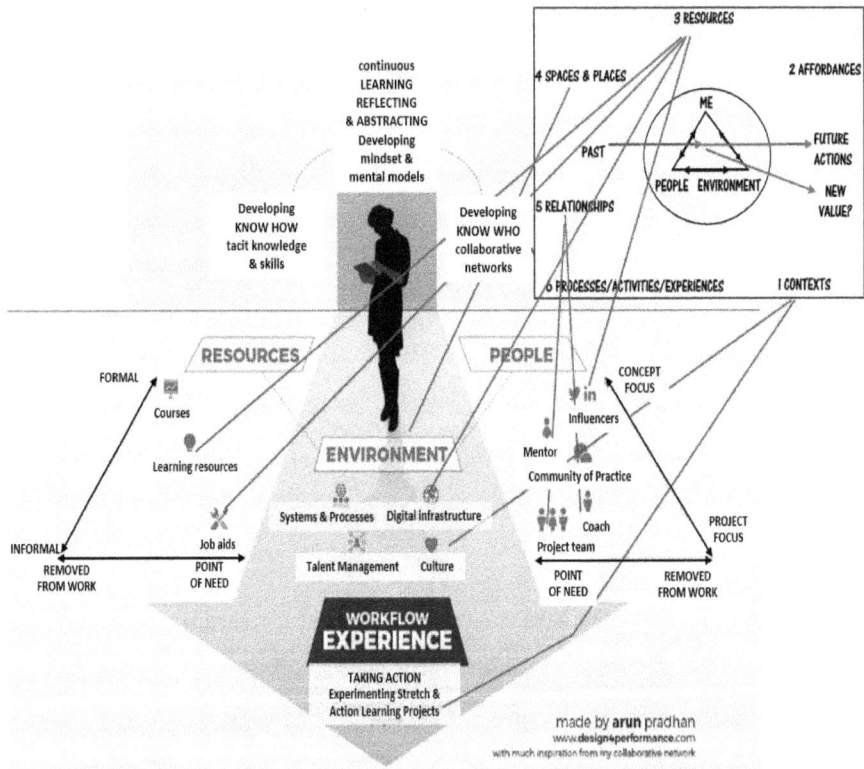

An individual's map of their ecology of practice could reveal exactly how and when an organization's learning support mechanisms were used within an individual's workflow learning as well as celebrating individual's resourcefulness in finding their own learning support. Such maps could provide those responsible for designing and providing resources in support of workflow learning with information about how, why and when such resources are being used within a workflow and provide evidence of their impact on enabling an individual to achieve their goals.

Pradnam stresses the importance of experience and thinking about what was learnt through the experience in his model of workflow learning:

experience [is] at the heart of the model [which] prioritizes its interplay with a conscious process of reflection that bounds it....in my opinion, the relationship between experience and is the key driver of learning and change [in organizations]. Everything else, from training, performance support, to social learning, supports and scaffolds that key relationship.

Without a reflective process, the experience that lies at the centre of this model would be relegated to being 'stuff that happens'. I believe that reflective learning should focus on two elements:
• Mindset, or the underlying attitude and perspective that lies behind and informs behaviour
• Mental models, the conceptual frameworks and high-level linkages that are made between various experiences and elements" (Pradnam 2017a)

As we connect up the dots of our experiences we become more aware of how particular relationships and interactions motivate us or open up new possibilities, or conversely our dent enthusiasm or close down opportunities. The process engages with both the attitudinal and mental modelling dimensions of reflection and creates an entirely new paradigm within which learning, creativity and performance can be understood and discussed.

By making a map of our ecologies of practice we are trying to synthesize our experiences of interacting with people, our problems, challenges and opportunities in the particular social-cultural, material and emotional environments we are inhabiting in order to gain deeper understandings of ourselves, our effects on and in the world and the effects our world has on us. Alongside our map making we are also creating narratives to help us make sense of our world. Such narratives inform and shape our beliefs about how our particular world works and underpin our self-efficacy - our beliefs about what we are capable of achieving, which in turn influence future performance.

Once made, our map is an artefact that can be used, along with our narratives, to explain to ourselves and others the meaning that is our work. The type of learning we are developing through the process of making a map and the reflections it prompts, is an enhanced awareness that can be drawn upon in new situations in the future. With our map in front of us we can seek ways of becoming a better version of ourselves by asking, What have I discovered through assembling (or re-visiting) this ecology which should make me more effective in the future that I have been in the past"? *Professor John Cowan personal communication.*

APPENDIX 1

Questions to aid reflection on the ecological nature of learning and practice. These questions relate to the ecological heuristic (Figure 7.1)

- What is the nature of the ecosystem within which you are working? What is your role within the ecosystem?
- What purpose(s) did your ecology of practice fulfil? What were you trying to achieve?
- What were the important contexts in which you were working? What new understandings of context did you have to develop in order to achieve?
- What opportunities did you find or create for yourself that enabled you to achieve your goals? Who/what provided opportunities that you weren't expecting?
- What resources did you draw upon to achieve your goals, and what new resources did you create?
- What tools did you use or create to enable you to learn and achieve?
- What sort of physical, intellectual or emotional, spaces did you create in order to achieve your goals?
- Were particular places important in order to learn or accomplish something? How/why were they important?
- What processes/activities did you engage in or create in order to achieve/perform?
- What challenges did you have to overcome and what did you learn from engaging with these challenges?
- What mistakes did you make that you learnt something useful from?
- What important relationships did you form in order to achieve your goals? What did you learn through these relationships?
- How/where and when was your creativity involved in your ecology of practice? How was your creativity manifested?
- What do you now know about how the organisation works that you didn't know before?
- What forms of support for your learning did you gain through your organisation?
- What forms of support for your learning did you gain from sources outside your organisation?

What have I discovered through assembling (or re-visiting) this ecology which should make me more effective in the future that I have been in the past?

References

Amabile, T. M. and Kramer, S. J. (2012) *The Progress Principle: Using Small Wins to Ignite Joy, Engagement, and Creativity at Work.* Boston: Harvard Business Review Press.

Baker, P., Jackson, N.J. and Longmore, J. (2014) *Tackling the Wicked Challenge of Strategic Change: The story of how a university changed itself* Authorhouse.

Banks, J.A., Au, K. H., Ball, A.F, Bell, P., Gordon, E.W, Gutiérrez, K.D., Heath, S B., Lee, C.D., Lee, Y., Mahiri, J., Suad Nasir, N., Valdés, G., Zhou, M. (2007) *Learning in and out of school in diverse environments: Lifelong, Lifewide, Lifedeep.* The LIFE Center (The Learning in Informal and Formal Environments Centre), University of Washington.

Bandura, A. (1986). *Social foundations of thought and action: A social cognitive theory.* Englewood Cliffs, NJ: Prentice Hall

Bandura, A. (1986). Self-efficacy: The exercise of control. New York, W.H.Freeman

Bandura A. (1995) Self-efficacy in changing societies. Cambridge, MA: Cambridge University Press

Bandura, A. (2001) Social Cognitive Theory: An Agentic Perspective. *Annu. Rev. Psychol.* 52:1-26.

Barab, S. A., Cherkes-Julkowski, M., Swenson, R., Garrett, S., Shaw, R. E., & Young, M. (1999). Principles of self-organization: Ecologizing the learner-facilitator system. *The Journal of the Learning Sciences,* 8 (3&4), 349-390

Barab, S.A. and Plucker, J.A. (2002) Smart People or Smart Contexts? Cognition, Ability, and Talent Development in an Age of Situated Approaches to Knowing *Educational Psychologist* 37(3), 165-182

Barab, S. A., & Roth (2006) Curriculum-based ecosystems: Supporting knowing from an ecological perspective. *Educational Researcher,* 35 (5), 3-13

Barnett, R. (2007) *A Will To Learn: Being a Student in an Age of Uncertainty* Society for Research into Higher Education & Open University Press MaGraw Hill: Maidenhead

Barnett, R. (2011) Lifewide education: a new and transformative concept for higher education. in N. J. Jackson (ed) *Learning for a Complex World: A lifewide concept of learning, education and personal development.* Authorhouse 22-38

Barnett, R., and Coate, K. (2005) *Engaging the Curriculum in Higher Education*. Buckingham, UK: The Society for Research into Higher Education and Open University Press.

Barron, B. (2006) Interest and Self-Sustained Learning as Catalysts of Development: A Learning Ecology Perspective. *Human Development* 49:193-224 Available on-line at: http://life-slc.org/docs/barron-self-sustainedlearning.pdf

Bateson, G. (2000 reprint. First published 1972). *Steps to an Ecology of Mind: Collected Essays in Anthropology, Psychiatry, Evolution, and Epistemology*. Chicago, Illinois: University of Chicago Press

Bauman, R. (1986) *Story, Performance, And Event: Contextual Studies of Oral Narrative* Cambridge University Press (New York)

Baxter Magolda, M. B. (1992) *Knowing and Reasoning in College: Gender-related Patterns in Students' Intellectual Development*. San Francisco, CA: Jossey-Bass.

Baxter Magolda, M. B. (1999) *Creating Contexts for Learning and Self-authorship: Constructive Developmental Pedagogy*. Nashville: Vanderbilt University Press.

Baxter Magolda, M. B. (2001) *Making Their Own Way: Narratives for Transforming Higher Education to Promote Self-development*. Sterling, VA: Stylus.

Baxter Magolda, M. B. (2004a) Learning Partnerships Model: A Framework for Promoting Self-authorship. In M. B. Baxter Magolda and P. M. King (eds) *Learning Partnerships: Theory and Models of Practice to Educate for Self-authorship*, Sterling, VA: Stylus, pp. 37-62).

Baxter Magolda, M. B. (2004b) Self-authorship as the Common Goal of 21st Century Education. In M. B. Baxter Magolda and P. M. King (eds) *Learning Partnerships: Theory and Models of Practice to Educate for Self-authorship*, Sterling, VA: Stylus, pp. 1-35.

Baxter Magolda, M. B. (2007) Self-Authorship: The Foundation for Twenty-first Century Education. In P. S. Meszaros (ed.) *Self-Authorship: Advancing Students' Intellectual Growth, New Directions for Teaching and Learning*, San Francisco, CA: Jossey-Bass, Vol. 109, pp. 69-83.

Baxter Magolda, M. B. (2009) *Authoring Your Life: Developing an Internal Voice to Navigate Life's Challenges*. Sterling, VA: Stylus.

254

Baxter Magolda, M.B. (2011) Authoring your life: a lifewide learning perspective in N.J.Jackson (ed) *Learning for a Complex World: A lifewide concept of learning, education and personal development.* Authorhouse. 76-99

Baxter Magolda, M.B. (2014) The journey to self-authorship and a more meaningful life. Lifewide Magazine 9, 8-11 http://www.lifewideeducation.uk/uploads/1/3/5/4/13542890/lifewide_magazine_9.pdf

Berger, G. (1970) Introduction. OECD-CERI interdisciplinary - problems of teaching and research in universities. San Francisco: Jossy-Bass

Bishop, J. (2005) An ecological model for understanding and influencing behaviour in virtual communities, *Proceedings of the Post-Cognitivist Psychology Conference 2005,* Glasgow: University of Strathclyde [15] Rose, A. & Clarke, P.

Bishop, J. (2005) The role of mediating artifacts in the design of persuasive e-learning systems. *Proceedings of the First International Conference on Internet Technologies and Applications (ITA 05).* Wednesday 7th - Friday 9th September 2005. University of Wales, NEWI, Wrexham,

Blaschke, L.M. (2012) Heutagogy and Lifelong Learning: A Review of Heutagogical Practice and Self-Determined Learning The International Review of Research in Open and Distance Learning v13 56-71 Available at: http://www.irrodl.org/index.php/irrodl/article/view/1076/2087

Bloch, E. (1986). *The principle of hope* (N.Plaice, S.Place, & P.Knight Trans.). Cambridge, Mass: MIT Press. (Original work published in 1959)

Boekaerts M. & Minnaert, A. (1999) Self-regulation with respect to informal learning *International Journal of Educational Research* 31 533-544

Boisot, M. H. (1998) *Knowledge Assets: Securing Competitive Advantage in the Information Economy.* Oxford: Oxford University Press.

Bonwell, C. & Eison, J. (1991). *Active Learning: Creating Excitement in the Classroom AEHE-ERIC Higher Education Report No. 1.* Washington, D.C.: Jossey-Bass. ISBN 1-878380-08-7.

Boud, D. Keogh and Walker (eds.) (1985) *Reflection. Turning experience into learning,* London: Kogan Page. 170 pages

Bronfenbrenner, U. (1994). Ecological models of human development. In *International Encyclopedia of Education, Vol. 3, 2nd. Ed.* Oxford: Elsevier.

Brown, J. S. (2000) Growing Up Digital: How the Web Changes Work, Education, and the Ways People Learn Change March/April 2000Available at: http://www.johnseelybrown.com/Growing_up_digital.pdf

Cairns, L. & Stephenson, J. (2009) *Capable Workplace Learning: in the 21st Century*. Rotterdam: Sense Publishers.

Capra, F. (2007) Sustainable Living, Ecological Literacy, and the Breath of Life *Canadian Journal of Environmental Education (CJEE)*, Available at: http://jee.lakeheadu.ca/index.php/cjee/article/viewFile/624/507

Canole, G. (2011) The role of Mediating Artefacts in learning design Chapter 6 in G. Canole *Designing for learning in an open world* http://cloudworks.ac.uk/cloud/view/5410

Castells, M. (1996) *The Information Age: Economy, Society and Culture*, Vol. 1. Oxford: Blackwell

Cleary, T. J., & Zimmerman, B. J. (2001). Self-regulation differences during athletic practice by experts, non-experts, and novices. *Journal of Applied Sport Psychology*, 13, 185-206.

Cook, S. D. N. & Brown, J. S. (1999) Bridging epistemologies: the generative dance between organisational knowledge and organizational knowing. *Organizational Science* 10 (4) 381-400.

Crapoulet, E (2008) An Immersive Experience: Making a Classical Recording of Chopin's 4th Ballade in F minor Op. 52 in N J Jackson (ed) *Appreciating the Power of Immersive Experience Conference Programme,* University of Surrey p48-54 available at: http://immersiveexperience.pbworks.com/w/page/10471625/Power%20of%20Immersive%20Experience

Davenport, T. H., and Prusak L. (1998) Working Knowledge: How Organizations Manage What They Know. Cambridge, MA: Harvard Business School Press

Deal, T.E. & Kennedy, A.A. (1982) *Corporate Cultures*, Perseus

Deleuze, G. & Guattari, F. (2007/1980) *A Thousand Plateaus*. London: Continuum.

Dewey, J. (1916). Democracy and education An introduction to the philosophy of education. New York: MacMillan.

Dewey J. (1933) How We Think. Boston, MA: D. C. Heath and Co

Dewey, J. (2015) Experience and Education. New York: Free Press.

Di Stefano, G., Gino, F., Pisano, G., & Staats, B. (2014) Learning by Thinking: How Reflection Aids Performance *Harvard Business School Working Paper* 14-093 March 25, 2014 Available on line at: http://www.hbs.edu/faculty/Publication%20Files/14-093_4d4e874c-8e46-4054-84fd-df533e94ccd8.pdf

Dusenbery, D. B. (1992). Sensory Ecology. New York: W.H. Freeman.

Eberle, J. (2009). Heutagogy: What your mother didn't tell you about pedagogy and the conceptual age. In *Proceedings from the 8th Annual European Conference on eLearning*, October 29-30, 2009. Bari, Italy.

Education Council (2006) Recommendation of the European Parliament and the Council of 18 December 2006 on key competencies for lifelong learning. Brussels: Official Journal of the European Union, 30.12.2006

Edwards, M., McGoldrick, C., & Oliver, M. (2006) Creativity and curricula in higher education, in N.J. Jackson et al (eds) *Developing Creativity in Higher Education: an imaginative curriculum,* London and New York: Routledge 156-172.

Ellis, R & Goodyear, P. (2010) *Students experience of e-learning in HE: a sustainable ecology* New York: Routledge

Engstrom, Y. (1987) Learning by Expanding: An Activity - Theoretical Approach to Developmental Research Available on line http://lchc.ucsd.edu/MCA/Paper/Engestrom/expanding/toc.htm

Eraut, M. (1994) *Developing Professional Knowledge and Competence.* London: Falmer Press.

Eraut, M. (2004) Informal learning in the workplace *Studies in Continuing Education,* Vol. 26, No. 2, 247-273

Eraut, M. (2009) How Professionals Learn through Work. In N. Jackson (ed.) *Learning to be Professional through a Higher Education.* Online at http://learningtobeprofessional.pbworks.com/How-professionals-learn-through-work

Eraut, M. (2007) Learning from Other People in the Workplace, *Oxford Review of Education,* 33 (4), 403-422

Eraut, M. (2009) How Professionals Learn through Work. In N. Jackson (ed.) *Learning to be Professional through a Higher Education.* Online at http://www.lifewideeducation.uk/professional-learning.html

Eraut M (2010) Understanding Complex Performance through Learning Trajectories and Mediating Artefacts, Chapter A7 in N J Jackson (ed) *Learning to be a Professional,* Surrey Centre for Excellence in Training and Education available at: http://www.lifewideeducation.uk/professional-learning.html

Eraut, M. (2011) Improving the Quality of Work Placements. in N.J. Jackson (ed) *Learning to be Professional through a Higher Education.* Available at: http://www.lifewideeducation.uk/professional-learning.html

Eraut, M. & Hirsh, W. (2008) *The Significance of Workplace Learning for Individuals, Groups and Organisations* SKOPE Monograph http://www.skope.ox.ac.uk/wordpress/wpcontent/uploads/2014/12/Monogrpah-09.pdf

Ertmer, P. A. & Newby, T. J. (1996) The expert learner: strategic, self-regulated and reflective. *Instructional Science*, 24, 1-24.

Facer, K. (2011) *Learning Futures: Education, technology and social change*. London: Routledge.

Facer, K (2016) Using the Future in education: creating spaces for openness, hope and novelty in H Lees & N Noddings (eds) (2016) *Palgrave International Handbook of Alternative Education*, Palgrave Macmillan Available at: https://www.academia.edu/21661152/Using_the_Future_in_Education_Creating_Space_for_Openness_Hope_and_Novelty

Fraser, S. & Bosanquet, A. (2006) The Curriculum? That's just a unit outline, isn't it? *Studies in Higher Education*, Vol. 31, (3), 269-284

Fortheringham J., Strickland K, & Aitchison, K. (2012) Curriculum: Directions, decisions and debate. Edinburgh Napier University http://www.enhancementthemes.ac.uk/docs/ publications/curriculum-directions-decisions-and-debate.pdf?sfvrsn=8

Gettinger, M. & Seibert, K. (2002) Contributions of study skills to academic competence. *The School Psychology Review*, 31, 350-365

Gibson, J. J. (1982) The problem of temporal order in stimulation and perception. In E. Reed & R. Jones (Eds.), *Reasons for realism: Selected essays of James J. Gibson* (171-179). Hillsdale, NJ: Erlbaum.

Gibson, J. J. (1986) *The ecological approach to visual perception*. Laurence Erlbaum, Hillsdale, NJ.

Gibson, J. J. (1977). The Theory of Affordances. In R. Shaw and J. Bransford (Ed.), *Perceiving, Acting, and Knowing* (67-82). Lawrence Erlbaum.

Gibson, J. J. (1979). *The Ecological Approach to Visual Perception*. Houghton Mifflin.

Gibson, E. J. & Pick, A. D. (2000). *An Ecological Approach to Perceptual Learning and Development*. Oxford University Press, USA.

Goleman, D. (1996), *Emotional Intelligence. Why it can matter more than IQ*, Bloomsbury.

Gough, D.A., Kiwan, D., Sutcliffe, S., Simpson, D., & Houghton, N. (2003) A systematic map and synthesis review of the effectiveness of personal development planning for improving student learning. Report on-line at http://eppi.ioe.ac.uk/EPPIWeb/home.aspx?page=/ree/review_groups/EPPI/LTSN/LTSN_intro.htm

Graves, C.W. (1974) "Human Nature Prepares for a Momentous Leap" *The Futurist,* April, 1974, pp. 72-87 Available at: http://spiraldynamicsintegral.nl/wp-content/uploads/2013/09/Graves-Clare-Human-Nature-Prepares-for-a-Momentous-Leap.pdf

Greeno, J. G. (1994). Gibson's affordances. *Psychological Review, 101*(2), 336-342.

Gundem, B. B. (1998). *Understanding European didactics - an overview: Didactics (Didaktik, Didaktik(k), Didactique).* Oslo: University of Oslo. Institute for Educational Research. Reprinted in B. Moon, S. Brown & M Ben-Peretz (eds.) (2000) *Routledge International Companion to Education.* London: Routledge. 235-262.

Hannafin, K. & Hannafin, M. (1996) The ecology of distance learning environments *Training Research Journal* 1 49-70

Hase, S., & Kenyon, C. (2000). From andragogy to heutagogy. In *UltiBase Articles.* Retrieved from http://ultibase.rmit.edu.au/Articles/dec00/hase2.htm

Hase, S. & Kenyon, C. (2007). Heutagogy: A child of complexity theory. *Complicity: An International Journal of Complexity and Education, 4* (1), 111-119.

Haythornthwaite, C. (2012) New Media, New Literacies, and New Forms of Learning.International *Journal of Learning and Media* 4:3-4, 1-8.http://www.mitpressjournals.org/doi/abs/10.1162/IJLM_e_00097

Heckhausen, H., & Gollwitzer, P. M. (1987). Thoughts contents and cognitive functioning in motivational versus volitional stages of mind. *Motivation and Emotion,* 11, 101-120.

Holland, D. & Lave, J. (2009) Social Practice Theory and the Historical Production of Persons *Actio: An International Journal of Human Activity Theory* No. 2 1-15 available at: http://www.chat.kansai-u.ac.jp/publications/actio/pdf/no2-1.pdf

Hung, D. W. L. (2002) Metaphorical ideas as mediating artifacts for the social construction of knowledge: implications from the writings of Dewey and V ygotsky *Int. J. of Instructional Media* 29 (2) 197-214 Available on-line at: http://www.andrews.edu/~rbailey/Chapter%20Nine/6766208.pdf

Ingold, T. (2000) Hunting and gathering as ways of perceiving the environment. *The Perception of the Environment. Essays on livelihood, dwelling and skill* Routledge, 2000

Jackson, N. J. (Ed) (2011a) Learning for a Complex World: A lifewide concept of learning, education and personal development. Authorhouse

Jackson, N. J. (2011b) An imaginative lifewide curriculum. In N. J. Jackson (ed) *Learning for a Complex World: A lifewide concept of learning, education and personal development.* Authorhouse. 100-21

Jackson, N.J. (2011c) The lifelong and lifewide dimensions of living, learning and developing. In N. J. Jackson (ed) *Learning for a Complex World: A lifewide concept of learning, education and personal development.* Authorhouse 1-21

Jackson, N.J. (2014a) Lifewide Learning and Education in Universities & Colleges: Concepts and Conceptual Aids in N Jackson and J Willis (eds) *Lifewide Learning and Education in Universities and Colleges* Chapter 1 available at: http://www.learninglives.co.uk/e-book.html

Jackson, N.J. (2015) Personal Learning Networks an Ecological Perspective Lifewide Magazine 14 available at: http://www.lifewideeducation.uk/uploads /1/3/5/4/13542890/lifewide_magazine_14.pdf

Jackson, N.J. (2016) Exploring creativity in the Social Age through #creativeHE. Creative Academic Magazine #3, 6-10 Available at: http://www.creativeacademic.uk/magazine.html

Jackson, N.J (2020) Ecologies for Learning and Practice in Higher Education Ecosystems, in R.Barnett and N.J.Jackson (Eds) Ecologies for Learning and Practice: Emerging Ideas, Sightings, and Possibilities, London: Routledge

Jarche, H. (2014) The Seek > Sense > Share Framework Inside Learning Technologies January 2014, *Posted Monday, 10 February 22 014* http://jarche.com/2014/02/the-seek-sense-share-framework/

Jones, D. M. (2013) Finding Your Authentic Voice Will Set You Free to Express Who You Really Are *Huffington Post* http://www.huffingtonpost.com/dennis-merritt-jones/authentic-voice_b_4241021.html

Jonker, L. (2011) *Self-regulation in sport and education Important for sport expertise and academic achievement for elite youth athletes.* Doctoral Thesis University of Groningen Available on line at: https://www.rug.nl/research/portal/files/14646058/Proefschrift_digitaal_incl._st _1.pdf

Jonker L, Elferink-Gemser M T & Visscher C (2011)The Role of Self-Regulatory Skills in Sport and Academic Performances of Elite Youth Athletes *Talent Development & Excellence* Vol. 3, No. 2, 2011, 263-275

Kegan, R. (1982). The evolving self: Problem and process in human development. Cambridge, MA: Harvard University Press.

Kegan, R. (1994). *In over our heads: The mental demands of modern life.* Cambridge, MA: Harvard University Press.

Kelly, A.V. (2009) The Curriculum: theory and practice (6th edition) Sage

Kitsantas, A, Winsler, A. & Huie, F (2008) Self-regulation and ability predictors of academic success during college: A predictive validity study. *Journal of Advanced Academics*, 20, pp 42-68

Knowles, M. (1975). *Self-directed learning: A guide for learners and teachers.* United States of America: Cambridge Adult Education.

Kornell, N. & Metcalfe, J. (2006) Study efficacy and the region of proximal learning framework. *Journal of Experimental Psychology: Learning, Memory and Cognition*, 32, pp 609-622

Kroeger, M. (2016) The creative expression of process management. Blog post at https://medium.com/@Mattpkroeger/the-creative-expression-of-process-management-f3c86fc9665c#.hwu9zz4p5

Laloux, F. (2014) *Reinventing Organizations: A Guide to Creating Organizations Inspired by the Next Stage of Human Consciousness.* Nelson Parker. pp. 381. ISBN 978-2960133509.

Land, R., Rattray, J., & Vivian, P. (2014) Learning in the liminal space: a semiotic approach to threshold concepts *Higher Education* 67:199-217

Lave, J. (1988) *Cognition in Practice: Mind, Mathematics and Culture in Everyday Life* Cambridge University Press, Cambridge, 1988.

Lave, J. (1997) The Culture of Acquisition and the Practice of Understanding, in D. Kirschner and J. Whitson (Eds), Situated Cognition: Social,Semiotic and Psychological Perspectives pp. 17-35. Mahwah, NJ: Lawrence Erlbaum Associates, 1997.

Lave, J. & Wenger, E. (1991) *Situated Learning: Legitimate peripheral participation*. Cambridge University Press.

Law, R. (2008) *Get a Life - an Introduction to Explorativity.* Lulu.com.

Levinson, D. J. (1978). *The Seasons of a Man's Life.* New York: Knopf.

Leach, J. & Moon, B. (2010) *The Power of Pedagogy* Sage

Lemke, J. L. (1994) Discourse, Dynamics, and Social Change.*Cultural Dynamics* Leiden, Brill 6(1): 243-275.

Lemke, J. L. (1995) *Textual Politics: Discourse and Social Dynamics*. London: Taylor & Francis.

Lemke, J. L. (1997) Cognition, Context, and Learning: A Social Semiotic Perspective" in D. Kirshner and A. Whitson, Eds., *Situated Cognition: Social, Semiotic, and Psychological Perspectives.* (37-55). Hillsdale, NJ: Erlbaum.

Lemke, J. (2000) Across the Scales of Time: Artifacts, Activities, and Meanings in Ecosocial Systems. *Mind, Culture and Activity 7*(4), 273-290 available on-line at http://www.jaylemke.com/storage/Scales-of-time-MCA2000.pdf

Lindeman, E. C. (1926). *The Meaning of Adult Education.* New York: New Republic, republished in 1989 by Oklahoma Research Center for Continuing Professional and Higher Education. [Online version from:http://archive.org/details/meaningofadulted00lind.

Luckin, R. (2008) The Learner Centric Ecology of Resources: a Framework for Using Technology to Scaffold Learning. *Computers and Education* 50, 449-462

Mahon, C. & Crowley, U. (2013) Promoting Self-Regulation Skills in Undergraduate Students Using a Group-Based Training Programme

McLoughlin, C. & Lee, M. J. W. (2008) The Three P's of Pedagogy for the Networked Society: Personalization, Participation, and Productivity *International Journal of Teaching and Learning in Higher Education* 20, 1, 10-27 available at http://www.isetl.org/ijtlhe/ ISSN 1812-9129

McPherson, G. E. & Zimmerman, B.J. (2002) Self-Regulation of Musical Learning: A social cognitive perspective. In R Colwell and C Richardson (eds) The New Handbook of Research on Musical Teaching and Learning. Oxford University Press

McWilliam, E. (2009) Teaching for creativity: from sage to guide to meddler. *Asia Pacific Journal of Education* v29, 3, 281-293 Available at: http://www.vcu. edu/ cte/workshops/teaching learning/2011 resources/sagetoguidetomeddler.pdf

Merino, A. & Aucock, M. (2014) The role-modelling of self-regulated learning strategies and skills through enrichment tutorials, *Curtin University Teaching and Learning Forum* Available on-line at: https://ctl.curtin.edu.au/events/conferences/tlf/tlf2014/refereed/merino.pdf

Meyer, J. H. F., & Land, R. (2005). Threshold concepts and troublesome knowledge: Epistemological considerations and a conceptual framework for teaching and learning. *Higher Education,* 49, 373-388

Mezirow, J. (Ed.). (2000). *Learning as transformation: Critical perspectives on a theory in progress.* San Francisco, CA: Jossey-Bass.

Miller, N. and Boud, D. (1997) Working with Experience: Animating Learning (format: restricted e-book, .pdf). London: Routledge

Nicol, D. (2010) The foundation for graduate attributes: developing self-regulation through self and peer-assessment Quality Assurance Agency (Scotland) Available on-line at: http://www.enhancementthemes.ac.uk/docs/publications

Nicol, M. & Macfarlane-Dick, D. (2005) Formative assessment and self-regulated learning: A model and seven principles of good feedback practice. *Studies in*

Higher Education 31 191-218 Available on-line at
http://www.psy.gla.ac.uk/~steve/rap/docs/nicol.dmd.pdf
Norman, D. A. (1990) *The design of everyday things.* New York: Doubleday.
Nye, B. D. & Silverman, B. G. (2012). Affordance. In N. M. Seel
(Ed.),Encyclopedia of the Sciences of Learning (pp. 179-183). New York, NY:
Springer. Available at: http://repository.upenn.edu/cgi/viewcontent.
cgi?article=1682&context=ese_papers
Oliver, M. (2002) Creativity and the curriculum design process: a case study.
LTSN Generic Centre Working Paper Available at:
http://78.158.56.101/archive/palatine/files/1037.pdf
Pendleton-Jullian, A. (2015) Keynote at Relating Systems Thinking and Design 4
Symposium https://www.youtube.com/watch?v=sJefLlnb3pk
Pendleton Julian, A., & Brown, J. S. (2016) Pragmatic Imagination available at:
http://www.pragmaticimagination.com/
Piaget, J. (1950). The Psychology of Intelligence. London: Routledge
Poli, R. (2011) Steps towards an explicit ontology of the future. *Futures, 16*(1), 67-
78.
Pradhan, A. (2017a) Reframing 70:20:10, The Anatomy of Workflow Learning
Posted January 28, 2017
http://design4performance.com/2017/01/28/reframing-702010-the-anatomy-of-
workflow-learning/
Pradhan, A.(2017b) Learning in a High-Performance Ecosystem Linked in post
May 2017 https://www.linkedin.com/pulse/learning-high-performance-
ecosystem- arun-pradhan/
Puccio,G. J., Murdock, M. C., & Mance, M. (2005). Current developments in
creative problem solving for organizations: A focus on thinking skills and styles.
The Korean Journal of Thinking & Problem Solving, 15, 43-76.
QAA (2002) Guidelines for the HE Progress File (www.qaa.ac.uk /crntwork/
progfileHE/contents.htm 25th November 2002).
QAA (2009) Personal development planning: guidance for institutional policy and
practice in higher education Available on-line at: http://www.qaa.ac.uk/en/
Publications/Documents/Personal-development-planning-guidance-for-
institutional-policy-and-practice-in-higher-education.pdf
Redecker, C., Leis, M., Leendertse, M., Punie, Y., Gijsbers, G., Kirschner, P.
Stoyanov, S. & Hoogveld, B. (2011) *The Future of Learning: Preparing for
Change.* European Commission Joint Research Centre Institute for
Prospective Technological Studies EUR 24960 EN Luxembourg: Publications

Office of the European Union http://ipts.jrc.ec.europa.eu/
publications/pub.cfm?id=4719

Redecker, C. (2014) The Future of Learning is Lifelong, Lifewide and Open. Foreword in N. J. Jackson, & J. Willis, (eds) *Lifewide Learning and Education in Universities and Colleges. Lifewide Education* available at: http://www.learninglives.co.uk/e-book.html

Rogers, C.R., (1961) *On becoming a person.* Boston: Houghton Mifflin

Rogers, A. (2003) *What is the difference? a new critique of adult learning and teaching,* Leicester: NIACE.

Savin-Baden, M. (2008) *Learning Spaces: Creating Opportunities for Knowledge Creation in Academic Life* Maidenhead: McGraw Hill / Open University

Schön, D. (1987) *Educating the Reflective Practitioner,* San Francisco: Jossey-Bass. 355 + xvii pages.

Schulman, L. (2005a) The Signature Pedagogies of the Professions of Law, Medicine, Engineering, and the Clergy: Potential Lessons for the Education of Teachers. Transcript of a presentation Delivered at the Math Science Partnerships (MSP) Workshop National Research Council's Center for Education Available at:
http://www.taylorprograms.org/images/Shulman_Signature_Pedagogies.pdf

Schunk, D. H. & Zimmerman, B. J. (1994) *Self-regulation of learning and performance: Issues and educational applications* Hillside NJ: Lawrence Erlbaum Associates.

Schunk, D. H. & Zimmerman, B. J. (1997) Social origins of self-regulated competence. *Educational Psychologist 32,* 195-208.

Schunk, D. H. & Zimmerman, B. J. (1998) *Self-regulated learning: from teaching to self-reflective practice.* New York: Guilford Press.

Schunk, D. H. & Zimmerman, B. J. (2003) *Educational Psychology: A Century of Contributions* Routledge

Seimens, G. (2007) Connectivism: Creating a Learning Ecology in Distributed Environments in T. Hug (Ed) *Didactics of Microlearning: Concepts, Discourses and Examples* Munster; Waxman 53-68

Shaw, R., Turvey, M. T. & Mace, W. M. (1982). Ecological Psychology: The Consequence of a Commitment to Realism. In W. Weimer & D. Palermo, *Cognition and the Symbolic Processes II. Pages 159 - 226.* Hillsdale, NJ: Lawrence Erlbaum Associates, Inc.

Smith, M. K. (2000) Curriculum theory and practice. *The encyclopedia of informal education,* www.infed.org/biblio/b-curric.htm

Soylu, M. Y. (2014) Exploring self-regulation of more and less expert college-age video game players: A sequential explanatory design *ETD collection for University of Nebraska - Lincoln.* Paper AAI3615276. http://digitalcommons.unl.edu/dissertations/AAI3615276

Staron, M. (2011) Connecting and integrating life based and lifewide learning. In In N. J. Jackson (ed) *Learning for a Complex World: A lifewide concept of learning, education and personal development.* Authorhouse 137-159

Staron, M. (2013) Learning Ecology a Matter of Trust. *Lifewide Magazine* #7, 7-8 available at: http://www.lifewidemagazine.co.uk/

Staron, M., Jasinski, M. and Weatherley, R. (2006) Life-based Learning: A Strength-based Approach for Capability Development in Vocational and Technical Education. Australian Government Department for Education Science and Training and TAFE NSW. Online at http://learningtobeprofessional.pbworks.com/w/page/32893040/Life-based-learning

Stefano G. D., Gino, F., Pisano G.P., Stats B.R. (2016) Making Experience Count: The role of reflection in individual learning Working Paper 14-093 Harvard Business School

Stodd, J (2012) *Exploring the World of Social Learning* SmashWords https://www.smashwords.com/profile/view/JulianStodd

Stodd, J. (2014a) Exploring the Social Age and the New Culture of Learning. *Lifewide Magazine* Available at: http://www.lifewidemagazine.co.uk/

Stodd, J. (2014b) Scaffolded Social Learning Blog post Nov 5 2104 https://julianstodd.wordpress.com/2014/11/05/scaffolded-social-learning/

Swenson, R. (1999). Epistemic ordering and the development of space-time: Intentionality as a universal entailment. *Semiotica,* 126 (1), 1-31

Tansley, A. G. (1935) The use and abuse of vegetational concepts and terms. *Ecology* 16:284 -307

Tremblay, N. A. (2000) Autodidactism: an exemplary model of self-directed learning. In G A Straka (ed) *Conceptions of self-directed learning, theoretical and conceptual considerations.* New York, Waxman p207-220.

Thomas, D. & Seely Brown, J (2009) Learning for a World of Constant Change: Homo Sapiens, Homo Farber & Homo Ludens revisited (paper presented at the 7th Glion Colloquium by JSB, June 2009)

Thomas, D. & Brown, J. S. (2011) New Culture of Learning: Cultivating the imagination for a world of constant change http://www.newcultureoflearning.com/

Thomson, P., Hall, C., Jones, K. & Sefton-Green, J. (2012). The Signature Pedagogies Project: *Final Report. Newcastle: Creativity Culture and Education* Available at: http://www.creativitycultureeducation.org/wp-content/uploads/Signature_Pedagogies_Final_Report_April_2012.pdf

Tobin, W. (2014) Personal Inflection Points Shift the Trajectory Kaufman Fellows Report v5. http://www.kauffmanfellows.org/journal_posts/personal-inflection-points-shift-the-trajectory/

Todd, P.M. (2001) Heuristics for Decision and Choice in International Encyclopedia of the Social & Behavioral Sciences

Tough, A. (1971) *The Adult's Learning Projects: A fresh approach to theory and practice in adult learning.* Available at: http://ieti.org/tough/books/alp.htm

Turner, V. W. (1967) Betwixt and Between: The Liminal Period in Rites de Passage. In *The Forest of Symbols: Aspects of Ndembu Ritual,* 93-111. Cornell University Press

van Lier, L. (2000) From input to affordance: Social-interactive learning from an ecological perspective in (eds) 245-59 In *Sociocultural Theory and Second Language Learning.* Oxford: Oxford University Press. 155-177

Vygotsky, L. S. (1978) *Mind in Society.* Cambridge MA: Harvard University Press.

Vygotsky, L. S. (1998) Imagination and Creativity in Childhood. *Soviet Psychology* 28 (10) 84-96 (originally published in 1930)

Williams, R.T., Karousou, R., & Gumtau, S. (2008). *Affordances for learning and research* (Final project report for the Higher Education Academy). Retrieved from http://learning-affordances.wikispaces.com/Project+Report

Warger, T and Dobbin, G (2009) Learning Environments: Where Space, Technology, and Culture Converge ELI Paper 1: October 2009http://net.educause.edu/ir/library/pdf/eli3021.pdf

Wiles, J. (2008). *Leading Curriculum Development.* Thousand Oaks, CA: Corwin Press

Zimmerman, B. J. (2000) Self-regulatory cycles of learning. In G A Straka (ed) *Conceptions of self-directed learning, theoretical and conceptual considerations.* New York, Waxman 221-234

Zimmerman, B. J. (2002) Becoming a Self-Regulated Learner: An Overview *Theory into Practice* 41, 2, 64-70

Zimmerman, B. J. (2003) Self-regulating Intellectual Processes and Outcomes: A social cognitive perspective. In D Y. Dai and R J Sternberg (eds) *Motivation, emotions and cognition: Integrative perspectives on intellectual functioning and development.* Mahwah, NJ: Lawrence Erlbaum.

Zimmerman, B. J. (2008) Investigating Self-Regulation and Motivation: Historical Background, Methodolgical Developments and Future Prospects *American Educational Research Journal*, 45, 1 166-183

Zimmerman, B. J. & Schunk, D. H. (eds) 1989 Self-regulated learning and academic achievement *Theory, Research and Practice* Springer-Verlag New York

Zimmerman, B. J. & Schunk, D. H. (2008) Self-Regulating Intellectual Processes and Outcomes: A Social Cognitive Perspective. In D Y Dai and R J Sternberg (eds) *Motivation, emotion and cognition. Integrative Perspectives on Intellectual Functioning and Development* Lawrence Erlbaum: New Jersey 323-349

Lifewide Education

This book is part of a strategy to explore the ideas and practice implications of a lifewide approach to learning, development and achievement in higher education. The project is being implemented by Lifewide Education, a not for profit, community-based, educational enterprise whose purpose is to champion and support a lifewide approach to learning, personal development and education. Our vision for a more complete education is captured in the words of Eduard Lindeman 'the whole of life is learning therefore education can have no ending.' A more complete education unites and integrates formal education with learners' own attempts to develop themselves through their lifewide experiences.

Our community is open to anyone who is interested in these ideas. You join the Lifewide Education community by subscribing on the home page of our website.

Further information, including our magazines and books can be found at http://www.lifewideeducation.uk/

All proceeds from the sale of this book are used to support the Lifewide Education & Creative Academic http://www.creativeacademic.uk/ open educational enterprises.

Norman Jackson
Founder Lifewide Education @lifewider
Founder Creative Academic @academiccreator

Ecologies for Learning and Practice: Emerging Ideas, Sightings, and Possibilities
Ronald Barnett and Norman Jackson (Eds)

Ecologies for Learning and Practice provides the ideal introduction to the history of learning ecologies and locates the concept within the context of the contemporary world. Considering the ways in which individuals and society are being presented with new kinds of learning challenges arising from fluidities and disruptions that extend across all domains of individuals' lives, this book unpacks the emerging ways of understanding and living purposively with this new fluidity.

Providing an insight into the research of a range of internationally renowned contributors, this book explores diverse topics from the higher education and adult learning worlds, these include:
- perspectives on the challenges faced by education systems today
- thinking ecologically and the creation of ecologies for learning and practice
- an exploration of the different eco-social systems of the world - local and global, economic, cultural, rational, practical, technological and ethical
- how adult learners must create and manage their own ecologies for learning in order to sustain themselves as learners.

Recognising how learners consider themselves, their personal development and their learning spaces, *Ecologies for Learning and Practice* is an essential guide for researchers and students who seek to conceptualise and analyse the learning processes that will form the foundation of future learning.
Published November 2019 London: Routledge